D1357107

JIMMY REID

A SCOTTISH POLITICAL JOURNEY

JIMMY REID

KENNY MacASKILL

Biteback Publishing

First published in Great Britain in 2017 by
Biteback Publishing Ltd
Westminster Tower
3 Albert Embankment
London SE1 7SP
Copyright © Kenny MacAskill 2017

ISBN 978-1-78590-279-6

10 9 8 7 6 5 4 3 2 1

A CIP catalogue record for this book is available from the British Library.

Set in Sabon

Printed and bound in Great Britain by
CPI Group (UK) Ltd, Croydon CR0 4YY

MIX
Paper from
responsible sources
FSC
www.fsc.org   FSC® C020471

CONTENTS

INTRODUCTION

Jimmy Reid died in Inverclyde Royal Hospital, Greenock, on 10 August 2010. He had suffered from ill health for several years and a brain haemorrhage sadly brought his life to an end at the age of seventy-eight. He'd moved to Rothesay on the Isle of Bute and it was there that he passed away with his family by his side. Both press and public were quick to eulogise him. Papers and news broadcasts carried obituaries and lauded his contribution to Scottish life. Even the right-wing press that had espoused policies he deplored and castigated the socialist views he cherished were fulsome in their praise of the one-time communist. Many commentators described him in the numerous obituaries as the 'best MP Scotland never had'.

A private service in Rothesay was followed by a public service in Govan Old Parish Church in the heart of the community where he had grown up. There was no death-bed conversion for this atheist to the end; the church was required due to the size of the crowd wishing to attend. In attendance were Alex Salmond, the then First Minister of Scotland, Gordon Brown who had recently demitted office as Prime Minister of the United Kingdom and other leading politicians from various parties. Sir Alex Ferguson, who had grown up in Govan, and Billy Connolly, who had worked in the shipyards, both got to know Jimmy over later years, and regaled the congregation with humorous and poignant tales of Jimmy from years gone by. Police assistance was provided for the funeral cortege, despite Jimmy never having held senior elected office. Union leaders and celebrities attended, along with former shipyard workers and countless ordinary people who gathered to pay their respects. It was all testimony to the influence and effect Jimmy had upon so many both within and far beyond Scotland.

Jimmy's life was a political journey, starting in his early teenage years in the Labour League of Youth and the Young Communist League (YCL), from which he progressed to the Communist Party and ultimately to the Scottish National Party (SNP) in his later years. Yet in many ways, while his political affiliations shifted, his views remained constant. Throughout his life, he remained committed to the cause of socialism and to a Scottish Parliament. What changed was simply the political vehicle of choice for expressing those views. In many ways Jimmy was never entirely comfortable in any party. He was a free thinker and a free spirt and political orthodoxy weighed heavily on him, despite accepting both the democratic centralism of the Communist Party of Great Britain (CPGB) and party discipline in later ones.

Jimmy's was a political journey that he did not make alone, although he was in the vanguard of it. Few had been with him in the Communist Party, though sympathy abounded for what he argued. But many later followed him from the Labour Party to the SNP. Some, like Jimmy, were driven by contempt for New Labour and Tony Blair, and condemned Blair for leading the nation into war in Iraq. Others followed Jimmy to the SNP in the cascade that followed the unsuccessful referendum on independence for

Scotland in 2014, which Jimmy did not live to see but would have supported vigorously had he still been alive.

It was a political journey made in a country that itself changed dramatically over Jimmy's lifetime and in a myriad of ways. Its economy, society and culture altering significantly, though, as with the man himself, many values and attitudes remained constant. Some changes were welcome and long overdue, such as the clearances of the slums and single ends that existed in the Govan Jimmy knew. Others, however, such as the demise of the manufacturing base Jimmy worked in Govan and in Clydebank, were bitterly lamented. The poor immigrants from Ireland who lived in streets near where he was raised were replaced by new ones from Eastern Europe and south-east Asia. The industrial heartlands of the west of Scotland diminished and the powerhouses that were steel, coal mining and shipyards all but disappeared. Oil and financial services grew. New industries developed, as did new towns. People shifted to them and from the west to the east coast.

Equally, the communities Jimmy knew changed as council housing was replaced by home ownership and private rental. Slum tenements were cleared with great hope and anticipation. Yet, sadly, some of the housing schemes created in their place became slums themselves as poverty and unemployment soared. The challenges Jimmy and others faced have changed, but the struggle for that better society he believed in continues to this day.

The power and influence of the unions Jimmy knew reduced substantially. Once union leaders were household names and their views held considerable sway, not just with governments but amongst the public. But the Scotland of men working in overwhelmingly heavy industry died and a new one was born with the service sector and other enterprises. Now the majority of the population work in non-unionised industries and their say in the public sector is limited. However, political activism remains and has shifted from the workplace to the community. That was shown during his lifetime with opposition to the poll tax, the Iraq War and, after his death, in the referendum on independence and the Yes campaign.

As Scotland changed and developed, so did Jimmy and countless others as Calvinist Scotland became a much more cosmopolitan country, but the issues of poverty and unemployment remained. The challenges faced continued with a 21st-century backdrop and new complications replacing what went before. The struggle he engaged in continues to be carried on by others, who lament his passing and are inspired by his contribution.

Jimmy was an iconic figure in Scottish public life throughout the latter part of the twentieth century and had a public profile not unlike that of a famous footballer or musician. Despite never being elected to Parliament or senior office and remaining on the fringe of British party politics, Jimmy was one of the most popular politicians of his time.

Though a communist for many years, he was respected by almost all, irrespective of their political allegiance. Even the right-wing press that had castigated his politics throughout his life hugely respected him. Renowned for his oratory, he was able to communicate difficult and often unpopular political ideas to ordinary people in a manner that they understood and appreciated. He challenged if not changed perceptions of the Communist Party. Many ordinary people who baulked at his creed greatly liked and admired its most able and articulate exponent.

His profile grew immensely along with his prestige, following the Upper Clyde Shipbuilders' (UCS) work-in. It's that for which he's perhaps understandably best remembered. He played a leading role along with the other shop stewards in a major industrial dispute that inspired public support across Scotland. His firebrand address to the assembled workers about to occupy the yard and fight for their very livelihoods is remembered by all who were alive at the time. The grainy black and white footage is symbolic for many of a Scotland with shipyards, coal mines, steel mills and other heavy industry for which it was famed around the world. It captured a moment in Scottish history and life.

It jettisoned Jimmy into public prominence and is seared in the soul of those on the left in Scotland.

Jimmy had been involved in industrial action before during an apprentices' strike on Clydeside. There were several such disputes in the west of Scotland over the decades spanning from 1912 through to 1937, 1941, 1952 and 1960. Though prominent in the dispute in 1952, Jimmy's profile was lower then, even if his name was mentioned in the papers and talked about in the union and the political world. It would, however, be formative for future actions, proving to be a breeding ground for many future union leaders both locally and nationally. Not only Jimmy, but others such as Gavin Laird and Alex Ferry went on to have significant roles in the trade union movement. Dick Douglas was later to become a Labour MP and make the transition to the SNP.

That year also saw Jimmy elected as the National Chairman of the YCL which he had joined after initially being a member of the Labour League of Youth. Disenchantment with the Labour government and a dislike of careerism within the Labour Party led him to switch to the Communists. In 1958 he became full-time

National Secretary of the YCL, which saw him move to London. He stayed there until 1965 when he returned to Scotland and became the Secretary of the Scottish District of the Communist Party of Great Britain (CPGB). He remained in that post until he stepped down in 1969 and returned to work in the shipyards.

Soon after, he quickly became involved in trade union affairs and was elected as a shop steward at John Brown's. It was there that he came to prominence with his role in the occupation of the yards in 1971, which pushed him into the limelight even more. Chat shows and other opportunities to promote his views and philosophy came along and he was nominated for the post of Rector of Glasgow University. Despite his working class and communist roots, he saw off other challengers to be selected in an institution then more noted for its conservatism than its radicalism.

His address when installed as Rector is viewed as one of the great speeches of the twentieth century. It resonated well outside Scotland, with the *New York Times* reporting it in full and describing it as 'the greatest speech since President Lincoln's Gettysburg Address' – an incredible accolade, given America's hostility to communism and the shadow of the Vietnam War ongoing at the time.

His campaigns to be elected to Parliament saw him stand several times under the Communist banner in Dunbartonshire and once as the Labour candidate in Dundee. The election in Dunbarton in February 1974 was rough, to say the least. His 15 per cent share of the vote was the largest for a Communist Party candidate in many years, but it wasn't what many, and perhaps he, had hoped for following the UCS work-in. Reid himself called out the tactics of his Labour opponent and made an assertion of 'Falangism' given the activities of some. Many viewed that as a fall from grace for a man otherwise courteous to opponents, irrespective of their views.

He contested the election in October of that year, but he wasn't to remain long in the Communist Party thereafter. It was heading even deeper into the wilderness from which it had never really managed to extricate itself in the UK. In many ways, he had become bigger than the party. Disagreements on various policy issues and management styles also rankled. Perhaps there was even an understandable desire to contribute in high office, for which he was eminently capable, but which he could never attain with a Communist label. He therefore left the party in 1976.

The following year, he joined Labour and stood as their candidate in the Dundee East seat held by the SNP in the election of 1979. Though he increased the Labour vote, he was unable to oust the sitting Nationalist MP. That, too, had been a high-profile and rough campaign, but again an unsuccessful one. Thereafter, though he initially remained politically active in the left of the Labour Party before subsequently joining the SNP, he was never again to seek political office. He was to remain for many 'the best MP Scotland never had'.

His position as a shop steward was well known after the UCS, but he also sought elected office within the Amalgamated Engineering Union (AEU). That was less well publicised, but given the hugely important position that trade unions still held in Scottish and British public life, it still carried clout and merited significant coverage. The Engineering Union was one of the most powerful of the large trade unions that then existed. Given Scotland's heavy industrial base, it had a significant role in the wider political scene both north and south of the border.

In 1975, he stood for the Scottish seat on the union's National Executive Committee (NEC) but was beaten by fellow Scot Gavin Laird. Shortly after that, he lost out in an election for the post of Scottish organiser. He never contested for union office again. It appears that in union politics as in party politics, his Communist Party membership cost him some support that otherwise might have been available. Unfortunately, he was destined never to achieve high office.

Instead, he moved out of the shipyards and away from involvement in party and union politics into a career as a journalist and broadcaster. There he was able to express himself sometimes with humour but always with great clarity on the important issues of the day. Despite never having trained in journalism or even having gone to college or university, Jimmy's broadcasting was exceptionally articulate and rousing.

His TV programmes on Russia saw him win two BAFTAs that many more experienced broadcasters could only envy. His columns, however, did cause controversy when he denounced the leadership of Arthur Scargill during the ill-fated miners' strike. Jimmy criticised the union leader's tactics and predicted that the price to be paid by the members would be immense. In that, he was sadly proved correct. Jimmy was denounced by many former colleagues on the left for breaking ranks, even though he was simply publicly expressing what others were saying privately. It did, however, sour the view some former allies had, even if events showed him to be prescient in his analysis.

Latterly, Jimmy joined the SNP, disgusted by the direction taken by New Labour under Blair and appalled by the Iraq War. Wooed by the SNP leader Alex Salmond, he joined the party in

2005. Age and ill health unfortunately limited his ability to be active and participate as he once had, but he still retained that aura and mystique people found so likeable, and he was elected President of their Trade Union Group in 2006. In the Glasgow East by-election in July 2008, he was rolled out delightedly by the SNP in support of their candidate John Mason, who went on to narrowly win the seat for the Nationalists.

As his active political participation waned, greater energy was given to *Scottish Left Review*, a magazine he and others had established in 2000 to put forward the views Jimmy had subscribed to since boyhood. That occupied him to his final days as he continued to articulate his political views for socialism and Scotland.

Jimmy's profile was greater than most who were elected to high office. Though his major political career was on the margins of British politics with the Communist Party, his influence was far greater than many of those in larger parties. And throughout it all, he remained rooted in the community from which he came. At the end of his life, he retained the respect and affection of ordinary people across the land of his birth – something that was displayed at his funeral: quite an astonishing achievement.

However, while Jimmy was in the public eye, much remained unknown and undocumented. He touched upon some aspects of his early life and formative influences in his semi-autobiographical book, *Reflections of a Clyde-built Man*, and a collection of his writings was published in 1984. He also wrote a myriad of musings on Scottish politics throughout his life and much has been written on both the UCS and the Communist Party. But there has never before been a biography of the man, which is quite surprising, given his high profile and longstanding prominence.

Where did his parents come from? What was his childhood like? What influenced him in his formative years? What motivated him throughout his life? Why did he remain in the Communist Party despite his opposition to the Soviet invasion of Hungary and Czechoslovakia? What motivated him to join the Labour Party and then the SNP? How did he make the transition to journalism? Why did he speak out against Scargill during the miners' strike? What of his family and friends? Ultimately, who was Jimmy Reid, the best MP Scotland never had?

Moreover, what of that political journey made by him and taken by countless others in Scotland who followed in his wake? His commitment to socialism and a Scottish Parliament stayed unwavering throughout his life, though his party affiliations changed. Many since have followed in his footsteps and hold him up as a shining light along their political path.

The story of Jimmy Reid is not just about UCS and an iconic political figure, but also about Scotland and its changing society. It's about how Scotland transformed from Jimmy's communist days to a land where a referendum on independence would see much of Red Clydeside vote 'Yes'. It's the story of a country that shifted politically in sixty years from 1955 when the Conservatives gained an absolute majority, to 2015 when the SNP won fifty-six out of fifty-nine seats after many decided that the British road to socialism was ending and Scottish independence was the way to achieve a socialist society. There has been a Tory revival in the elections since where they've won seats in mainly rural Scotland from the SNP and overtaken Labour to become the major opposition party. However, the SNP still remain dominant in seats and votes at all levels of government whether local authority, Holyrood or Westminster. Moreover, the contrast with south of the border remains, as Scotland once again has a Tory government that it didn't vote for.

This, then, is the story of Jimmy and that of the political journey he and others made.

CHAPTER ONE

THE RED CLYDESIDE INHERITANCE

Jimmy Reid grew up in Clydeside, a region around the city of Glasgow made up of other towns and villages that sit along the banks of the River Clyde as it flows from Lanarkshire down to Inverclyde. The coal mines native to the region were used to fire steel works in the nineteenth century, thus making it the hub of industrialisation in Scotland. The mines provided fuel for the shipyards and other heavy engineering plants which grew alongside them. People flocked there in search of work from all over Scotland, Ireland and beyond. Communities and were forged by whichever industry was there. Many of those settlers were extremely poor and experienced enormous hardship, which led to early trade union and labour movements being formed. It was an area with a socialist tradition and charismatic radical leaders: an inheritance that Jimmy was to be proud of.

The area was given the name Red Clydeside – and with good reason. From the years just before the First World War until the early 1930s, Clydeside became synonymous with radicalism both in the workplace and in the community. Left-wing groups proliferated. The ILP, affiliated to the Labour Party but with its own distinct socialist agenda, had been formed. Particularly

1

strong in Scotland, it was more radical in many ways than the larger organisation under which it sheltered and, as such, it was often viewed as its socialist conscience. Other socialist groupings were numerous, smaller but intense in their activism and beliefs. Some of them ultimately coalesced into the Communist Party that was formed in 1920 with a significant Scottish and Clydeside input.

The First World War split the socialist movement asunder. The Labour Party supported the war though many members opposed it, mirroring the divide in other major socialist parties across Europe. Indeed, the ILP and smaller socialist groups tended to be vehemently against it. Political activism continued unabated on the Clyde during the war.

The Clyde Workers' Committee (CWC) was formed early on during the First World War to coordinate activism. It brought together the shop stewards in the major industrial sites to oppose the war and protect workers' conditions. Such was the establishment's concern that both Lloyd George, the Prime Minister, and Arthur Henderson, the Labour leader, came north to meet them – however, to no avail. Their opposition to the war and, in particular, to restrictions on engineers leaving their workplace remained relentless. Several leaders were even imprisoned for their anti-war activities, which carried on regardless.

Radicalism was present in the community as much as in the workplace. Slum conditions during the war were compounded by rent rises, which led to a rent strike in Govan in May 1915. It soon spread across the city to other areas as support for the action grew and mass demonstrations took place. Confrontations with police and sheriff officers occurred when evictions were attempted. Trade unions threatened industrial action in support of the activists unless action against the rent strikers was called off. By the November, 20,000 tenants were withholding their rent and the crisis was escalating. The Secretary of State for Scotland had the Cabinet urgently legislate to control rents.

When the war ended, peace brought fresh challenges for governments and revolution in Russia caused alarm for authorities across Europe. Both those who had endured on the battle field and those who had suffered at home were seeking a better world. It was, after all, the war to end all wars, and the sacrifice of so many was meant to herald a better future for all. However, the lands to which they returned were struggling to cope. Unemployment was rising and housing and social conditions were deteriorating. Discontent led to agitation for change. Political activism grew as tension simmered across the European continent.

The Clyde was at the forefront of the agitation across the UK. Driven by fears of a significant rise in unemployment through the demobilisation of soldiers and sailors with the war ending, workers were seeking improvements in their working conditions and, in particular, were campaigning for a forty-hour week. Allied to that were concerns over a reduction in military contracts of which the area, including the shipyards, had been a major recipient.

In January 1919, the trade unions organised mass rallies in George Square, Glasgow, in support of a strike that had been called by the shop stewards' movement for the forty-hour week. Estimates vary, but up to 90,000 people rallied to the call. The Red Flag was memorably raised in the crowd that had gathered in the packed city centre. As the strike gained momentum, the authorities panicked. Protesters were attacked by the police and a riot ensued in what became known as the Battle of George Square.

Such was the concern about revolution that local troops stationed at Maryhill in the city were confined to barracks. The government was fearful that Glaswegian and West of Scotland soldiers would disobey orders if instructed to act against their fellow citizens. Instead, soldiers from around the country were hurriedly despatched to what was then described as the second city of the Empire. Tanks and troops were even deployed on the streets to deter any would be revolutionaries and assuage the evident fear in the establishment. The strike leaders were charged with instigating a riot and sentenced to five months' imprisonment. Revolution was never sparked though some like Willie Gallacher, Chairman of the CWC and later to become a Communist MP, felt that a revolutionary moment had been missed, regretting that they hadn't marched to the barracks and called on the soldiers to support them.

Change, though, was still demanded by the people and agitation continued unabated. The mood of militancy in the workplace and the community remained. However, the focus in the west of Scotland moved to action through the ballot box. The ILP moved to the fore in Scotland. The year of 1922 saw a breakthrough in Parliament and the election of a grouping of left-wing MPs, including John Wheatley, James Maxton, Davy Kirkwood, George Buchanan, Manny Shinwell and Tom Johnston. Along with Neil McLean, who had been elected in 1918 and was re-elected in 1922, their radical demands earned them the name the Red Clydesiders.

All of them were elected as ILP MPs, showing its grassroots strength in the area. They were united in their opposition to the war for which many had been imprisoned, a more radical agenda than the broader Labour grouping in the House of Commons and an unequivocal commitment to Scottish Home Rule. Able and articulate, they were active in Scotland and vociferous in the House of Commons. Some would serve as ministers in Labour governments legislating for social improvements, while others remained firebrands on the backbenches and kept the flame of socialism burning. It was a period that included the General Strike and the start of the Great Depression both of which left indelible marks on the area and these MPs both earned and lived up to their Red Clydeside moniker throughout that decade and beyond.

The Labour Party, including the ILP, was trounced in the 1931 election following the split over Ramsay MacDonald's formation of a coalition National Government. The Red Clydesiders, as with almost all their colleagues, had uniformly rejected MacDonald. However, Labour was reduced to just fifty-two MPs in the UK, and only seven in Scotland. Clydeside was not immune from that cull, with five seats being lost in Glasgow alone. That drew the period of the Red Clydesiders to an end.

The divide that had developed within the wider Labour parliamentary grouping under MacDonald spilled over into the ILP the following year (1932) as they split over whether to become an independent party, rather than a grouping under the Labour umbrella in Westminster. James Maxton was to leave and lead the formally separate ILP, but others such as David Kirkwood chose to join the Labour Party. They remained active, though, and the spirit of Red Clydeside lived on. And it was this year that James 'Jimmy' Reid was born and inherited his red legacy.

The leading figures were known throughout the land and es-pecially in Clydeside, where many were revered. Jimmy grew up hearing of their exploits, and later met and worked with some of them. So who were these people in whose footsteps Jimmy followed?

WILLIE GALLACHER

Willie Gallacher was chairman of the CWC during the First World War. Born in Paisley in 1881 he was the grand old man of the Communist Party. He had been sentenced to six months' imprisonment under the Defence of the Realm Act during the war for an article he had written in the CWC magazine *The Worker*. After the George Square demonstrations in 1919 where he felt a 'revolutionary moment' had been missed, he was jailed again for five months along with other leaders. They weren't to be his only spells in prison, as in 1925, along with other senior communists, he was sentenced to twelve months' imprisonment under the In-citement to Mutiny Act. His campaigning, however, continued undiminished upon his release. Elected Communist Party MP for West Fife in 1935, he was to be one of only four ever elected on the ticket. He retained the seat until defeated by Labour in 1950. The viciousness of that campaign between Labour and Communist, with accusations of interference from the pulpit by the Catholic Church, were to be redolent of Jimmy's campaign in February 1974 in Dunbartonshire. Gallacher subsequently became Party President from 1956 until his death in 1963, when Jimmy was working for it.

He wasn't the first Communist MP to be elected in Scotland.

That distinction went to Walton Newbold who was returned for Motherwell in the general election of 1922. Newbold was born in 1888 in Lancashire, not the Lanarkshire he was to represent. After studying at Manchester University, he became a lecturer in history and politics. He was a conscientious objector during the First World War, though he escaped punishment as he was unfit on medical grounds. He fought for election under the Communist Party though with Labour Party endorsement, and was one of two Communist MPs elected in the UK. Newbold only held the seat until the following year, when he was defeated by a Unionist.

DAVE KIRKWOOD

Gallacher had been ably supported on the CWC by many, including Davie Kirkwood who was elected the ILP MP for Dumbarton in 1922, which then included the growing community of Clydebank. Kirkwood was born in the east end of Glasgow in 1872. After attending the local Parkhead School, he trained as an engineer in Parkhead Forge. Now a well-known shopping centre, it was then the site of the largest steelworks in Scotland. Covering twenty-five acres, it employed over 20,000 men at its height during the First World War. Kirkwood was convenor of the shop stewards there and became a Glasgow town councillor for four years before his election to parliament. However, when the ILP officially disaffiliated from the Labour Party, he resigned and took the Labour whip. He remained an MP until 1951. Made a Baron, he went to the House of Lords until his death in 1955: an institution, however, that Jimmy would disdain throughout his life.

MANNY SHINWELL

Manny Shinwell was another figure that helped paint the Clyde red. He was born in 1884 in London to parents who were Jewish immigrants from Europe. They moved to Glasgow, where his father ran a small drapery. He became a union activist in the city and in 1911 helped organise the National Sailors' and Firemen's Union during a national strike. The following year, he became the local secretary of the British Seafarers' Union. He came to prominence in the events that unfolded in Glasgow during 1919 over the forty-hour week and, like Gallacher, served five months in prison.

He was subsequently elected to parliament as an ILP member in 1922, though for Linlithgowshire rather than Clydeside. Defeated in 1924, he won it back in a by-election in 1928 only to lose it again in 1931. He was returned to the House of Commons for a Durham seat in 1935 as the Labour Party candidate, defeating Ramsay MacDonald standing as the National Labour MP following the party split. It was a seat he retained until he stepped down in 1970. Similarly to Kirkwood, he accepted a peerage and became Baron Shinwell of Easington and was active in the House of Lords until shortly before his death at the ripe old age of 101.

JOHN WHEATLEY

John Wheatley was another member of the cadre. Many believed that he and not Ramsay MacDonald should have led the Labour Party in 1922 and that history may have turned out differently, but it was not to be. Less well known, new to parliament and from the more radical ILP, he deferred to the former leader and member of the mainstream organisation. Wheatley was born in

County Waterford, Ireland. in 1869 and came to Scotland as a child with his parents. Initially following his father down the pits at the age of twelve, he subsequently made a career in printing where he ran a successful publishing business, specialising in many left-wing works. He was a prominent Glasgow councillor, campaigning against the war and supporting the rent strikes.

Elected as MP for Shettleston in 1922 which he held until his sudden death in 1930, he was seen as an intellectual heavyweight, adding ballast to the mainly industrial shop stewards he worked alongside. He was also the first chairman of the Catholic Socialist Society. Minister of health in Ramsay MacDonald's short-lived minority Labour government in 1924, he introduced the Housing Act that was to become his greatest legacy. It allowed for the construction of public housing that was essential for providing work at a time of high unemployment and making affordable rented homes available to those on low incomes. By 1933, three years after Wheatley's death, over half a million homes had been built across the UK. The genesis for which had no doubt been the rent strike that took place in Glasgow during the war and in which he had been actively involved. Like his colleagues, he had opposed the war and campaigned against conscription. A vocal critic of Ramsay MacDonald's actions in steering the Labour Party rightwards, he found himself excluded from ministerial office when the second Labour administration was formed in 1929. He died the following year at the age of sixty before the splits occurred between Labour and the ILP.

JAMES MAXTON

James Maxton, born in Glasgow to two teachers in 1885, was

highly charismatic and became a darling of the left. After attending Glasgow University, he became a teacher himself and joined the ILP in 1904. During the war, he was a conscientious objector and was made to work on barges. He became involved with the CWC and he was charged with sedition and imprisoned during the war. Elected to parliament in 1922 for Glasgow Bridgeton, he retained the seat until his death in 1946.

A highly gifted orator, he was respected by his opponents – Churchill describing him as 'the greatest parliamentarian of his day'. Very supportive of a Scottish Parliament, he was president of the Scottish Home Rule Association for a period. A committed socialist (he even wrote a biography of Lenin), he was a pivotal figure at the time when the ILP formally split from Labour in 1932. Maxton's dislike for Labour's drift to the right led him to support the ILP, a move which, though it left him a revered figure on the left, made him politically isolated. Membership plummeted and the ILP declined in influence. However, in the 1945 election the ILP returned three MPs – including Maxton – all of whom were in Glasgow constituencies. His death the following year was a body blow for the party, even though the seat was retained in the by-election. However, his successor and his former colleagues were to join the Labour Party in 1947 and the ILP ceased to be an electoral force.

GEORGE BUCHANAN

Another of the Red Clydeside activists, and one who initially sided with Maxton in the ILP's formal split from Labour, was George Buchanan. Born in Glasgow in 1890, he became a patternmaker by trade. Vice-chair of Glasgow Trades Council, he was a Glasgow town councillor before his election as MP for the Gorbals in 1922.

Though he had gone with Maxton at the outset, he subsequently changed his mind and re-joined Labour in 1939. He was to serve as an Under-Secretary of State for Scotland in Clement Attlee's government of 1945 and was later minister for pensions. In 1948, he left parliament and ministerial office to become chairman of the National Assistance Board. He died in 1955.

NEIL MCLEAN

Neil McLean was first elected in Govan in 1918 and was returned with his ILP colleagues two years later. An organiser in the Scottish Co-operative Wholesale Society, he had also been a conscientious objector during the war. He did, however, split from Maxton and the ILP to remain a Labour MP in 1932. On his retiral in 1950, he declined a seat in the House of Lords and died in 1953. He was the local MP when Jimmy first became interested and active in politics, and had lived nearby.

TOM JOHNSTON

Tom Johnston, who arguably became Scotland's greatest ever Secretary of State, was another member of that first contingent of Red Clydeside MPs. Johnston was born in 1881 in Kirkintilloch, Dunbartonshire, where his father was a grocer. While studying at Glasgow University, he helped launch the left-wing paper *Forward*, the media channel for the Red Clydesiders, and ultimately became its editor. He was also an accomplished author and wrote *Our Scots Noble Families*, a scathing indictment of the aristocracy in Scotland, and *The History of the Working Classes in Scotland*, a socialist appraisal of Scottish history. The latter book deeply affected Jimmy when he read it as a young man.

Elected to Parliament as an ILP member in 1922 for Stirling and Clackmannan on the fringes of Clydeside, Johnston lost the seat in 1924, though was re-elected later that year in a by-election in Dundee. He returned to win the Stirlingshire seat in 1929, although he lost it again in the electoral wipe-out in 1931. He had vigorously opposed Ramsay MacDonald's move to the right, but disagreed with Maxton over disaffiliation from Labour. Accordingly, when he won the seat back in 1935, he served as a Labour Party MP until he retired from Parliament in 1945.

Johnston served briefly as Lord Privy Seal in Ramsay MacDonald's second Labour government, but he's best remembered as the war time Secretary of State for Scotland. In that role, he was radical and progressive not just when dealing with the requirements of war, but also when seeking to effect social and economic change. He was a strong supporter of Home Rule and he oversaw the establishment of the North of Scotland Hydro-Electric Board and the Scottish Council of Industry. Action was also taken to regulate rent and address health issues before the NHS was introduced by Attlee's post-war Labour government. Committees were created to address issues ranging from agricultural matters to youth offending. After stepping down from Parliament, he chaired the North of Scotland Hydro-Electric Board that he had established, as well as the Scottish Tourist Board and the Forestry Commission. In those posts, he was equally innovative in bringing development to remote areas and jobs to the entire country. He died in 1965.

PATRICK DOLLAN

The radicalism of the contingent in Westminster was matched in the council chamber, where some had served prior to their election to Parliament. Prominent amongst them and a key ally of the Red Clydeside MPs was Patrick Dollan. Born in Baillieston on the eastern edge of Glasgow in 1885, he was a miner's son who quickly followed his father down the pits before becoming a journalist with *Forward* in 1911. Elected to Glasgow Council just before the war as an ILP councillor for the Govan Central Ward, he was imprisoned for anti-war activities and was an activist in the rent campaigns. He was the chair of the ILP from 1920 until the decision in 1932 to disaffiliate from Labour saw him leave and join the party. In 1938, he became the first Lord Provost of Glasgow from Irish Catholic roots. He was knighted for campaigning against fascism in the war and, after retiring from the council in 1946, he became the chair of East Kilbride Development Corporation, where his name adorns several public buildings. He died in 1963.

JOHN MACLEAN

At the fore in the early years of the Red Clydeside movement was John Maclean. Born in Pollokshaws, Glasgow, in 1879 he attended Glasgow University and graduated with a Master of Arts. He became a teacher, but was sacked for his anti-war activities. He was appointed Bolshevik Consul in Scotland in January 1918 after the October Revolution and, in the April of that year, he was sentenced to five years in prison for sedition. His speech from the dock in his own defence entered socialist folklore in Scotland. After being force-fed during a hunger strike, he was released following an amnesty coinciding with the armistice. On his return to Glasgow from Peterhead prison, he received a tumultuous reception. He never really settled in any political party. He stood as the Labour candidate for the Gorbals in Glasgow in 1918 but was defeated and left shortly afterwards. Following disputes with the CPGB, he sought to establish a Scottish Communist Party and stood in the 1922 election in the Gorbals as an Independent Communist. He eventually formed the Scottish Workers Republican Party in an attempt to marry communism and Scottish independence. However, he died prematurely in 1923 from pneumonia was brought about by his political activism and compounded by the forced feeding during his hunger strike. His name is recalled in several well-known Scottish socialist folk songs that Jimmy and others would gustily sing in later years.

MARY BARBOUR

Mary Barbour and other working-class women came in to their own politically when the men went to war. Barbour was born in 1875 in the nearby Renfrewshire town of Kilbarchan. Her father was a carpet weaver and, leaving school at fourteen, she also entered the mills. In 1896 she married David Barbour, an engineer, and they moved to Govan. Her political activism started there in the Co-operative Guild. However, it was her involvement in housing matters that brought her to the fore in Red Clydeside. She was an activist in the South Govan Women's Housing Association and was active in the rent strike that broke out during the war. In 1920, she was elected as a Labour councillor for the Fairfield Ward on Glasgow City Council and remained on it until 1931, becoming Glasgow's first woman baillie (civic officer).

The radical calls in the workplace, community and Parliament were not simply for social and economic rights but also for

Scottish Home Rule. Individuals such as Mclean had called for it, and parties such as the ILP stood for it. A Scotland Day event on Glasgow Green, organised by the Scottish Home Rule Association in 1923, attracted a crowd of 35,000 campaigners. The resolution from a variety of parties represented on the platform was 'to work steadily for national self-government until the Scottish people regain full control over their own affairs'.

The Home Rule being sought was substantial and significantly greater than the devolution gained in 1999 and since added to with further powers. It has to be seen in the context of the time when the British Empire was still in existence and the European Union had not been established nor British withdrawal from it countenanced. It was also a time before globalisation and when international affairs conducted outside of the Empire were of much less importance in many ways, than discussions within it.

Those campaigning for Home Rule weren't seeking the revolutionary path pursued in Ireland with the Easter Rising. They were pursuing the democratic path chosen by Charles Stewart Parnell and John Redmond that had sought similar type status for Ireland through peaceful measures. The dominion status afforded to the Irish Free State after the treaty in 1922 afforded an option though other models were available. However, it was most certainly envisaged by the more radical Maxton and the more restrained Johnston that it would be full control over the economy and social affairs albeit remaining within the Empire.

Though Scottish Home Rule had been discussed in Parliament back in the 1890s at the time of Gladstone's push for Irish Home Rule, the Red Clydesiders were to push for it with new zeal. In 1924, during the period of the first Labour minority government,

George Buchanan introduced a Scottish Home Rule Bill. He indicated that his efforts were the twentieth such attempt over numerous years. His proposals were relatively modest, envisaging a Parliament with 148 members from seventy-four constituencies. It would have control over pensions and employment as well as the power to vary imperial taxes. Though institutions such as Customs and Excuse and the Post Office would remain British organisations, part of the taxes raised would be returned for the Scottish Parliament to do with as it liked. A joint board between Scotland and London would officiate on any areas of dispute with a final appeal to the Judicial Committee of the Privy Council. What would happen to Scottish representation at Westminster was never fully outlined, though Buchanan stated that Scottish MPs wouldn't vote on English-only matters. Some like Johnston envisaged it continuing but, as the Empire faded, as they predicted it would, ultimately reducing.

Though the Labour Secretary of State William Adamson accepted that it was wanted by the overwhelming majority of the Scottish people, it ran out of procedural time in the Westminster Parliament and fell. Despite pledging to support it, Ramsay MacDonald hadn't attended to show support, though Johnston had seconded it. MacDonald's absence had diminished its importance, and Kirkwood in particular was loud in his denunciations of the outcome. The issue caused rancour within Parliament as well as beyond it and nationalists became bitter and resentful of the failure of the Labour government.

But try again they did. In 1927, the Rev. James Barr, the ILP MP for Motherwell, introduced another bill – the twenty-first such effort. Barr was a minister of the United Free Church of Scotland in

1924. His bill was more radical than Buchanan's, as it put forward that all taxes raised in Scotland would fall to the Scottish Treasury. Moreover, the memorandum to his bill envisaged the withdrawal of all Scottish MPs from the Imperial Parliament. The military and the Foreign Office were designated joint services and to be shared between the two Parliaments. The king would be represented by a Lord High Commissioner as with Canada's Governor General. A joint council would be established between the two countries to decide on any issues of dispute. Barr was supported by his colleagues and not just Buchanan, Johnston and Maxton but by Adamson and Wheatley who had been Labour ministers on the last occasion. However, the bill still fell. The majority of Westminster MPs showed little interest in returning powers to Scotland.

The cause remained notionally supported by Labour and more keenly by the ILP. However, the flame began to dim in the corridors of Westminster and in the main left-wing political parties. It was kept alight in the community, however, through campaigning and cultural activities. Political nationalism, though, was a fringe force and would remain so for many years to come. With the demise of the ILP and Labour focusing on other issues, the Home Rule agenda lessened – though it never went away. Jimmy would have a prominent role in ensuring that the Communist Party was fully committed to self-government when he became Scottish Secretary in the 1960s and political nationalism was on the rise once again.

Those tumultuous times and the individuals within and beyond Parliament were recalled with pride within communities that were still radical. These characters would become well-known to Jimmy and he even got to know some of them personally as his political activism developed.

It's no wonder that, given the impact these Red Clydesiders had on his formative years along with his work in the shipyards that Jimmy's autobiography was entitled *Reflections of a Clyde-built Man*. Now it's time to look more closely at who Jimmy was, what he was like and why he followed the path that he did.

CHAPTER TWO

EARLY DAYS IN GOVAN

Govan, a working-class community on the banks of the River Clyde, is where Jimmy grew up and his political views were forged. It has a long history: it formally became a Burgh in 1864 but a community had existed there for centuries before. It takes pride in its own identity, distinct from the City of Glasgow, of which it now forms part. In the early days of industrialisation, textile mills and coal mines sprang up. However, it was shipbuilding that was going to have its greatest impact on the community. Yards grew and developed along the banks of the river and cranes began to loom large overhead. Napier became Beardmores, which was then sold to Harland & Wolf; Elders and Pierces subsequently became Fairfield's; and Stephens at Linthouse and many more. The community made ships and shipbuilding made the community.

In 1864, Govan had a population of just 9,000 but by the turn of the century it had increased tenfold, becoming the seventh largest town in Scotland. In 1912 it became part of Glasgow, but its distinct identity lives on and remains to this day. Jimmy, like others, was to remain a proud Govanite.

The population continued to grow as people flocked to Govan for work. Both Protestants and Catholics came from Northern

Ireland in the 1850s to work in the yards, starting when the Great Famine afflicted Ireland and continuing on thereafter. Other immigrants came seeking work from south of the border and from Eastern Europe, fleeing pogroms or poverty. Even more arrived from elsewhere in Scotland. The 1911 census showed in Scotland that 78 per cent were born in Scotland and 11 per cent were Irish, 7 per cent Russian or Polish and 4 per cent English, with a scattering of others from elsewhere.

They crowded into the tenements that had sprung up around the yards. Tens of thousands lived in these crammed conditions with sometimes as many as sixteen or eighteen people in one small apartment. It was a very poor community with a great deal of slum housing. Jimmy's early years were to be no different to those of so many of his contemporaries. His earliest recollections were of a two-room and kitchen flat with an inside toilet. Crowded for a growing family but superior, he recalled, to the single ends with outside toilets that many families occupied.

Jimmy was born on 9 July 1932 to Leo and Bella Reid. Jimmy was the youngest of seven children but three died in infancy, leaving two brothers and two sisters. The three who died had chronic chest infections – no doubt brought about by the poor housing conditions. Jimmy could recall seeing his mother weep over the death of an elder sister, and that sadness remained with his mother for the rest of her life. Another had died on Hogmanay and the festivities were a constant reminder of a life loved and lost, with the family always having to make sure that Leo and Bella were never left alone that night of the year.

Leo didn't have a trade and depended on picking up casual work often as a docker or a bookies runner. Income would vary from day to day. Although he cared deeply for his family and he was generous and open-handed when he had money, he was a heavy drinker and a gambler. A family tale recounts Bella fretting about what could be put on the Christmas table when a commotion was heard outside. Leo had won handsomely at the bookies and had bought food at the butchers, not just for his family but for the entire stair, and bedlam ensued. He claimed to have invented the pools, but had apparently been unable to commercialise them due to a lack of savings and funds. The family were sceptical, but humoured him all the same. Though a dubious claim to fame, it was indicative of a very bright and rather gallus* Glaswegian who, while limited by his lack of education, aspired for the best for his children. He was keen for them to succeed in life and always encouraged them to achieve their full potential. Leo died in the early 1960s.

His mother, Isabella Mclean, known to all as Bella, had her family roots in the Isle of Mull before they moved to Govan. She had a very hard upbringing, as her parents died when she was young and she was required to look after her five younger siblings. These poor orphans had to endure a spell in the workhouse. Fortunately, Bella moved to Glasgow later on and became a tram car conductress. When she married Leo, she needed to manage the family budget on the very limited income she and Leo could obtain. Hunger was not unknown, and Jimmy spoke in later years of seeing his mother eating just a piece of bread after she'd fed the family with what little she had. She was a gentle and quiet soul who, despite her rudimentary schooling, made up for

---

* A Scots word that means 'bold' or 'cheeky'.

her lack of education with love for her children. Bella lived well into her eighties, although she suffered from bouts of depression throughout her life – which is understandable, given what she had endured during her life.

From his father, Jimmy inherited quickness of mind and that Glasgow gallusness which enabled him to speak and perform as he did. He also took from him an open-handedness and generosity of spirit that was also to be a mark of him. Like his father, he became fond of a flutter, a dram and a song. Leo was eager that his children should be able to play instruments and read music, despite the financial challenges that faced the family. As such, Jimmy played the trumpet in a brass band and his brother the saxophone. Leo also took Jimmy to the races from an early age. It was an outing that young Jimmy loved and he enjoyed a bet and the races throughout his life. Like Leo, Jimmy was good company and could be the life and soul of a party.

Bella gave Jimmy the ability to love his children deeply and openly. Showing affection was something that not all Scotsmen of his generation did, but Jimmy was a very loving father. He sometimes even showed it in public when he had a high public profile, which, though it may have been embarrassing for his children, it never was for him. Whether cavorting in busy Sauchiehall Street or pretending to be in the RAF band and leading grandchildren around the house like the Pied Piper, he was always relaxed and comfortable with his family and doted on them throughout his life.

Despite the trenchant views he held and the robustness of debates he could participate in, Jimmy always had time for ordinary people. He never showed any malice or condescension to anyone, no matter how trivial the question or point may have been. He invariably listened and answered politely. That generosity of spirit was, perhaps, something that he took from his mother. Unfortunately, however, he also inherited his mother's propensity for melancholia and depression. While his condition was undiagnosed as many were at the time, Jimmy would simply go quiet and introverted for a while and could take to his bed for days on occasions. However, it never stopped him from working and columns would still be filed. Even if privately tormented or doubtful, he never failed to deliver messages in an upbeat and charismatic way.

The early years for Jimmy were spent on Whitefield Road in Ibrox, just a stone's throw from Rangers' stadium. He lived in one of the 'Wheatley' houses, so called because they had been built following the legislation brought in by the Red Clydesider John Wheatley in the 1920s. His parents had moved there from the even more crowded and deprived Gorbals when the slum clearances began. Jimmy sometimes wondered whether, if they had moved there earlier, his siblings who died may have survived. It was a two-room and kitchen flat with an inside toilet: far from salubrious, but by no means in the worst area. Many other houses had outside toilets and catered for far larger families. So, in many ways, they considered themselves fortunate.

The family then moved to Kintra Street in Govan, where Jimmy shared a room with his older brother John. Infant mortality in the UK was amongst the highest in Europe and diphtheria, tuberculosis and rickets abounded. These diseases fortunately didn't affect Jimmy or his surviving brother and sisters, although the memory of his sister's death along with other neighbours' children who died remained with him throughout his life. The poverty was grinding for both his families and most others in the community and these tragedies served as a constant reminder of the human consequences of deprivation.

Govan was viewed as a tough area and there were some hard men around. Jimmy, however, always felt that the image portrayed by the book *No Mean City* was false. He walked to the Gorbals for his band practice and felt the violent image of that area was vastly exaggerated. The violence was more between gangs rather than against ordinary people and he never felt threatened or intimidated by it.

While Jimmy's parents were Catholic and he was to attend the local Catholic primary school, St Saviours, and St Gerrard's Secondary school, religion played little part in the family's life. There was inter marriage between Protestants and Catholics within it and prejudice was abhorred. His father had no great interest in religion and the death of his third child brought any limited church attendance to a halt. Bella, however, did take the children to church in their early years but wasn't particularly active in her faith. While Jimmy protests against ever having been a choir-boy, as his family joked, he was to remain respectful of religious faith throughout his life and was an admirer of the moral code of Christianity.

Religious sectarianism existed in the community, but the Reids, as with many others, despised it. It was more extensive back then than it is now, with there being both fewer laws against it and greater acceptance of it. Openly sectarian and neo-fascist political organisations, such as John Cormack's Protestant Action, had sprung up in Edinburgh that were openly sectarian and neo-fascist. The Churches themselves were much less ecumenical than now and doctrine and hostility between the faiths more common. Discrimination existed in some of the labour market, and Orange and Hibernian Walks took place in Govan as elsewhere in Scotland.

Moreover, though the religious divide in football existed then as now between Celtic and Rangers, it was less pronounced in many ways. Football strips and colours were not worn and travelling to away games was unusual, since so many men worked in the morning. Often people would simply go to the local team – and, for Jimmy Reid, though notionally a Celtic supporter, Ibrox was the nearest ground. He later regaled the family with tales of having busked by tap dancing outside the stadium as a boy. Rangers were his local team and some friends and relatives supported them. Jimmy even went to some old firm games with family members of both faiths. The fixture in his young days could see friends socialise after the match, especially following the traditional New Year's Day fixture. However, the tribal divide still existed and could be raw. He grew to dislike the matches between the clubs intently in his later years as the bitterness continued.

It was at school that Jimmy's strong political convictions began to emerge. Leo was a committed socialist and he often spoke to his son about politics and socialism. Jimmy recalled his father almost crying with joy when the Labour government was elected in 1945. He and Bella, though not members of a political party, were supporters of the ILP, which dominated in the area. Memories were long in the family as in the community of the likes of John MacLean and Mary Barbour. The ILP and later Labour MP Neil McLean lived nearby. Leo later joined the Communist Party for which, by that time, his son was working.

The political seeds sown were further nurtured by Jimmy's extensive reading. He started reading before he even went to school and thereafter became a voracious devourer of books. Though he was a quiet boy, he had a wide circle of friends. Like most children, he spent a lot of time playing football and other games in the streets and the back yards. However, it was reading that he really loved and took to with a passion that was to become lifelong. There weren't many books in the home as they were expensive, so Govan Library became a regular haunt. Stories abound amongst locals of a small boy who used to traipse home with a pile of books under his arm. He'd head to his bedroom to the concern of his mother who was barely literate and worried about his devotion to it. Anything and everything could capture Jimmy's attention and he had a genuine thirst for knowledge. He loved Stevenson, Scott and Dickens and by the age of fourteen he had read Marx's *A Contribution to a Critique of Political Economy*. George Bernard Shaw also influenced him greatly.

Despite being very bright and able and sailing through his eleven plus exams, Jimmy left school at fourteen years old. The rote learning required for Latin, French and Greek, however, was a huge turn off for him and a suggestion by one teacher about going to university wasn't even considered. As far as Jimmy was concerned, university was for others, not for working class lads from Govan like him. The world of work awaited him, as it did for the rest of the community. Despite these perceived limitations, he still felt that the school had failed him. That was doubtless a big driver behind the ongoing self-education that he was to maintain throughout his life.

On leaving school, that desire to learn and thirst for knowledge was further unleashed. From his first pay packet, he bought a copy of Tom Johnston's *The History of the Working Classes in Scotland*, which had a huge effect upon him. It recounted a significantly different history of Scotland and its people than had been taught in school. It both angered and motivated him, driving him to investigate more and further fuelling his political convictions.

His reading raised his awareness of his Scottish heritage as well as inspiring his socialism. Lewis Grassic Gibbon's *Scots Quair* and James Barke's *Land of the Leal* were later recalled by him as influential books. Delving into Rabbie Burns led him on to Robert Fergusson and modern Scottish poets such as Hugh McDiarmid and Sydney Goodsir Smith. The extent and breadth of Jimmy's reading was huge, ranging from economics to philosophy, history to poetry, literature to politics. Later, when he was working in Glasgow city centre, he enjoyed browsing through second-hand book shops, a pastime he kept up for the rest of his life.

His love of reading and his passion for socialist politics meant it wasn't just books he read assiduously, but also papers and periodicals. He used to read *Forward*, the left-wing periodical at the library and, once he started working and had an income, he ordered the *Daily Worker* and the *Daily Herald* from his local newsagent. His reading led him to start participating. When working up town, he attended the Workers Open Forum, a group mainly made up of older men who discussed politics and philosophy. Jimmy didn't really contribute, but soaked up what was said or argued over. He was already reading Marx by then and was interested in the likes of Adam Smith and Jean-Paul Sartre. In Jimmy's early teens, he would note down names of philosophers that he'd never heard of and read up on them later. Jimmy was trying to stretch himself intellectually as well as challenge himself philosophically. It was another occupation he continued throughout his life.

It's no great surprise, then, that he joined the Labour League of Youth, which gave him an introduction to socialist philosophy as well as to political debating. Jimmy became involved with the youth parliament based at the Iona Community that had been established in Govan by George MacLeod (later to become Lord MacLeod of Fuinary). Jimmy was a precocious member, becoming Chancellor of the Exchequer on the Labour benches at just fifteen and putting forward a radical budget. One of Jimmy's youth parliament peers, Gregor McKenzie, went on to become the Labour MP for Rutherglen between 1964 and 1987 and also served as a minister in the Scottish Office.

However, not long after joining, Jimmy soon left the Labour League of Youth. Attlee's Labour government was moving too far to the right on both economic and foreign policies for his liking. Moreover, Jimmy tired of the careerism of many members who he thought simply aspired to be councillors and then acquire safe parliamentary seats. He felt they were pursuing their own ambitions and ignoring the plight of the poor or the greater needs of humanity. Unlike them, Jimmy believed that politics was both a mission and a dedication.

Alongside these intellectual and political endeavours pursued in his free time, it was out into the world of work for Jimmy when he left school at fourteen. His first job was as a grocer's delivery boy for Galbraith's. What most surprised him about it was that they provided him with a bike – he hadn't ridden before, as there hadn't been the money for one. However, the job only lasted four weeks. Since it required working on a Saturday, which interfered with his love of watching football, and it neither stretched his mind nor sated ambitions, alternative employment was sought.

His next job was at a stockbroker, right at the heart of the capitalist system. It was the Labour Exchange in Govan that had sent him there. The firm, Kilpatrick and Robertson, was located in the city centre, and Jimmy's duties involved recording the share sales from the previous day's trading and then making his way round to the other brokers' offices to have them initial the records collated by him before entering them into a ledger.

Jimmy's spark and intellect meant that he thrived in the office. Most doing similar type jobs were considerably older and sometimes grown men, but by the age of fifteen, Jimmy was responsible for the monthly reconciliations for those transactions. David Robertson, the owner of the company, was a prominent Conservative who took a shine to his young office boy, notwithstanding Jimmy bringing his left-wing papers and journals to the office. The old stockbroker even laughed when his young prodigy had light-heartedly challenged the lecturer at a course about the Stock Exchange. Told that the stockbroking jobs would last as long as the current capitalist system, the would-be firebrand retorted that they deserved better job security than that. The older man indulged the young radical and even paid him a significant bonus if he found errors before him, as they tallied the books together.

When Jimmy turned sixteen and said that he wanted to leave and take an apprenticeship in industry, his old employer sought to persuade him to stay. He extolled the benefits of staying in stock broking and said that by eighteen he could have his own clients, and by twenty-one even a junior partnership. He was even advised that his ardent socialism wasn't an obstacle, even if no socialists were known to be working in the business. But, as Jimmy himself said, he had no intention of becoming the first! He genuinely liked the old stockbroker and, although they disagreed on politics, he respected his integrity, as well as no doubt appreciating his indulgent attitude towards him.

So, it was off for an apprenticeship at the age of sixteen for Jimmy, as so many of his school friends would also do. It wasn't in the shipyards, but an apprenticeship in the tool room at an engineering firm. Scottish Precision Castings was located in Hillington in the west of the city. By then, the Reids had moved to Priesthill, a new housing scheme that had recently been built in the south-west of the city, near to Govan. It drew many families from that area as it was accessible for work and socialising in Govan, and the homes were an improvement on the tenements that many families had previously lived in.

Scottish Precision Castings was a small company but it was highly unionised, and on Jimmy's first day he joined the AEU. As was the case across many engineering factories in the west of Scotland, the senior shop steward and others were all Communist Party members. They made a considerable impression on Jimmy. Thoughtful and considerate, they helped guide his thinking whether in critiques of the Labour government or wider views on politics and society. They also listened to him and encouraged him in this thinking.

Through them, he joined the Junior Workers Committee of the AEU that met in Paisley, which later led to him being invited to attend the Govan Young Communist League. The Iron Curtain, as Winston Churchill coined it, had descended and the Cold War was beginning. However, memories of the Soviet sacrifice in the Second World War were still fresh. Jimmy, like many, was deeply marked by the loss of over 20 million Soviet lives during the conflict. He recalled cheering along with others at Pathé news clips shown in the cinema of the Red Army confronting the Nazis. Not just the communists, but the British government and much of British society had praised the Soviet sacrifice and lauded Uncle Joe, as Stalin was the affectionately known.

Moreover, Jimmy was enraged by the poverty he saw around him and had a strong belief in the better world that had been fought for. While there were concerns about Soviet activity in Eastern Europe, likewise there had been the British crushing of the Greek communists. Decolonialisation was coming to the fore with the British and French Empires facing demands for independence; and the nuclear arms race was about to commence. The Soviet Union was considered vital to social and economic progress, despite qualms about its actions both at home and abroad. It was a bulwark against the unbridled power of the West and offered the hope of a socialist society.

It was the message of communism rather than the ethos in the Soviet Union that appealed to Jimmy. Jimmy was more inspired by what communism could offer in a future society, as opposed to what was offered in the Soviet Union. In terms of this distinction, Jimmy was no different to many on the left. The likes of George Bernard Shaw and Sidney and Beatrice Webb, whose writings Jimmy had read, had visited Russia and met Stalin. They were impressed and sympathetic to the cause.

Jimmy was committed to the socialist cause. His reading of Marx at an early age had provided him with a prism through which to see and interpret the world and he accepted the Marxist analysis of the economy. Jimmy was also partial to the visions of society offered by Plato and Milton. Under that wide philosophical view Jimmy sought to change the world in which he lived. That would be achieved through the working class and socialist movement, of which the Communist Party was its vanguard.

The cyclical economic problems befalling the British economy and the Western world justified Jimmy's belief in the communist cause. The economic depression amid which Jimmy had been born was part of a pattern created by the system which had been and would be repeated unless something drastically changed. He believed that capitalism put profit before people. The way in which the rights and needs of individuals could be jettisoned and ignored repelled him. There had to be a better way, and Jimmy believed that communism offered a way forward. Jimmy was always clear that it was the social and economic conditions in Scotland that made him a communist rather than events in the Soviet Union. The memories of the hungry thirties ran deep, and Jimmy intended never to allow such poverty to afflict the communities ever again. The misfortune Jimmy had witnessed within his own family and on the surrounding streets was burned deep in his soul.

Additionally, Jimmy was greatly impressed by the integrity and humanity of the communists he met. They were well-read and had wide-ranging interests, which must have appealed to a young mind eager to learn. It was a time in which many felt that they had to be as educated as the employers they sought to confront. Self-education and self-improvement was a hallmark of the cause, and the passion and commitment of these fellow communists encouraged Jimmy's insatiable thirst for knowledge. They also rejected the careerism that Jimmy saw in the Labour Party and were far removed from those on the left who championed the working class but were also contemptuous of them or avoided their company. Jimmy genuinely enjoyed the company of ordinary working people. The communists, therefore, seemed to Jimmy to have much more in common with his own roots, and appeared to strive to achieve the society he sought.

In many ways, Jimmy was a deeply moral man who sought to live as he preached. He remained a man of great integrity even when moving political parties. Later in life, he would be incandescent when Bill Clinton flew to Arkansas during his presidential campaign to oversee the execution of a murderer who was mentally impaired simply to protect his own political ambitions. Clinton's actions disgusted Jimmy in terms of both the sanctioning of the death penalty and pursuing publicity for being tough on crime. Jimmy's willingness to speak out caused him problems throughout his lifetime; however, when he felt strongly about something, he often felt unable to remain quiet.

It was natural, therefore, that Jimmy saw many kindred spirits in the Communist Party. They put the cause above themselves, had wide ranging interests and a deep desire for a better world. And so he joined the YCL at the age of sixteen and it wouldn't be long until he became secretary of the branch.

Meanwhile, Scottish Precision Castings went into liquidation and Jimmy had to transfer his apprenticeship to Weirs, a large engineering firm on the south side of Glasgow. However, he was sacked by a foreman, which Jimmy believed was down to his politics and personal dislike by a man who had acted as a mini tyrant. What Jimmy had been accused of was a relatively minor indiscretion done by many others and apprentices were rarely dismissed for anything aside from gross misconduct.

The communist stewards and the wider party rallied to his support and Jimmy obtained a third employer for his apprenticeship at Daniel Varney's. That was a happier place to work and he enjoyed his time there until the company decided to close the factory and relocate to Wishaw in Lanarkshire. The apprentices were offered the choice of moving to the new place of work or transferring their apprenticeship to British Polar Engines in Govan. It was a simple choice for Jimmy. British Polar Engines was on his doorstep. After making the move, the memories of how he and his colleagues had been treated and made to feel dispensable stayed with him and helped strengthen his commitment to fighting for workers' rights.

Finally, at his sixth place of employment, Jimmy entered the shipyards. It was a marine engineering firm, though from time to time he and colleagues would go to a ship for installation or repairs. He again joined the AEU and was active in setting up an apprentices' committee. It was here that Jimmy was going to have his first involvement in an industrial dispute and which would further raise his profile both within the party and the Union.

There had been several apprentices' disputes over past decades and a major strike in 1937, which had seen over 12,000 apprentices on Clydeside involved for over a month and resulted in apprentices obtaining recognition and union rights. Wages for apprentices everywhere were miserable. It was seen as almost a rite of passage to be endured on the way to becoming a time-served tradesman. It was a form of exploitation of young people that was sadly accepted for far too long, despite the same young men being sent to fight in conflict zones such as Korea and Malaya as part of their national service. In 1952, Jimmy participated in another strike that was to bring him to the fore of championing workers' rights.

The previous year had seen a very modest pay increase awarded to engineering apprentices. This incensed the young workers who were feeling the economic pinch as the post-war economy struggled. As anger mounted, a Young Engineers Clydeside Conference was called for late January 1952. The Glasgow event was attended by 114 apprentices from thirty-one firms and Jimmy became the conference secretary. That meeting led to demands for strike action with supporting demonstrations across the country, as far away as Aberdeen, Manchester, Sheffield and London.

On 2 March 1952, an all-UK delegate conference in Glasgow voted overwhelmingly for a strike the following week if their demands for an increase in wages weren't met. The shipbuilding and engineering employers refused to settle and the strike proceeded. Monday 10 March saw 5,000 Clydeside apprentices walk out. In the coming weeks, they were joined by over 20,000 apprentices striking in England, Northern Ireland and elsewhere in Scotland. Unions sympathised but there was no strike action in support of the apprentices.

During the strike, several demonstrations were held in Glasgow that saw up to 5,000 young apprentices march through the city. At one, near the end of the dispute there were conflicts with the police as the march sought to take a route that hadn't been approved. Confronted by lines of police, Jimmy and other leaders tried to turn the demonstration around. However, with crowds of boisterous young men still pouring down the road behind them, it descended into a general melee. As Jimmy tried to resolve matters and extricate himself, he and a few others were arrested by the police. He was bailed by colleagues, though was subsequently fined £1 for his troubles at a court hearing a few weeks later.

He humorously recalled that an officer processing him at the police station had called him a communist when he emptied his pockets and left wing leaflets and literature poured out. When another young man being processed with Jimmy identified himself as Karl Marx McCulloch, the officer thought he was mocking his authority. It took some time for the young man to persuade the policeman that it was his real name and that he had revolutionary parents who had called him that. At the time, however, Jimmy was more worried about what his mother would say. As it turned out, he had no need to be, as she was incandescent that her son had been arrested when, in her view, hooligans walked the streets.

The dispute also saw Jimmy enter battles with the union leadership as well as with the employers. During the dispute, he was a delegate to the Youth Conference of the AEU in Eastbourne. Back then, both youth conferences and the Union Movement as a whole were larger and more powerful than now. The attendance was substantial and it allowed Jimmy and other members to lobby and seek support for their actions. The chairman of the conference was Jack Tanner, who had been president of the AEU since 1939 and was a leading right-wing union figure, virulent in his anti-communism. Jimmy was to cross swords with him several times: a brave, though some might say foolhardy, thing to do given his age and the status of his opponent. But, then as ever, when believing he was right, Jimmy gave no quarter.

Jimmy had sought an emergency resolution to support the apprentices' actions, but it had been ruled out of order by Tanner. Seeking guidance on what would constitute an appropriate format, he'd been publicly slapped down by the old union baron. Not intimidated by the public reprimand, however, Jimmy returned with an appropriately worded resolution and gave an impassioned address to the delegates. That further angered the already irritated chair who openly attacked him. Undaunted, Jimmy got back up and berated Tanner for his inaction to date and failure to support the apprentices. The motion was carried overwhelmingly and bedlam ensued. The spat between the union boss and the young apprentice made press headlines the following day. The enmity between the two was reinforced when, at a delegate's dinner, Jimmy's talents were commented on by Tanner but allusions were made to keeping the right company for a future political or union career. The radical young delegate questioned what he was implying and a deathly silence descended for the rest of the meal. Jimmy, then as ever, was not to be intimidated or bought off.

After more than three weeks on strike, it was decided the apprentices would return to work to aid the ongoing negotiations. An increased payment was promised and, although it was not as much as most would have liked, it was still noticeable that a distinct award had been made for apprentices rather than simply tacking it on at the end of the settlements for other workers as was usually the case. It was a victory of sorts, but the mood remained militant.

It had given Jimmy and others their first taste of industrial action. Many gained their first campaign experiences in that strike and would go on to become senior union officials or politicians. Alex Ferry, who was to become General Secretary of the Confederation of Shipbuilding and Engineering Unions between 1978 and 1994, had been a leading activist. Another, Gavin Laird, was a man Jimmy was to contest unsuccessfully in later years, as union battles between Labour and Communists waged. Gavin went on to become General Secretary of the Amalgamated Engineering and Electrical Union (AEEU), as the AEU became, between 1982 and 1994. Yet another was Dick Douglas, who was later to become a Labour MP before joining the SNP at the height of the anti-poll-tax campaign in the early 1990s.

It was also to be a launch-pad for Jimmy's rise in the Communist Party. That year, 1952, he was elected National Chairman of the Young Communist League in Britain. He was to be a member of the Communist Party for twenty-eight years and a full-time official for eleven of them.

But, it wasn't all political and union activism for young Jimmy. There was still fun to be had with both his comrades and friends from school or work. Reading remained a favourite pastime but Jimmy also enjoyed other pursuits. Football remained a firm favourite, as his quick move from his first job as an errand boy at Galbraith's had shown. He often went to games and was a huge admirer of Hibernian's Famous Five of forwards: Gordon Smith, Bobby Johnstone, Lawrie Reilly, Eddie Turnbull and Willie Ormond. Though he'd been no great player himself, he became very knowledgeable about the game, as Sir Alex Ferguson recognised in later years.

Music remained another passion that Leo had nurtured and encouraged with the purchase of a trumpet in his teenage years.

Jimmy had played in a brass band and continued to do so during national service. He developed a love of jazz and he was a huge fan of Louis Armstrong and enjoyed the bebop genre of Charlie Parker and Dizzy Gillespie.

Jimmy regularly attended recitals given by the Scottish National Orchestra and often went to see plays performed at the Citizens Theatre. Jimmy was greatly disdainful of the notion that theatre and classical music were reserved for the elite members of society. He was as comfortable there as he was going to the pub, and he never lost that ability to be at ease in any company. He was though a creature of his time. When going out he'd invariably wear a shirt and tie, a habit he continued throughout his life.

Though he enjoyed a dram and a drink with his pals, there was never any hooliganism. It was part of his socialising and conviviality. Unlike his father, he never had a drink problem. A night with good company, song and political discussion was his way of relaxing. While Jimmy and his peers were anti-establishment and prepared to confront laws that they saw as unjust, they wouldn't countenance mindless disorder. Like many Scots he enjoyed a drinking session from time to time. A night with good company, song and political discussion was his way of relaxing as much as enjoyment; and it could often continue for quite some time. He did, however, start smoking and puffing through sixty to eighty cigarettes a day until an incident in 1975, which saw him spitting up blood. With an iron will he managed to quit, although he took up smoking cigars later in life – much to the chagrin of his family.

Between football and smoking cigars, Jimmy inhabited a very male-dominated society. Feminism was much more limited in its political impact back then, so it was only in later years that he refused to attend male only events at Burns clubs and so on. Prior to that, overwhelming male presence had simply been the norm and Jimmy, like others, had left it unchallenged. In that, he was simply a creature of his time.

Aside from socialising, there was still national service to be done. Young communist or not, it still applied. In 1953, Jimmy completed his apprenticeship and was called into Her Majesty's Forces. There, he was to be as rebellious as he had been in the factory. In October of that year, he reported to the Royal Air Force at Cardington Camp, near Bedford. He just about missed the deadline, having watched the England vs Hungary football match being shown on television with a local publican.

The initial days of national service involved a lot of 'square bashing', which must have been mind-numbingly boring along with intensive drills. Most moved on after three days of it, but Jimmy found himself there for six weeks. Knowledge of his Communist membership was known and a file on him had preceded his arrival. The RAF was unsure what to do with him. Though the idea of him being a Soviet spy seems fanciful, it has to be seen against the context of the time. The Cold War was underway and the Soviet threat was viewed as real. Communist spies were sought everywhere. Interestingly, the Soviet spies that were to surface over later years were not from poor backgrounds or industrial areas. Guy Burgess, Kim Philby and Donald MacLean along with Sir Anthony Blunt were from privileged and very establishment backgrounds. The Reds they were seeking were not in the unions or the Communist Party but in the very heart of the establishment and even British Intelligence.

However, as a consequence of the fears surrounding communism, Jimmy became the camp dogsbody. He even had to clean the toilets and do all sorts of menial tasks during the week when they were confined to barracks. When he was transferred to Bridgnorth he seemed destined for more square bashing and mundanity, but, fortunately, a corporal asked who could play music. Having played the trumpet, Jimmy volunteered and joined the regimental band. It suited both Jimmy and the Royal Air Force. It meant that he could enjoy the music with some extremely talented band members. Meanwhile, it meant that the RAF could keep their resident communist well away from military secrets or any other harm they thought he could do.

The RAF still had to endure Jimmy's politicking, albeit in a limited fashion. Current affairs lectures were held regularly for national servicemen, although they were right-wing political doctrine as far as Jimmy was concerned. They weren't meant to be questioned or challenged, but they hadn't reckoned on a young communist from Scotland being in the audience. Coincidentally, the first lecture Jimmy attended was on communism. An officer delivered what was both a factually inaccurate and excruciatingly boring talk on the dangers of the philosophy. He then asked if there were any questions. The officer was no doubt surprised when Jimmy asked about the basis of his claims. Jimmy then followed up with extensive quotes on the philosophical differences between Lenin and Trotsky, as well as other clarifications on the theory behind communism. This seemingly encouraged others to join in and the somewhat shell-shocked officer hastily brought the lecture to an end. From then on, Jimmy was to provide his own socialist lectures to fellow recruits that provided both an alternative to and a critique of the officer's propaganda.

Thereafter, Jimmy moved to a camp in Wales where the excruciating minutiae of military life continued. His quick thinking and way with words, however, were to come to his rescue. Pulled up by an officer for the stripes on his pyjama top not being directly in line with those on his pyjama bottoms, he had initially replied flippantly. He only avoided being placed on a charge by pointing out with a poker face the necessity in a service like the RAF for absolute attention to detail!

At one point, it seemed that Jimmy and his colleagues were destined to embark for Malaya, but at the last moment word came that he was going to Shrewsbury instead. Whether it was too much to send a young communist to a country where Britain was facing communist insurgency isn't known, but moving to Shrewsbury certainly suited Jimmy. There, he effectively became a full-time musician and the rest of his period of national service was spent playing at local community fetes and other enjoyable events. It was a blessed relief from square bashing and toilet cleaning.

Towards the end of Jimmy's national service, there was to be one more issue brought about by his political convictions. A dock strike was ongoing in London at that time and the young conscripts were to be sent to unload boats tied up by the strike. Concerned about being guilty of strikebreaking, Jimmy explained his concerns to the commanding officer. His colleagues feared he'd be taken away by the Military Police as Jimmy explained his concerns about being used for strikebreaking, adding that had he known about being used for strikebreaking when he agreed to do his national service, he would have been a conscientious objector. The senior officer responded that they weren't going to allow 'those bastards' to dictate to us. Jimmy asked who were the bastards they were referring to and his commanding officer confirmed that the bastards were the dockers and by 'us', they meant the nation. Jimmy took issue with that in a calm and analytical way which resulted in him and the commanding officer having a wide-ranging political discussion. It was clear that there was a file on Jimmy but that the commanding officer and others respected his courage and being prepared to speak out. They appreciated that it was a matter of conscience for him and he was excused from the London duties and he whiled away his remaining service playing the trumpet – despite most of his colleagues expecting him to be marched summarily to the guardhouse.

There was still time, however, for one last push at the parameters of military discipline. Two Young Communist friends were getting engaged and wanted Jimmy to come to their celebration party. Passes for conscripts were limited and restricted to forty-eight hours. Jimmy arranged for his friends to send a formal invite for him to take to the squadron leader and request leave. Jimmy had just given one of his alternative political lectures and, whether out of grudging respect or simply a desire to get him off the base, his leave was granted. Moreover, recognising that time was short to make it back up north for the function, a phone call was made by his commander to request a plane. Flying time needed to be put in by the pilots in the new Vampire planes that the RAF had acquired, so the squadron leader requested that they take Jimmy up to Scotland. Dressed in civilian clothes he was told that he had to be in uniform to fly, but the pilot kindly flung him a wing commander's flying suit. Upon landing at Edinburgh, the attendant ground crew immediately snapped to attention when they saw the insignia on the flying suit, although they made some acerbic comments about the youth of the apparent senior officer. Jimmy simply returned the salute and headed for the party. It's a story he loved to regale later in life and it demonstrates his mixture of charm and gallusness that had no doubt endeared him to the senior officers, despite his politics.

Though Jimmy's national service was over, his communist beliefs remained. In October 1955, he was discharged and returned to Glasgow and his work at British Polar Engines. By now, he was a time-served engineer, but it was the union work that most interested him. By the end of that year, he had become the convenor of shop stewards. His rise in the union and the party was just beginning.

CHAPTER THREE

JOINING THE
COMMUNIST PARTY

Jimmy joined the Communist Party for several reasons. The commitment and sincerity of the communist stewards he'd met had made a huge impression on him. Many were heirs to a tradition of Scottish working-class intellectualism and that resonated with him. They encouraged him to join the YCL and the wider Communist Party and it was there he found a political home with kindred spirits. He joined in 1948.

Jimmy was already a committed socialist when still at school. Tackling injustice and addressing poverty and inequality were fundamental to him, and would remain lifelong commitments. His social conscience was compounded by his anger at the rightward drift of the Labour government and his concerns about the careerism he perceived in some Labour League of Youth members. Like many, he had been a huge admirer of the early steps taken by Clement Attlee's Labour government, particularly the nationalisation of key industries and the establishment of the NHS. Rail, steel and coal (though not shipbuilding) were all brought into public ownership. But there were pressures within the Labour Party to avoid being too radical or politically controversial, and that worried Jimmy as he was eager to see the socialist policies not just maintained but extended. Progress was already being opposed or stymied by right-wing sections within the Labour Party. In later years, Jimmy would recall a particular case from the early 1950s of a reduction in the size of council homes being built. Rooms were made smaller and roofs lowered. That, along with other policy trimmings, troubled him.

He feared that there were some within the Labour Party who would curtail the progress made and was inspired by the communists who selflessly pushed for further action to be taken. It seemed to him that the Labour Party would shift to the right any time they were put under pressure by those with vested interests in their own agendas. As a result, he saw the Communist Party as the vanguard for socialism within the labour movement.

Jimmy was an idealist, but he was also a product of his time. In Britain, Europe and beyond, the centre of politics had moved to the left. Socialism was arguably the dominant post-war ideology. Not all governments were socialist, of course, but the philosophy was the fulcrum around which politics would pivot for many years, until the right regrouped. Jimmy wished to ensure that the drive for radical socialist policies was maintained and he believed the Communist Party was the vehicle by which to do it.

Both the collectivism brought about by a wartime economy and the sympathy elicited for the Soviet Union in its titanic struggle against fascism had boosted the party. Attlee's radical manifesto saw Labour win a landslide election in 1945 with a majority of 146 over the Tories defeating Winston Churchill, the wartime leader. Labour's re-election in 1950 saw them obtain only a majority of five seats but still outpoll the Conservatives by 1.5 million votes.

Despite its exciting beginnings, Attlee's government began to run out of steam. Internal divisions were starting to show as charges for NHS services required to meet the cost of the Korean War brought about the resignation of the minister for health, Nye Bevan, and a few others.

Attlee felt he needed an early election to try and win a clearer majority and impose some internal party discipline. King George VI, however, wanted to avoid an election when he was on his grand Commonwealth tour scheduled for the following year and so, accordingly, Attlee called an early election. As it transpired, the King never went on the tour due to ill health, and so Princess Elizabeth went instead. As a result, an election was called in 1951. Labour lost, but they still won the popular vote, polling just under 14 million votes: its highest ever recorded total, and a record that stands to this day. However, the 13,948,883 votes (48.78 per cent) brought Labour only 295 seats. The Tories, along with their National Liberal allies, polled 13,717,850 (47.97 per cent) and won 321 seats.

Such was the political shift when Attlee's government was defeated in 1951 that the incoming Tories made few changes to Attlee's social and economic policies. The social consensus forged during wartime remained intact and neither the health service and welfare state nor the nationalisation of coal, steel and mining was rolled back in any significant shape or form by Churchill's new Conservative administration. It was clear that Attlee's defeat owed more to the electorate's desire for an end to austerity, than a repudiation of the Labour government's social and economic policies.

The Tories were re-elected in 1955 and the benefits and changes brought in by the 1945 Labour government were again left unchallenged. The Tories benefitted from an expansion of the global economy recovering from the Second World War and were able to show an improving economy and further lessen the austerity that had been imposed by previous governments.

Moreover, while Labour's leadership was still in the hands of Clement Attlee who was then aged seventy-two, the Tories had a new leader. Under Anthony Eden, the Tories increased their majority, winning 345 seats to Labour's 277 and polling 13,310,891 (49.7 per cent) to Attlee's 12,405,254 (46.4 per cent). Labour wouldn't form a government again until 1964, when Harold Wilson formed a minority administration and brought thirteen years of Tory rule to an end. Even so, in the meantime, the NHS, welfare state and nationalised industries again remained unchallenged.

While still on the fringe of British politics, the Communist Party was neither as far from the centre of political debate nor so devoid of political influence as it would later become. Moreover, the Soviet Union and the communist bloc, together with non-aligned nations and anti-colonial movements, afforded visions and hope for young radicals. It was a time of radical change not just in Britain, but all over the globe. The old orders were being challenged and empires were being fragmented. Independence movements and revolutionary forces were fighting for radical change and social improvement. A better world, it seemed, could be obtained, if struggled for.

Jimmy, however, disliked the ultra-left who he felt were both unrealistic and often unsympathetic to the working class. Moreover, they had little base in trade unionism or in the community where he grew up. It seemed a doctrine for students or more affluent areas, so the choice was Labour or Communist for a young working-class radical like Jimmy. Jimmy had grown up in a socialist household amid the legacy of Red Clydeside. Socialism, however, wasn't dominant in the rest of the Scotland but heavily concentrated in the west-central belt where industry was concentrated and poverty was most grievous, and across broad swathes of Scotland conservatism and unionism dominated. The concept of an independent Scotland to end Tory rule was hard to imagine, even if the Red Clydesiders believed that more could be achieved in a Scottish Parliament than in Westminster.

The electoral divergence of Scotland and England hadn't yet occurred. It was only many years later that Scotland would become markedly more anti-Tory. The Labour Party was still a significant force in many areas of southern England that are now seen as Tory heartlands and the wider Labour movement a power in many areas. Working class solidarity was therefore with other industrial areas of England rather than rural parts of Scotland. Election results clearly showed that.

Labour had won the 1945 election in Scotland as it had across the UK. North of the border, Labour had polled 1,144,310 (47.9 per cent) votes to the Tories' 964,134 (40.3 per cent), thereby giving them thirty-seven seats to the Tories' twenty-seven. There were also three ILP MPs, and Willie Gallacher had been returned as a Communist. The Labour vote in Scotland shrunk in 1950 when Labour polled 1,259,410 (46.2 per cent) to the Tories' 1,222,010 (44.8 per cent), resulting in thirty-seven seats to thirty-one. But they were still the dominant party. However, the 1951 election saw Labour, albeit marginally, outpolled by the Tories and National Liberals, polling at 1,330,244 (47.9 per cent) to

1,349,298 (48.6 per cent). Though both parties tied with thirty-five seats each, the 1955 election saw the Tories win a majority in Scotland. They polled 1,273,952 (50.1 per cent) to Labour's 1,188,058 (46.7 per cent), though in seats it only gave the Tories thirty-six to Labour's thirty-four.

The Tories were to remain a significant electoral force in Scotland until the 1990s. The idea that independence would rid Scotland of the Tories for ever as suggested during the referendum on independence in 2014 was neither thought of nor credible at that time. Scotland in the 1940s and 1950s was very evenly balanced between Labour and Conservative. Clydeside may have been Red, but much of Scotland wasn't. Scottish socialism not only sought solidarity with the English working class ideologically, but required their support electorally. It was therefore a British road to socialism that Jimmy and his peers on the left sought to pursue.

Though Jimmy supported Home Rule, his priority still remained the change from a capitalist to a socialist system. The battlefield was in the factories that crossed the border and that required unity and cooperation. The ownership was often the same and common cause was needed. Moreover, Scottish nationalism was still very much a fringe movement. A sense of Scottish identity was strong across the land, but political nationalism was very weak. Jimmy never considered joining a non-socialist party and left-nationalist groupings were very minor indeed. The way to champion Home Rule was through the wider Labour movement.

So Jimmy's focus was on changing Scotland and arguing for communism in a British context, as detailed in the Communist Party programme, 'The British Road to Socialism'. Later, he would move towards the Eurocommunism line that was to be articulated in Italy in particular. He hugely respected the sacrifice the Soviet Union had made in the war against fascism and agreed with the ideology of communism. However, there were many aspects about it which concerned him as it was a vastly different society with little resonance to ordinary people in Britain. In many ways, his membership of the Communist Party was in spite of rather than because of the Soviet Union.

Jimmy outlined his communism in a talk he gave in Dundee in 1966[*] and gave a steer as to why he had joined the party. It laid out his idealism and belief in the better world it could lead to. He described communism as 'a world force, an ideological force, a political force on this planet, and it is also an international movement which has significantly contributed to all the social and political developments of the last fifty or sixty years'.

He went on to praise those who had inspired him through their commitment and condemn the careerists that had seen him leave the Labour League of Youth. He stated:

Communism seems to have this capacity to develop in people another incorruptibility, a dedication to the working class and the cause of Socialism, that cannot be intimidated nor bought. Consider Willie Gallacher, who all his life served the working class, served the cause of Socialism and died as a tenant of a two room and kitchen in a council house in Paisley.

Jimmy contrasted that with those he disdained throughout his life, saying:

---

[*] Jimmy Reid, *Reflections of a Clyde-built Man*, p. 47.

compare his life with those of some of his contemporaries, who were also involved in the struggle on behalf of the working class of Clydeside in the early part of this century, and who ended up, regrettably in the House of Lords, or living in the stockbroker belt in the south east of England.

He summarised communism as being a philosophy that had a sense of responsibility to fellow human beings and to the physical world. For a young idealist, it was a logical choice of political persuasion. It certainly wasn't done in the pursuit of any guaranteed electoral success or trade union advancement. The Communist Party had some council representation but it was small and often localised in areas such as Glasgow, east London, Tyne & Wear and the Rhondda. Willie Gallacher had lost his West Fife seat in the 1950 general election, so there was no communist representation in Parliament, although the party was able to exert some political influence on left-wing Labour MPs and the wider socialist movement. Especially in engineering with the AEU, in mining with the NUM and with the electricians' union ETU where they had a strong presence.

The Communist Party had only been formed in 1920 and the party had endured a turbulent start which was a sign of things to come. Its leaders had been imprisoned in 1926 when twelve were charged with sedition, including Willie Gallacher and Harry Pollitt, both of whom Jimmy would get to know well. Five were jailed for one year and seven for six months. They had made great inroads, however, and won much support for their work in the National Unemployed Workers' Movement during the depression. The fight against fascism also saw the party gain in profile and prominence. Its activities in supporting the Republican side in the Spanish Civil War were unstinting and the International Brigade saw many members enlist or support its cause. The actions of the Soviet Union in the Second World War gave another huge boost to the party cause and membership – its 18,000 members at the start of the conflict had risen to 56,000 by 1942.

Membership of the party was never substantial. It was at its height during the war years when sympathy for the Soviet Union was greatest, but it dropped thereafter with the Cold War. When Jimmy became chairman of the YCL in 1952, it's estimated to have had approximately 35,000 members. It was never to rise above that, falling significantly after the Soviet invasion of Hungary in 1956, though rising again slightly in the 1960s. Scotland, however, always remained one of the largest districts within it.

Peace and decolonialisation were all issues of the time and supported by the party. Apartheid would become one when working down in London. Both the party and its papers gave support to liberation movements that proliferated as the old empires frayed. However, it was on the industrial and community issues that Jimmy came alive and excelled. Jimmy sought to express his socialism in language that was intelligible and relatable to ordinary people. The rhetoric that some socialists used baffled working men and women and became a positive turn off to them. That was no doubt why Jimmy became so popular. He impressed people with the passion of his convictions, which were delivered in an engaging and disarming style. He was, of course, steeped in Marxist–Leninist theory and could hold his own in any ideological debate, as he was often to show at party congresses and in other formal party meetings. However, his forte was undoubtedly in engaging with the public and the party quickly recognised the star it possessed.

He was, however, never to be entirely comfortable in any party and that was to apply to the Communist Party. Throughout his membership, issues troubled him and he remained a free thinker, even if he accepted the strictures of democratic centralism that applied within it. That doctrine allowed for open debate on issues over a period of months. The discussions that followed could be fierce and intense. But, when the time for debate closed, a democratic vote was taken and acceptance of the agreed line was demanded. Policy discussions could be wide ranging and rumbustious but iron discipline thereafter applied to the approved party position.

Before Jimmy became a full-time Communist Party official, issues arose that caused him and many others to reflect on their membership. In 1956, the new leader of the Soviet Union, Nikita Khrushchev, detailed the evils of Stalin in a private session to Soviet party members which began to leak over coming months. It caused some turmoil within the ranks, not simply because of what was being exposed but also due to the party's previous unquestioning support for Stalin. However, Jimmy's communism was based on his support for its ideology rather than in defence of the Soviet Union and while the issues concerned him, he believed they could be overcome. The Soviet party also seemed intent on resolving matters there. It was British socialism he pursued, not the Soviet one and so he remained a party member in spite of the qualms Soviet communism caused.

The real crisis, though, was the Soviet suppression of the Hungarian Revolution that same year. That harmed the party badly and Jimmy had vehemently disagreed with it. He was not alone. Membership dropped substantially and it's reckoned that 7,000 members resigned or left that year. It also cost them the support of many leading lights and intellectuals, such as the historian E. P. Thompson. Others in the party, however, accepted the Soviet line. The divisions between the Eurocommunists and the Stalinists that would play out in later years were beginning to be set.

Jimmy knew the Soviets' actions were wrong and would be damaging. Like many, he agonised over it but decided to remain a member – something he was to regret in later life. The precise reasons why he stayed will never be known and he probably couldn't have fully explained them anyway. They would have been many and complex. They no doubt included his deep commitment to the belief in a better world. He was relatively new in the party leadership, but he was rising fast. Close friendships and alliances had been made and these, as he'd discover later, were a hard bond to break. The companionship and comradeship was deep and leaving would jeopardise, if not altogether fracture, these relationships. Had he left, he would have been looking to join a new party. He'd rejected the Labour Party before and nothing had changed to make him reconsider that decision. The alternatives were few and unattractive. So, there was some logic behind staying in the Communist Party, even if he had his qualms.

The Soviet invasion of Hungary has also to be seen in context of the time. While it was accepted as wrong by many, including Jimmy, he had argued against it at the time and made his point of view known within the party. However, what is often forgotten is that it occurred at the same time that Britain, France and Israel had invaded Egypt over Colonel Nasser's nationalisation of the

Suez Canal. The two international disputes almost entirely over-lapped. The Hungarian Revolution ran from 23 October until it was finally crushed by Soviet tanks on 19 November and, in the meantime, Israel invaded Egypt on 29 October, bombing by Britain commenced on 31 October and British and French para-troopers landed along the Suez Canal on 5 November. Many liberal commentators noted that the Suez invasion had deflect-ed criticism from the Soviet invasion of Hungary. However, for many Communist Party members, it no doubt justified why they had no option but to remain and seek to change from within. The actions of their communist allies had been wrong, but so had those of Britain and other Western allies.

The crises had nearly precipitated the Third World War, fur-ther fuelling the arms race in which Britain was working closely with its American allies. U2 spy planes were being deployed and the possibility of the nuclear arming of West Germany was being mooted; highly sensitive for generations reared in war with that country. In these circumstances, many such as Jimmy concluded that the lesser of two evils was to remain in the party and fight for change from within. To do otherwise would undermine a coun-terbalance to the USA and the West and threaten gains both made and being pursued. He remained troubled, though, throughout his membership by his acquiescence over Hungary.

The decolonialisation movements depended in many instances on the balance between East and West to be able to survive and succeed. It was the socialist countries that portrayed themselves as the friends of liberty from imperialism, with the Western coun-tries often seeming to either be the oppressor or give tacit support to them. Though decolonialisation was ongoing, there was still a legacy of conflict in places such as Kenya or Malaya and the on-going struggles of France in Indochina and Algeria would become even bloodier. The USA, with the Cuban Missile Crisis on the horizon, would soon replace the old empires as the main bulwark to liberation.

Moreover, the fight at home remained the battle between capital and labour. Despite the reported brutality, there was still a belief that the Soviet Union was delivering economic success and prosperity for working people. The brutality of the regime was still not fully exposed. The age of consumerism had not yet properly dawned and the gulf between the West and the East was less obvious to the eye than it is in retrospect. Jimmy and others thought that reform was possible and they were of the view that much of what was said against the Soviet Union was capitalist propaganda. Jimmy had been to the Soviet Union and had seen its potential, as well as some of the progress made. No doubt he and others had been shown only what the authorities wished them to see, which did not include the harshness of the oppression. Although they had their doubts, there was still a belief in the possibility of a better future.

However, Jimmy was still impressed by what had been done in very backward areas such as Central Asia where in health provision and social services, a third world society had been given first world services. In addition, the success in building up a huge industrial base from a very limited start was striking to someone reared in one. Though doubts remained there was still a belief in the possibilities of what might come from it.

Meanwhile, though, Jimmy's activism within the party and the wider labour movement remained relentless. To boost both membership and interest, he had sought to move shop steward meetings from dull and dreary halls to a hotel on a Friday night so that political conversation and debate would be interspersed with a drink and socialising. The meetings were to prove highly popular. They weren't without the occasional problem though, such as when he invited the former MP Willie Gallacher to speak. The old stalwart was an ardent teetotaller who had been briefed about the format but still complained about the alcohol being consumed. Jimmy had to appease the old man whose concerns traced back to the harm done to his family by an alcoholic father.

Those successful meetings and Jimmy's talents were noted by the party leadership, who took a shine to him and helped promote him. Bright and able, articulate and energetic, he was the working class advocate they were looking for. Jimmy's rise within the party was, therefore, quite meteoric: indeed, within four years, he was chair of the YCL.

In 1958, the call came to become a full-time worker for the party as national officer for the YCL. It came as a genuine surprise to him. He'd been very active but had never given any thought to becoming a full-time official and it would mean moving to London where both the YCL and the CPGB were based. Not only was it unexpected, but it came at an awkward time in his personal life, too, for he'd met Joan Swankie. She was from Clydebank and her family were original Bankies: her father was a welder in the shipyards and had worked on the construction of the Queen Mary, and her mother had grown up on Kilbowie Road. Other than a brief stay in the nearby Vale of Leven, Joan had lived there all her life.

In later years, Joan was fond of recounting how they had first met at a YCL Halloween party and she'd even sat on his knee.

However, she was still very young then and he had still to go off on national service. It was a good few years after their first meeting when she was nineteen that they struck up a proper romance. Jimmy had returned from the RAF and was working in the yards and Joan was employed in a fruiterer's in the town, where she'd gone to work after leaving school. After being persuaded by a friend to chum her to a Daily Worker Dance at the Woodside Hall in Glasgow, there she met Jimmy once again. A romance soon blossomed that was to be lifelong.

Joan was from a very musical family, with her father playing guitar and mother singing for friends and at special events. She sang in the YCL choir. Her sister Rena was very talented and together the pair occasionally sang as the Swankie Sisters, both locally and even in London. Joan also came from a political household. The Swankies were also Communist Party members, with her grandmother having been involved in the past rent strike. Though Joan's political activism was more the social side, it was still a political household. There was therefore a natural synergy as well as mutual attraction between the two.

Jimmy and Joan were preparing to get married and were looking for their first flat in her home town when the offer for Jimmy to work for the party in London came. It would mean moving to a strange city and also accepting a reduction in wages for the new couple. However, even though it was complicated both personally and financially, Jimmy was by then twenty-six years old and politics was in his lifeblood. To work full time for the cause was a calling. Despite the challenges that arose, Jimmy took the job.

CHAPTER FOUR

WORKING FOR THE
COMMUNIST CAUSE

So, in spring 1958 Jimmy headed off to London. Joan and her sister headed south the following weekend to meet him and see how he was settling in. After they arrived, having travelled overnight by train, he took them for breakfast and it was then that Joan recalled Jimmy opening his diary and asking her to pick a date. That was to be their wedding day. Romance and personal life needed to be scheduled around political commitments. Within nine weeks they were married and she had moved south to be with him.

Initially, they lodged with Communist Party members in London and it would be several years before they obtained their own first home at Foresthill in Lewisham, south London. Eileen, their eldest daughter, was born in 1959 in Scotland, where Joan as a young expectant mum had returned to be near her family for the birth – though Jimmy sometimes liked to claim that it was in case they'd had a son and he could play football for Scotland.

Life for the family was fun but challenging in many ways. Pay was low for Communist Party workers and they struggled financially. Prior to Jimmy joining, some members had to even depend on their own fundraising for their wages. Fortunately, changes had been made so that payment was made centrally for all. The pay was still low, however, and that combined with long hours meant that life could still be intense. The work was done out of commitment to the cause, rather than for the money in the weekly wage packet.

Although cash was limited, there was warmth in the communist family. Workers and members socialised together and they became great friends. Jimmy was especially close with Harry Pollitt and John Gollan and he also got to know Rajani Palme Dutt and Peter Kerrigan amongst many others. If home repairs or any support of any kind were required, then a communist joiner or electrician could be found. Holidays were still had even if money was never plentiful. Throughout the London years and into the late 1960s holidays were taken at Jimmy's sister's caravan in Girvan where they could relax and enjoy the west coast of Scotland once again.

Pollitt was very much the grand old man of the Communist Party. He was in his sixties by the time Jimmy moved south and he was extremely fond of the young Scot. He even babysat for him and Joan on occasions. Jimmy reciprocated the affection for the old man. He was hugely influential on Jimmy, who viewed him as a personal and political mentor.

There were similarities in both their upbringing and their idealism. Born in Lancashire in 1896, Pollitt was the son of a blacksmith. Like Jimmy, three of his siblings had died in infancy. That drove a passionate desire to change the conditions that inflicted such grinding poverty upon so many. Pollitt had trained as a boilermaker and had moved to Southampton, where he became a union activist. A founding member of the party, he was sentenced to a year's imprisonment for offences under the Mutiny Act in 1925 along with Willie Gallacher and others. He became party general secretary in 1929.

In the 1945 election, he narrowly failed to win the Rhondda seat, losing out by fewer than 1,000 votes. During the Stalin purges and the show trials, under pressure from Moscow, he had spoken out in support of the Soviet regime. He was, however, to show his independence when voicing his support for Britain's declaration of war on Germany a few years later. He was in agreement with his old colleague, Willie Gallacher, who thought that taking a position of neutrality was impossible to justify in the face of the *volte-face* from opposing fascism in Spain and elsewhere.

But the line was imposed by Moscow all the same and the majority of the executive committee followed suit. The pact between the Soviet Union and Nazi Germany saw the party go into reverse and oppose the war and the militarisation that they had previously been demanding. Pollitt was replaced by Palme Dutt, who was more closely aligned with Soviet thinking. However, upon Germany's invasion of the Soviet Union in June 1941, Pollitt was reinstated and remained in post until 1956. Khrushchev's revelations about Stalin, however, came as a great shock to Pollitt. By then, he was in poor health and the shock speeded up his death. On stepping down he became party chairman until his death in 1960.

After his funeral, which was attended by the American communist and famous singer Paul Robeson, Pollitt was succeeded as general secretary by John Gollan. He was another Scot, though from Edinburgh. Born in 1911, Gollan, though younger than Pollitt, was still considerably older than Jimmy. A painter by trade from Edinburgh, he had become politically active during the general strike in 1926. He joined the YCL in 1927 and went on to become its general secretary – a post that Jimmy would take up more than twenty years later. In 1931, he was jailed for six months for distributing anti-military leaflets. He later became secretary for the Scottish District in 1941; again, a role Jimmy would later perform. Gollan died in 1977, the year after Jimmy resigned from the party.

He also took young Jimmy under his wing and, as with Harry Pollitt, the affection was mutual. In many ways Gollan, supported by Pollitt, helped sponsor Jimmy's rise through the party ranks. It was Gollan in particular to whom Jimmy was drawn and with whom he formed a close relationship. Jimmy also warmed to Gollan because of what he saw to be his constant anti-Stalinism. Jimmy felt able to speak privately with Gollan about his concerns about democracy and the prominence of the Soviet Union within party thinking. Gollan assuaged some of Jimmy's doubts, though many were to remain constant until he finally left. These confessions further forged the bond between the old mentor and the party's rising star.

Other communists Jimmy met and worked with in London included Johnny Campbell, Rajani Palme Dutt and Peter Kerrigan. Campbell was yet another Scot. Born in Paisley in 1894, he was another founder member of the CPGB. Decorated for his service in the Royal Navy during the First World War, on his return he became active in the CWC before heading to London in 1924. There, he became editor of the party paper, the *Workers' Weekly*. The following year, he was another member of the leadership convicted of Incitement to Mutiny and imprisoned. Along with Pollitt and Gallacher, he was one of the most prominent communists during the inter-war years. He wrote a defence of the Moscow show trials, having been in the Soviet Union as the foreign editor of the *Daily Worker* and subsequently became that paper's editor. However, along with Pollitt and Gallacher, he opposed the *volte-face* when the Nazi–Soviet Pact was signed and was removed. He wasn't reinstated until the war broke out, and he served as editor until 1959 and died in 1969.

Palme Dutt was very much the party theoretician and intellectual. Born in 1896, the same year as Pollitt, he was the son of an Indian doctor and Swedish mother. She was a relative of Olaf Palme who became Sweden's Social Democratic Prime Minister in the 1970s. He had a brilliant mind, and was awarded a first class honours degree from Oxford University. He founded the magazine *Labour Monthly* and edited it until his death in 1974. He also edited the *Daily Worker* for some years. His links to Moscow were very close and he was very much a hardliner, which goes some way to explain his switch when the Nazi–Soviet Pact was signed, as well as his later disagreement with CPGB's opposition to the invasion of Czechoslovakia. Though he and Jimmy worked together, they were never particularly close. In terms of both their background and temperament, they were vastly different. Moreover, Jimmy was moving towards Eurocommunism while Dutt remained an irredeemable hardliner.

Kerrigan was yet another Scot in a senior position in the Communist Party who became a very close family friend. Again, he was significantly older than Jimmy but he was a Glaswegian. Born in the Gorbals in 1899, he had been both a railwayman and a soldier. An activist in the AEU, he had been appointed the party's Scottish organiser in 1930 before serving as the CPGB's representative to the Comintern and also as commissar to the English-speaking volunteers in the International Brigade. When Jimmy moved to London, Kerrigan was the National Industrial Organiser and remained in the post until retiring in 1965. He died in 1977.

Jimmy was the only full-time official working for the YCL. However, the organisation shared offices with the Communist Party and by 1959 he'd been elected to the National Executive Committee (NEC) of the party itself. He was also voted on to its Political Committee which set the political direction and was its key body. Jimmy sat on that alongside Harry Pollitt, Johnny Campbell, Peter Kerrigan, Willie Gallacher and others. Very much the youthful face of the Communist Party, even as he began to approach his thirties, it was an opportunity for Jimmy to be groomed for future leadership roles. He was very much at the centre of the party in London.

Jimmy worked hard and was pushed constantly. There were mundane administrative tasks to complete and a lot of campaigning to be done. As with the Communist Party, the YCL had its paper, *Challenge*, which needed to be written, edited, printed and distributed and sold across the country. That in itself was a challenging task. It was a critical vehicle for spreading the communist message to new and existing members, even if circulation was only in the region of 10,000. Jimmy had managed to increase sales from the 6,800 he had inherited on arrival and he covered considerable distances across London and the rest of the country in his visits to YCL and other communist groups.

It was during this time that it became clear that Jimmy was an outstanding orator. He was sought after to speak about both the YCL and other issues to motivate existing members and recruit new ones. The ongoing battle between capital and labour in the workplace was still going strong, as was the fight for a fairer society. Jimmy voiced his support for pensioners' rights and he spoke passionately about anti-colonialism, the arms race and apartheid.

The Communist Party and YCL may have been small numerically but the membership was highly active. Speaking both to them and to groups with whom they were aligned took up a great deal of his time. Platform speakers were often needed; and again Jimmy was in demand. CND, anti-apartheid and numerous other groups had meetings aplenty and a desire for quality speakers. With communications being much more basic, face-to-face meetings were needed. Moreover, with broadcasting and the media being much more limited and much less available, public meetings were more common and much better attended. Distances were considerable and the journeying exhausting.

While speaking to groups across the country was exhausting, Jimmy was eager to raise the profile of the party and extend its influence. The Campaign for Nuclear Disarmament (CND) was on the rise, but some party members viewed the nuclear weapons debate as a side-show to class politics and perceived the organisation itself as petit bourgeois. Jimmy thought this was wrong and believed in forging alliances wherever possible. His common-sense position prevailed and, along with many other party members, he joined the marches that took place at Aldermaston and at the Holy Loch on the Clyde.

His main report to the 23rd Congress of the Young Communist League in October 1960 held in Finsbury Town Hall set out the work done and the challenges to take up. He narrated the issues as he saw them, starting with the theme of 'Youth and Peace', and then looking at the fight against the nuclear policies of both the Tory government and the right-wing Labour Party leadership. He then moved to consider opposition to a third world war that would lead to the end of humanity through the use of nuclear weapons. A call for Britain to renounce the nuclear bomb, close all American bases on its soil and halt the policy of giving nuclear weapons to West German militarism.

He moved on to the social and economic issues that faced the country, such as the demand for higher wages, better working conditions, the right to a decent job with a future, trade training, better and equal educational opportunities for all. Championing trade unionism amongst young people and seeking to support it, by establishing youth committees and youth sections within it. In addition, arguing for social opportunities for young people on everything from sufficient football pitches to swimming pools; local issues that might help draw young people into the wider trade union and labour movement. It required campaigning and recruitment not just in the workplace but where young people gathered.

Finally he indicated the need for solidarity with the colonial peoples in their struggles. The suffering of people in the former colonies was detailed and the legacy of imperialism held to blame. Continued liberation struggles were extolled. It was why they supported the Youth section of the Movement for Colonial Freedom and why members were active in the Anti-Apartheid Movement. The oppressors of the colonial peoples were the exploiters of the British working people. The common enemy was imperialism.

The report also highlighted the challenges the organisation faced. The number of full delegates at the congress was 152, made up of 115 men and thirty-seven women. Membership was reported as showing a significant increase of almost 50 per cent since the previous congress and that year alone had seen 800 new members. However, it still stood at only 2,600. It was hoped that a recruitment drive might push that up to 3,000 for the Communist Party congress due to be held in Easter the following year. Achieving that target was to be through sales of *Challenge*. In his report, Jimmy sought to ensure that the paper had popular appeal and he rejected calls from members to reduce or even abandon the content on music, films and sport, arguing that would make it an 'internal journal for erudite young Marxists'. What was needed, he argued, was a mass circulation paper which catered for all aspects of youth interest. For communists, he stated, politics embraced every aspect of life with political points to be made about sport, films, music and art as well as on jobs, higher pay and peace.

The old-time communist thinking was still extolled to encourage young comrades to continue to fight against inequality, condemn the rich becoming richer, denunciate the low pay and limited prospects for so many working-class youngsters and disavow the plenty that was available for the affluent in contrast to the poor. Jimmy stated:

> Their ideas don't correspond to reality as it is experienced by young people. Our ideas do. Their philosophy offers nothing to youth, except utter selfishness, corruption and national treachery. Ours holds out the prospect of a new and wonderful world. Their principles are rotten and corrupt. Ours are the finest ever conceived by man.

London was made up of great wealth as well as abject poverty. The contrast between the East End and Chelsea and Kensington was just as stark then as now. Campaigning for social justice was carried on at grassroots level with trade unionists, tenants' groups and pensioners' organisations, as well as with Labour MPs and other political groups. While Jimmy always felt that the London working class were less collectivist in their view of society than the Scots, he met many kindred spirits, particularly amongst the Jewish community in London's East End.

When he travelled away from home, Jimmy would most often stay with party comrades, often in the valleys of the Welsh coalfields or the manufacturing centres of northern England. Jimmy had huge respect for the grassroots comrades with whom he stayed. Political victories continued to elude the party then as later, but it still had a significant influence on the trade union and labour movement, in terms of both ideas and action.

The Soviet Union was secretly funding the party, though its method was complicated. Money was given in cash by the Soviet Embassy to the party's assistant general secretary, Reuben Falber. It didn't appear in the books and was undeclared. Senior party members knew of the donations but the precise details appear to have been kept secret. In addition to the direct funding, the Soviet Union also bought substantial copies of the party paper, the *Daily Worker*, later retitled the *Morning Star*. During the 1960s, the sums amounted to £100,000 per annum. That declined in the 1970s and, according to Falber, ended in 1979 at the request of the British Party.

Jimmy knew that financial support was being provided by the Soviet Union. Given his seniority and the committees on which he served, it couldn't have been otherwise. He wasn't particularly happy about it and the extent of the financial support seemed to surprise him when it was made public. He had assumed more funds had come in from unions and supporters than the reality of significant Soviet support. However, he was passionate about the work he was doing and while he'd argue about political issues, he never openly challenged or questioned the structures. They had remained largely unchanged for many years, if not since its inception. In many ways, the bureaucracy of the party bored and frustrated him, but he didn't want to undermine an organisation whose cause he believed in so fervently.

The party operated not just through democratic centralism but under intense pressure from without. Some need for secrecy therefore remained. It seems that Jimmy and many other comrades may have turned a blind eye to the Soviet funds and left the minutiae of the administration and regulation of the party to others. Secrecy over the party's income was later compounded by mystery over ownership of its assets. The party paper and its headquarters became matters of dispute after Jimmy had resigned, and were found not to belong to them at all. Many of those at the heart of the party organisation seem never to have fully understood the complexities. Revelations about ownership and structure were staggering for many. There seems to have been those who were out campaigning in the country for the cause, while there were others who were ultimately stitching up the party structures from its headquarters.

The truth is the party needed funds. It couldn't have been maintained without Soviet financial backing. Like others, Jimmy just accepted it – he had a job to do and he got on with it. His views on the Soviet Union were more forgiving in those days, since less information was available about its sins back then and greater hope still existed in its possibilities. All the same, Jimmy was prepared to confront the Stalinists in the party on occasions. Once, he even exploded at Palme Dutt who had described Stalin's reign as a blot on the sun. Jimmy was incensed that the deaths of 20 million people could be so lightly treated.

The party was being monitored and was under intense pressure from British security services after the Cold War period. Jimmy always believed that the headquarters were bugged and he was proven right. In the 1960s, MI5 tracked senior communists as well as tapping their phones and offices. The suggestion that spying was a one-way street by KGB agents on the British was fanciful: it worked both ways. Jimmy and his colleagues were subjected to it, though greater interest would always be on their Soviet contacts.

MI5 even recruited agents to work for the CPGB and had infiltrated the party. Olga Gray, who worked as Harry Pollitt's secretary, as well as carrying out other tasks for the party, was recruited in 1931. She was unable to cope with the double life, however, and dropped out in 1935. She subsequently emigrated to Canada and complained bitterly about apparently receiving a severance payment of only £500 from MI5, despite the personal cost sustained by her.

John Gollan's leadership was also spied upon. Julia Pirie had been recruited by MI5 to infiltrate the party by becoming his secretary. It is suggested by some that Pirie was the inside source for revelations on several operations, as detailed in Peter Wright's book *Spycatcher*. She continued to work for the party until 1978 and her efforts for the British security services continued thereafter with her involvement with operations against the Provisional IRA. Jimmy had always found her quiet and withdrawn and he found her constant complaints after accompanying John Gollan on trips to Eastern Europe deeply suspicious. Jimmy used to humorously recall that she even continued to receive a pension from the party, despite her going on to work for the British security services.

Life in London was exhausting for Jimmy. He had an incessantly busy political schedule to maintain and a young family to support. Another daughter, Shona, came along in 1962 and the family moved to a maisonette in Lewisham. Despite the limited pay, life was still enjoyable and the London years were looked back on fondly by the family.

However, it couldn't continue for ever. Jimmy was by now in his early thirties and his tenure at the YCL would soon come to an end. An opportunity arose to leave the King Street headquarters and return to Scotland. It is suggested by many that Jimmy was being groomed for the role of general secretary, but Johnny Gollan was not retiring any time soon and others were ahead of him in the hierarchy. He was, however, most certainly future leadership material, and the party wished to maintain him and prepare him for further promotion.

Jimmy was tiring of the strictures being imposed at Party HQ even though he hugely admired Gollan. He felt his friend and mentor was unable to make the internal changes that the party badly needed. While he was highly skilled, he was rather shy and unable to command the authority necessary for the radical transformation that was required. Jimmy admitted later that he had found it difficult to raise some of his concerns with Gollan,

despite their close friendship. Though they had talked of the in-
iquities of Stalinism, there was no line of open questioning of the
party direction or challenging of the more doctrinaire wing. In
many ways, returning to Scotland was the escape route from the
stifling orthodoxy that existed in the party's London HQ.

Moreover, neither Jimmy nor especially Joan ever truly settled
in London. There were aspects of life there that they enjoyed,
such as their friends, grand parks and museums. But it wasn't
home. Joan in particular felt it more than Jimmy. As a Clydebank girl, she missed the walks over the hills from Clydebank to
Carbeth where her granny had a hut. She found the scale of the
city daunting and overwhelming and she was eager to get back
to her family and roots, especially now she had young children.
Jimmy was less affected by the size of the city but still missed the
Clydeside camaraderie and needed a change. So, it was time to
return home to Clydeside.

CHAPTER FIVE

RETURNING TO CLYDESIDE

Jimmy returned to Clydeside in anticipation of being elected secretary of the Scottish District in 1965. The post was available as Gordon McLennan, the incumbent, was moving south to become National Organiser and Jimmy was duly elected the following year. Given the Scottish party's membership and its considerable influence in unions such as the NUM (National Union of Mineworkers) and AEU, it was an important post, even if it was away from the headquarters in King Street. It allowed him to continue his political campaigning away from the stifling atmosphere in London.

When they returned, the Reids initially moved in with Joan's parents in Clydebank. It was where they had been intent on moving, before they had gone south to London. It was an area they knew well. An industrial town adjacent to Glasgow but with its own distinct identity, like Govan it had been forged by the shipyards and had a distinctly industrial tradition. In the early 1870s, J & G Thomson shipyard in Govan needed to expand but was unable to do so due to its being surrounded by other yards and buildings. The company bought land further down the River Clyde on the opposite side of the bank to allow for larger vessels to be built. Work started constructing the new Thomson yard in

1871. Initially, workmen were brought to the yard from Govan up the river by paddle steamer. However, this soon became an unsustainable way of commuting, and pressure mounted for homes to be built closer to the yards. The company built tenements nearby and a township began to form. It was quickly expanded as others settled and churches and a school were established. In the early 1880s railway lines connecting Glasgow with the yard and town were constructed. Shortly afterwards followed the opening of the Singer Company factory, which was located only half a mile from the yard. With these growing workplaces, the population of Govan was expanding fast and in 1886 the town of Clydebank was formally established. Over the following years, it grew to envelope neighbouring villages including Faifley, where Jimmy would later move to.

In 1899, J & G Thomson's shipyard was bought by John Brown's which, along with Singer's, remained the main employers in the town and in many ways the town revolved around them. The sheer scale of the companies (at their peak, they each employed nearly 15,000 workers) meant that start and finish times had to be staggered to avoid public transport becoming overwhelmed by the sheer number of bodies. While these companies brought work and wages to the town, they also inspired union organisation and socialist activism.

A strike took place at Singer's in 1911 and it marked one of the first events to begin to paint Clydeside red. Almost 11,000 workers downed tools following the suspension of some female colleagues who had been protesting against changes resulting in longer hours for lower pay. Management responded by locking them out of the building. The dispute dragged on for a while, but many drifted back to work. When it ended, 400 workers were sacked, including the principal leaders of the dispute. Many of them had belonged to the Industrial Workers of Great Britain (IWGB). It was an offshoot of the International Workers of the World (IWW) that had been formed in the USA in 1905. Often referred to as the 'Wobblies' they're revered in many American folk songs by the likes of Woody Guthrie or Pete Seeger. The IWGB had been established in Britain in 1909 by socialists who advocated political activity through trade unionism – including many of the workers at Singer's and other nearby factories. The IWGB was ultimately superseded after the war by the newly established CPGB to whom many members flocked. Arthur McManus, one of the strike leaders at Singer's in 1911 who was sacked at the end of the dispute, became the first chairman of the CPGB when it was established in 1920. As with other parts of Clydeside, that political activism continued on into the First World War and beyond. Not simply in the workplaces but in the community where housing as elsewhere was a critical issue and into opposition to the war itself.

Clydebank was to be home to the Reids for many years to come. They obtained a council house in Faifley, one of the many small communities that had been enveloped as the town had grown over the decades. It was a small top-floor, two-bedroom flat that had views over the town below. It was far from salubrious: space was limited and there was a huge pylon facing them as they looked out of their front windows. Meals had to be eaten on laps in the living room, since there was neither a dining area nor space in the kitchen. Despite the tight fit, friends and family would visit regularly. Political discussion together with a drink and a singalong was a common occurrence. They lived there for many years and the family remember it fondly.

Jimmy was based at the Communist Party's central offices in Glasgow, in Albert Street in the south side. There, he worked with a team of volunteers and a small band of full-time workers. Besides Jimmy, there was a Scottish Organiser who spent a great deal of his time on the road and workers for the Lanarkshire, Glasgow, Edinburgh and Dundee areas. One woman in Aberdeen ran a boarding house at the same time as being almost a full-time worker for the cause, even if not on the official payroll.

While people's commitment was inspiring, the bureaucracy and the paperwork suited neither Jimmy's temperament nor talents. His interests lay with campaigning in the communities and factories while administration was a chore that he never really took to. He was frustrated by the amount of time he had to spend compiling statistics, many of which showed the party in far from good health. By the end of the 1960s, membership of the party across the UK had dipped to approximately 30,000 people. Scotland was one of the larger districts but there were still many moribund branches. On occasion, Jimmy acted independently of the instruction coming from the London HQ which, though it brought about some limited success, must also have caused some tension within the party.

Jimmy felt the party had to be active not just in the workplace but in the community. Accordingly, he soon stood for and was elected to the Town Council in Clydebank for the ward covering Faifley. The town already had a contingent of communist councillors – Finlay Hart, Jock Smith and Arnold Henderson – and Jimmy was to bring their number up to four. Finlay Hart, as with

Pollitt and Gollan, was considerably older than Jimmy but they became close. Born in the town in 1901, he had started work at Beardmore's Shipyard and had been a founding member of the Communist Party. A hard working and community-minded man, he was popular in the town. Hart and the others stood for the type of activism that Jimmy wished to see the party pursue more widely.

As one of the most prominent communists in the country, Jimmy was subject to surveillance. He never took it personally nor did he let it trouble him. He believed his phone was tapped and other surveillance equipment may have been installed. There had been workmen out on the roof that seemed unusual and could never be traced to any specific repair work. It never interfered with his work though, and he just got on with his life. Indeed, sometimes the extent of it could be humorous for family and friends. A Soviet official visited him at the house in the early 1970s. As the visitor, Jimmy and his daughter went for a walk through the area and down to the town, a black car slowly trailed them along the streets. It was unmistakably following them. Car ownership was still low, especially in an area like Faifley. No doubt, it was a member of the British security services seeking to monitor the Russian diplomat and impose similar routine harassment on him as endured by officials in Moscow. Jimmy's children later humorously recalled shouting to their dad when they saw the same diplomat on the television a few years later, when the UK expelled Soviet Embassy staff for alleged spying.

Jimmy carried the CPGB banner beyond local council elections to parliamentary ones. Jimmy contested the Dunbartonshire East seat for the Communist Party, which then included Clydebank.

The CPGB put up fifty-seven candidates across the country. Jimmy fared better than others, but only marginally so. In 1966, he gained 1,548 votes (2.45 per cent) in a seat that was won comfortably by Labour. Jimmy had actually contested that seat when he was still in London in 1964 and he'd polled 1,171 votes (just 1.98 per cent). The seat again was won comfortably by Labour with 55.6 per cent of the poll.

Meanwhile, the party continued its campaigning in both the workplace and the community. Wages and standards of living were the most pressing issues against a backdrop of escalating tensions in the Cold War and the arms race. Foreign policy remained topical as the British and French empires were receding, but American involvement in Vietnam was beginning, as was apartheid in South Africa. Amid this dramatic global scene, the notion of a Scottish Parliament was not forgotten. The SNP was beginning to rise in the polls, though its growing popularity was not reflected in the results of the election of 1966 when the SNP won no seats and received just 5 per cent of the national vote. The following year, however, saw the by-election victory of Winnie Ewing in Hamilton, which caused a political earthquake in Scotland. This increased interest in Scottish independence corresponded with the efforts of writers and poets such as Hugh MacDiarmid, whose use of the Scots language promoted Scotland's distinct culture and heritage over the years.

Living in England for ten years only strengthened Jimmy's belief in the importance of Home Rule. He felt it absurd to campaign for the self-determination of other small countries around the world and forget about Scotland. General support for Home Rule within the party, however, was lukewarm, with many members subscribing to the view that there were only class divisions, not national differences; and that an engineer on the Clyde was no different to that on the Mersey. Indeed, in the 1930s it had been more a case of King Street in London imposing a policy of Parliaments for Scotland and Wales, rather than support coming from within the local districts. Nevertheless, Jimmy strongly supported the policy and, as Scottish secretary, sought to make it a more pressing issue within the party.

Jimmy, like the poet Hugh MacDiarmid, was proud of his Scottish identity and of what working-class Scots had achieved. He understood that they had been products of particular aspects of Scottish society and parts of its history from the reformation through the Enlightenment to the industrial revolution. Creating the literacy, thirst for knowledge and belief in education that allowed many able young Scots to prosper and contribute greatly. He admired the likes of Thomas Telford and James Watt both from relatively humble backgrounds who transformed his own world of engineering. The quote by the French philosopher Voltaire that 'we look to Scotland for all our ideas of civilisation' was also something that he took pride in. While the 'lad o'pairts' mythology was something he knew was not entirely accurate, there was still more than a grain of truth in it. The success of both individuals and the country was something Jimmy believed should be celebrated.

This emphasis on national pride didn't obscure Jimmy's belief in the importance of class and the cause of socialism. Hence support for Home Rule didn't mean an acceptance of the policies of the SNP. Indeed, he was a trenchant critic of that party then. It was a vastly different party though to the more left of centre social democratic party it was to become in later years. At that time it sought to appeal to all classes and ignored the divide between the interests of capital and labour that Jimmy was rooted in. That was an anathema to Jimmy fired years before by Tom Johnston's book on the history and making of the Scottish working class; and where the ruling class in Scotland were the principal enemy.

Jimmy felt that the labour movement's power and influence was necessary for achieving a Scottish Parliament. However, he also felt that it was best achieved through a broad base of support. As with his willingness for alliances on issues such as nuclear weapons he thought it also applied in Home Rule. Several decades before the Scottish Constitutional Convention saw political parties and civic Scotland brought together to build the base and momentum for the restored Parliament in 1999, he was calling for common cause to be found. He wished not just the Scottish labour movement and the Communist Party to be campaigning for it but for them to be working in support of it along others, including with Liberals and Nationalists.

Moreover, in many ways, Jimmy would have liked an autonomous Scottish Communist Party as opposed to the Scottish District of the CPGB. Indeed, he thought likewise for trade unions in Scotland. However, the situation at the time precluded that. It would have allowed greater room for manoeuvre and more appreciation of distinctive Scottish issues.

Jimmy worked hard to gain the party's support for Scottish Home Rule. His two main supporters on the Scottish Committee of the Communist Party to whom he now turned were two English women: the writer Honor Arundel and Mabel Skinner, an Inverness councillor. Together they managed to win over the party, despite some continued opposition. However, though the battle was won within the Communist Party, there was still the wider labour movement to convince. A deep antipathy towards nationalism existed in the Labour Party. Jimmy and the Communist Party were to be pivotal in ultimately securing support in the Scottish Trades Union Congress (STUC) and the wider left for a Scottish Assembly.

In 1968, the STUC were seeking to move a motion in support of a Scottish Parliament. Labour, no doubt bruised by Winnie Ewing's by-election victory and SNP success in local government elections, was opposed to it. Had the motion gone forward, it would have been defeated. Accordingly, the Communist Party, through the NUM, arranged for it to be remitted to keep alive the opportunity to win it, as they did just a few years later. A defeat could have put the cause of a Scottish Assembly back for many years.

Even when Jimmy left his full-time position within the party, he continued his efforts for Scottish Home Rule. In the early 1970s, he co-authored the Communist Party's submission to the Kilbrandon Commission. That had been established initially under Lord Crowther in 1969, following the victories of both Winnie Ewing for the SNP in Hamilton in 1967 and Gwynfor Evans for Plaid Cymru the year before. When Crowther died in 1972, he was replaced by Lord Kilbrandon and the report was to look at the constitution in the UK and consider the options for devolution within it. Though the Commission was divided, it did lay the path for the unsuccessful Labour attempts to bring devolution to Scotland in the late 1970s.

Jimmy's position remained consistent throughout. He believed that Scotland was a nation in its own right with its own distinctive culture and laws. In a speech given during the October 1974* election, he insisted that:

From the sixth century, there has always been a Scottish people. From the end of the tenth century, the territorial boundaries have been practically the same as they are today. From the beginning of the eleventh century, we have seen the emergence of Scotland as an entity by the amalgamation of regions and principalities bound by, albeit primitive, economic ties. Scotland was a completely independent nation. It developed its own constitutional form of Parliament and this survives to the present. Scottish law differs in certain aspects from that practised in other parts of the United Kingdom. Scotland is a nation and its history and traditions conform to any definition of nationhood that I've heard.

He placed his belief in a Scottish Parliament in the context of the longstanding support given for it by the Red Clydesiders, arguing that:

The pioneers of the labour movement were always in favour of a Scottish Parliament. At the Labour Party conference in 1948 – when that party lurched disastrously to the right and created the climate for the return of the Tories in 1951 – Herbert Morrison argued for dropping the demand for a Scottish parliament. This was carried. The labour movement has paid

---

* Jimmy Reid, *Reflections of a Clyde-built Man*, p. 119.

for that wrong decision. Just like the aristocrats who framed the Treaty of Union. Labour leaders cannot obliterate reality. All they did then was to create a vacuum in relation to the aspirations of the Scottish people for their national rights and their national identity.

Jimmy, however, was still scathing about the SNP. Some years before he gave that speech, and at a time when he was arguing within the Communist Party for Scottish Home Rule to be given its due recognition, he wrote a piece published in the *Morning Star* in February 1968.[*] In it he criticised the failure to take sides on whether it was left or right and its proposal to leave fundamental decisions until after a Parliament was restored. Condemning the nationalists' failure to recognise class as an issue he wrote:

Is it seriously suggested that there are no conflicting classes in Scotland? No exploiters and exploited, only Scots?

The landed nobility is no figment of the imagination. It exists and on the basis of false title deeds owns millions of acres of Scottish land. Feudal in outlook, it stands in the way of social progress, particularly in the Highlands.

The problem of the Clyde's shipbuilding industry in the thirties and in the sixties, is not London rule, but Lithgow rule.

Scotland First, is a neat slogan, but it begs the question, Which Scotland? As a product of the Scottish Working class, I am more kith and kin with a London Docker or a black African miner than with the Countess of Sutherland or Sir Alec Douglas Home.

---

[*] Jimmy Reid, *Reflections of a Clyde-built Man*, p. 75.

Jimmy found the SNP position both unacceptable and unrealistic for the challenges of the age. He sought to marry the socialist argument for economic change with the argument for self-determination by invoking the spirit of those early pioneers in the Labour Party and the ILP who had argued for it. The intention was to create a powerful Parliament for a distinct nation that also retained links across the working-class north and south of the border to deal with the economic struggles. Much the same as had been argued by the Red Clydesiders two generations before.

While Jimmy's position might make it seem as though he was advocating federalism, his actions have to be seen in the context of the time. Britain had joined the EEC but the EU had not yet been established. The age of globalisation had not yet dawned, although multinational companies were growing. The struggle for capital and labour was constant and the unity of the latter was seen as essential. Jimmy's commitment to creating a devolved Scottish Parliament simply reflected the social, economic and political conditions of the time.

In the meantime, however, an international event brought crisis to the party while Jimmy was the Scottish District Secretary. In 1968, the Soviet Union and Warsaw Pact allies invaded Czechoslovakia, in a move that was reminiscent of Hungary just twelve years before. The invasion of Hungary had been something Jimmy had disagreed with but he hadn't acted upon it. This time, however, the party opposed the actions of the Soviet Union. As a full-time official and a member of the executive committee, Jimmy was at the heart of the debate that ensued.

CPGB had very close links with its Czechoslovak colleagues. Some Czech emigres during the Second World War had stayed in the UK and had made friends with their British communist counterparts. In many ways, the Czechs were the closest of the Eastern European communist parties politically to the British Party. The British Party had started to move away from its previous Moscow-orientated position. The Khrushchev revelations about Stalin had set people thinking, but it was a slow burn. Criticisms of Soviet actions, such as the imprisonment of dissidents, were being made. Khrushchev was removed and replaced by Brezhnev, and he was also openly questioned by the British Party. The rift between the Soviet and Chinese parties saw the UK ostensibly try to pursue its own independent line, even if it still depended on funds from Moscow.

The Czechoslovak crisis was to accentuate that. The executive committee of the Communist Party, including Jimmy, opposed the actions of the Soviet Union, and only one member voiced any opposition. As the crisis deepened and the Soviet position hardened, so did the CPGB's opposition to it. A heated meeting took place in London between a leading representative of the British Party and the Soviet ambassador. It was clear that not only was international law being violated but they were being lied to by their Soviet comrades. The Executive Committee, including Jimmy, agreed to issue a statement condemning the actions, though the phrase 'intervention' rather than 'invasion' was used to try and placate some hardliners within the party. Gordon McLennan gave media interviews expressing the British Party's disagreement, which gathered considerable publicity.

The Soviet Union was angered by the British Party's criticism and even cancelled orders for the *Morning Star* for a period. Dissent broke out within the party as not all could be placated. A battle raged and Palme Dutt and others continued to adhere to a pro-Soviet line. The debate was bitter and seemed a prelude to the almost civil war that would break out in the years after Jimmy left the party. Only two of the eighteen districts across Britain opposed the executive committee's actions. They were both in the south of England and in 1977, many of them would leave for a more Stalinist party. In Scotland, the vote on support for the executive opposition to the Soviet actions broke down 126–54 – a comfortable majority for the leadership, but it still showed a significant opposition within it.

What the Soviets had done was wrong and Jimmy expressed that. He knew their actions would further harm the party's already limited prospects for electoral success in this country. Despite CPGB's condemnation of it, they were associated with the Soviet Union in the minds of the public. As a full-time official, Jimmy had to fight from within the party. The party had taken the correct position as he saw it, even if political damage was inflicted and the internal dissent would continue.

It wasn't only the British Party that spoke out against the Soviet actions in Czechoslovakia. Most parties across Western Europe felt the same way. Jimmy was already more comfortable with the political views of his colleagues from the likes of Italy than those in the Eastern Bloc. It would only accelerate his support for a different type of communism from that operated in Russia and its satellites.

If anything, it seemed to confirm to Jimmy that Eurocommunism was the way forward. It was a political ideology in its infancy but one that would be given impetus by the rejection of Soviet methods. He was hugely impressed by this new wave of communism and considered many of these politicians to successfully marry liberal democracy with socialism. The Leninist concept of the political vanguard and dictatorship of the proletariat was seen as wrong and irrelevant in British society.

Despite the political crisis caused by Czechoslovakia, his day work as the Scottish Secretary continued. Colleagues remember him as being bored by the minutiae of both the party and council work but coming alive in meetings and in the community. His strength lay in his ideas and activism, as well as his outstanding advocacy. He was able to relate to people and people to him, and he was good natured and friendly – attributes that made him popular within the party and with the wider community.

By the time Julie, his third daughter, was born in 1969, financial pressures were mounting. There were no savings to fall back on and a growing family to provide for. Jimmy decided that it was time to leave and get a full-time job. The Communist Party sought to keep him – after all, he was the rising star and being groomed for high office. John Gollan even offered a wage increase to try and retain him. But, his mind was made up. While his reason for leaving the party was mostly to do with his own financial situation, it was still a political decision. He was wearied by the monotony of some of the party administrative work and was frustrated with the bureaucracy of the party. He wanted out.

It was still a difficult decision to make and a wrench to leave. He had worked for the party for over a decade and in addition he was very close to John Gollan. They were friends and Jimmy admired him. It was a matter of personal sorrow to him, but the time had come. Jimmy was going to leave and return to the shipyards on the Clyde. Unfortunately, as it would transpire, it was an inauspicious time to return, as British shipbuilding was sinking.

CHAPTER SIX

SINKING BRITISH SHIPBUILDING

British shipbuilding had been slowly sinking and so it was a troubled time to be entering the industry. Storm clouds were gathering, even though the noise of hammers and rivets still reverberated across the Clyde. The industry's peak in Scotland and elsewhere in the UK had passed and troubled industrial relations between management and workforce were often cited as the cause of its demise. Though far from helpful and certainly casting a shadow over the workforce, bad industrial relations were not the reason for the collapse. Poor management and a failure to invest in the industry had brought about the decline. However, in 1969 no one, and certainly not Jimmy, could have envisaged the near wipe-out of the shipyards that would occur across the UK.

Despite these difficulties, the industry was symbolic of manufacturing industry within Scotland. Clydeside was the industrial heart of Scotland and shipbuilding on the Clyde was its major artery. Coal mining, steel and railway production were large and important, but shipbuilding had a profile and prestige like no other. HMS *Queen Mary*, HMS *Queen Elizabeth* and HMS *Queen Elizabeth II* had all been built there. The term 'Clyde-built' was in common parlance and referred to the expert craftsmanship in these yards.

The prestige of the yards had grown over generations. In the nineteenth century, at the dawn of the industrial revolution and the expansion of trade driven by the British Empire, the Clyde boomed. Allied to that was a change in maritime construction, with shipbuilding moving from wooden hulls to iron and steel. The Clyde and the shipbuilding yards in the north-east of England produced the majority of the ships launched in the UK. Indeed, the Clyde was the leading shipbuilding river in the world and in the early 1900s it accounted for one fifth of world production. The proximity of steel and coal manufacturing along with the suitable depth of the water made west Scotland and Tyneside prime shipbuilding sites. While industry was dwindling in the 1970s, the Clyde still retained its shipbuilding fame.

This decline was a long time in the making. During the First World War, the yards were unable to cope with resupplying the number of vessels being sunk. And following the war, the industry faced severe challenges both at home and from abroad. Competition from the rising economies in Japan and Germany was intense. Diesel propulsion was taking over from coal-fired engines and British shipyards were behind the curve. It allowed for others to gain on them.

Then, in the 1930s, the Great Depression meant that unemployment in the yards, as in the rest of the country, was rife. By 1933, unemployment in British shipbuilding hit 63 per cent and a tonnage of only 131,000 was launched. That contrasted with a boom that had occurred post war in 1920 that saw 2 million tonnes launched in the year before economies around the world began to sink.

Action was needed. A company called National Shipbuilders Security Ltd was set up under the chairmanship of James Lithgow. It bought up yards considered to be redundant and closed many firms that had been associated with the river for generations. The doors of Archibald McMillan & Son in Dumbarton, Napier and Miller in Old Kilpatrick and Beardmore's yard in Dalmuir all clanged shut.

Then the Second World War saw a boom in the yards on the Clyde, as elsewhere with a war economy. The shipyards remained in private hands throughout and significant profits were made by the companies still operating. However, sadly not a great deal was put into reinvestment in the industry. Allied bombing of the yards in Japan and Germany had put the UK in pole position for shipbuilding in the aftermath of the war. Although shipbuilding areas had suffered dreadfully from the war – and Clydebank in particular after the devastating Luftwaffe air raids on the yards in 1941 – they were still in a better place than their former competitors, which had almost entirely been destroyed. In 1949, yards in the UK produced 45 per cent of world tonnage and employment rose to levels that hadn't been seen since 1914. The post-war economy began to boom and, while the UK yards did well, they did not profit as much as they should have done. An opportunity to capitalise on the demise of competition elsewhere wasn't taken. Underinvestment followed as profits were retained by the shipyard magnates and their shareholders rather than being reinvested in preparing the yards for the changes that were to inevitably come. In particular, oil-tanker construction was commencing and it was to be an area of industry that the Clyde and the rest of the UK would lose out on. The yards on the Clyde and elsewhere were constrained by limited space and river depth but dredging, relocation and other actions were not taken as they should have been. Accordingly, by 1956, the UK share of world tonnage had fallen to just 21 per cent and the country had been overtaken by Japan as the world's largest shipbuilder.

As the 1950s turned into the 1960s, the decline continued. The post-war Labour government had not nationalised the industry despite its pivotal role in the war. Rail, steel and coal had been taken over but the yards remained in private hands. Poor management, continued underinvestment and the government's failure to support the yards all played their part in the slow but steady decline of the once-great industry. Many foreign competitors received government subsidies and saw direction for local purchasers to use home-based yards. Those policies were forsworn by the UK at that time, though that would subsequently change – but it would be too little too late.

The 1960s saw further closures. This time great names such as Dennys of Dumbarton and Barclay Curle of Whiteinch passed into the history of the Clyde. They not only had been longstanding but had contributed greatly to maritime engineering. The former having been the inventor of ship stabilisers and the latter in the building of dredgers. Moreover, Harland and Wolff, though more synonymous with Belfast, closed their Govan yard. Others also closed including some such as Henderson's at the mouth of the River Kelvin who had a history going back through the centuries. By 1963, British tonnage output had fallen below 1 million tons and its share of the market to just 11 per cent. A global shipbuilding boom in the mid-1960s barely touched the Clyde. Much of the demand was for giant tankers and bulk carriers which were less costly to construct and more efficient to operate, but that opportunity had sailed by the Clyde.

In October 1965, Fairfield's yard in Govan went into receivership despite launching three ships and booking £131-million-worth in outstanding orders. The yard had recently been modernised, and so its failure sent waves of concern rolling along the banks of the Clyde. If it could happen there, then it could hit any of them. Unlike other closures, the workforce at Fairfield's yard decided to oppose it. Yard meetings took place and a summit was called by the STUC and attended by the UK government minister. Such was the influence of the unions and the importance of the shipyards at that time.

The workers and the wider labour movement mobilised for action and the government was obliged to step in. The following month, an advance of £1 million was paid to keep the yard operating and, at the same time, they entered into discussions with potential buyers. Support was required for any incoming purchaser, though outright nationalisation was ruled out by the government. The union's agreement to make some changes in working practices saw a deal concluded. The yard was sold to new owners, but the mobilisation of the workers was a portent of things to come.

Concerned by that and about the wider situation in the industry in 1965, Harold Wilson's Labour government established the Geddes Committee. It was tasked to investigate and report on what was happening and what might be done to make improvements. R. M. Geddes was a businessman whose expertise had been in the soft drinks sector. In his report the following year, he and his colleagues proposed rationalisation, amalgamation and centralisation. This they believed would deliver higher productivity, although closures and job losses would be incurred by these means.

The recommendations were accepted by the government and were put in practice over the coming years. They included the establishment of a Shipbuilding Industry Board to oversee the process that would be required. The Clyde yards were restructured into two larger consortia covering the Upper and Lower Clyde which came into existence in February 1968. Though nationalisation had been ruled out, the government still had a share interest of over 48 per cent.

The Upper Clyde yards were split into four sections and covered three divisions that mirrored historic areas on that part of the river. They were Clydebank, Scotstoun and Govan, with that last area comprising two yards. Clydebank was based on the famous John Brown's yard that had been opened in 1870 by the Thomson Brothers and was later sold to the Sheffield Steelmakers whose name it thereafter bore. In its heyday and before the end of the Second World War, it was famed for having built both the world's biggest liner and the world's largest aircraft carrier.

Scotstoun was the home of the shipbuilding company Charles Connell & Co. which had been there since 1861. It had been labelled the 'convict yard' in its early days in response to the desire of its well-intentioned owner to employ convicted felons. It had made its name through fast sailing ships and like several others accordingly did not have its own engine works.

The Govan division consisted of Fairfield's and Stephen's yards. The former had acquired the premises of John Elder and latterly William Pierce both names now synonymous with Govan though a park and an institute. The Fairfield's yard had acquired much of its reputation through the early design and construction of steam ships. Stephen & Co. had a history spanning two centuries. The family whose name it bore began shipbuilding on the Moray Firth in the north east of Scotland. Subsequent generations then expanded to Aberdeen, Arbroath and Dundee before Alexander Stephen opened a yard in Glasgow in 1851. He leased the Kelvinhaugh shipyard before buying the estate land at Linthouse on the other side of the river and heralding the opening of Stephens of Linthouse which became world renowned.

A fifth yard, Yarrow's, was part of the consortium but operated somewhat tangentially. Yarrow's, a name now redolent of the Clyde, actually had its origins in London. It was founded in 1865 by Arthur Yarrow and was based in Poplar in London before moving to Cubitt Town in 1898. It built many of the Royal Navy's first destroyers and also developed a boiler known as the 'Yarrow Boiler' used in many ships. As costs in the city grew and the yard needed to expand, the company relocated to Glasgow at what was in 1906 a greenfield site in Scotstoun. There it continued its expertise in building destroyers, and it also constructed merchant ships specialising in riverboat vessels for use in the southern hemisphere. In 1964, it took over the Blythswood yard to its east that had itself been established in 1919. It came out of the UCS consortium in February 1971 months before the occupation of the yards began.

By 1969, when Jimmy was returning to shipbuilding after more than a decade away from the yard, the industry was in decline. While the yards still dominated the Clyde and Ken Douglas, the new managing director of the UCS, was popular and spoke out strongly about the viability of the industry, the following year was to see UK tonnage slip to just 5 per cent of world production. Despite these dubious prospects, Jimmy was just glad to be earning a proper wage again and be out of the stifling atmosphere of the Communist Party offices. He was returning to the yards.

CHAPTER SEVEN

A RETURN TO THE YARDS

So, in 1969, Jimmy finally entered the shipyards he had known as a boy in Govan and had visited when working at British Polar Engineering. The Communist Party had helped him to find employment. They had been genuinely sorry to see him go and, in any event, he still remained a leading party figure and sat on the main committees. With their contacts in the yards and engineering industry, they were able to advise where jobs were available. Though blacklisting did occur in sectors of the engineering trades and especially in the construction industry, it didn't affect the shipyards in the west of Scotland where the Communist Party was already deeply rooted. So it didn't take long to find a place to start.

It was to the Upper Clyde that Jimmy Reid returned in 1969 and he initially worked as a fitter at Fairfield's in Govan, although he moved to John Brown's shortly afterwards. Working in the yards provided more pay than his work as a full-time Communist Party official, but money was still tight for the family. Joan had done a secretarial course at Clydebank College and would go on to work for a consultant at the Western Infirmary in Glasgow. In the meantime, Jimmy's earnings from the yards would still be essential.

Jimmy was soon elected as convenor of the AEU and Chairman of the Outfit Trades at John Brown's. That was to be the base from which his role in UCS would follow. Senior steward positions were full-time roles within the shipyards, as in other industries. There was sufficient work negotiating between management and workforce to justify it and wages were paid by the employer in recognition of that. It still applies today in sectors that remain unionised. It saw him swap his boiler suit for a jacket and tie, though the family often joked that Jimmy, who was far from a handyman around the house, was never suited to one anyway.

It wasn't long after Jimmy had moved to John Brown's that a crisis began to loom in the yards. Though the five yards had been restructured into UCS in February 1968, they were significantly undercapitalised to meet the challenges. Though a £5.5 million interest free loan had been granted at the establishment of it, £3.5 million went in clearing existing losses. Of the £2 million that remained for investment, over half went in building a covered yard for Yarrow's, which would leave the consortium in February 1971. Shipbuilding required materials to be acquired and wages to be paid before the financial return on the ship being constructed could be fully realised. The Geddes Committee had anticipated that it would be several years before the yards could be made profitable, although others thought it always doomed to fail. Borrowings had to be made and it was paying out £2 million per annum in loan interest without funds necessarily coming in. No matter what management or the workforce did, the ship was slowly sinking along with the cargo of debt it was carrying.

The Labour government refused to countenance increased

capital for the enterprise and declined to acquire the remaining shares in UCS belonging to John Brown's, when they were offered to them. That would have meant the government having a majority stake and it becoming to all intents and purposes nationalised industry. This meant that the company and the yards ploughed on into the waves that were beginning to lap over them.

By 1970, the problems were such that workers were already getting jettisoned overboard to lighten the load. The boilermakers had to accept 3,500 redundancies. Moreover, Alexander Stephen & Sons ceased shipbuilding and became a steel fabrication plant. Management and workforce hoped that those sacrifices would steady the ship. Older unprofitable contracts had been finished and new orders had been acquired that would generate a profit. Industrial relations had improved immeasurably, especially in demarcation between trades that had plagued the industry – an issue that had infuriated management and painted an unfavourable picture with much of the public.

However, it appeared there might be some calmer waters ahead, if the yards could only reach them. Indeed, some suggested that they could have been profitable by as early as 1972. By 1971, UCS had worked through the previous loss making orders and construction of unprofitable specialised ships had ceased, which included the flagship *Queen Elizabeth II*. Moreover, it was one of the few yards in the world with an order book of ships being constructed at current not historical prices; amounting to almost £90 million in total for thirty-four ships. The type of ship being built had also changed. The emphasis was now on the construction of standardised bulk carriers and general cargo vessels: less complex and more profitable.

However, it was not to be. Harold Wilson, the Prime Minister, called a general election that June, in 1970. Polls had him leading and the narrow Tory victory that came about was unexpected. It was to have profound consequences for the UCS yards. One of the early actions of the Tory government was to end the practice of guaranteeing yard owners against possible losses on orders.

Even worse was to follow. The Technology Ministry was merged with the Board of Trade and the Secretary of State in charge of the new Department of Trade and Industry was John Davies. He had been the Director General of the CBI and in November 1970 spoke in the House of Commons setting out the course he was to chart and the concept of 'lame ducks' in industry entered the political lexicon. By that, it was meant that governments would not bail out businesses that they felt couldn't survive on their own account. Other factors such as social costs and wider economic impact were to be ignored.

In early February 1971, Rolls Royce the car and aerospace manufacturer ran into difficulties. The production of the RB211 advanced jet engine had proved fraught and they hit financial turbulence. Davies had previously implied that the government wouldn't become involved or bail them out. However, on 4 February Davies announced to the House of Commons that a receiver had been appointed. And, more importantly, Davies said that due to Rolls Royce's importance for national defence, the government would be nationalising the company.

What applied to the aerospace industry was not, however, going to be replicated in the shipyards. With UCS facing cash flow problems and needing an injection of cash, several approaches were made by management to the government between October 1970 and February 1971. Given the 'lame duck' position being adopted, direct investment wasn't sought. Government guarantees that would have allowed for continued borrowing to be obtained were requested, but that call was rejected and, as a consequence, orders couldn't be accepted or wouldn't be awarded, given lack of credit for the yards and the suppliers' lack of confidence.

But, a decision had already been made by the government and they were operating according to a plan, unbeknown to those in the yards at that time. Those in management had been genuine in their approaches, and hoped that their pleas and arguments would be heard. However, the Ridley memorandum had already been written and was the template being operated to. It had been prepared in 1969 while the Tories were still in opposition and was compiled by Sir Nicholas Ridley, who became a junior minister in the Heath administration. He was later to gain notoriety for a similar type of plan a generation later, when Margaret Thatcher's government confronted the miners. His tactics then were to build up coal supplies before confronting the unions, which came to pass with calamitous consequences for the industry and the workforce. His proposals for shipbuilding, penned in 1969 when the Tories were still in opposition, envisaged the UCS being carved up. Firstly, by separating off Yarrow's yard and thereafter by selling off the others, to whoever would buy them. It was kept secret.

On 11 February, the week after the Rolls Royce announcement, John Davies made a further statement to parliament – this time about UCS. Advising that both the UCS and Yarrow (shipbuilders) faced cash flow problems, his action was to transfer the UCS consortium's 51 per cent share of Yarrow (shipbuilders) to Yarrow

& Company Limited giving the latter 100 per cent of the company. No payment was involved and it effectively hived Yarrow's off, as Ridley had suggested in private. Davies's reasoning was that they were primarily a naval yard and were important for the Royal Navy. In light of that, they were also to be supported by public funds through the Ministry of Defence who would provide £4.5 million of working capital over the next few years to support them. But, as Davies made clear, the UCS would be denied additional funds or further credit support. They appeared expendable, regardless of the cost to the communities on the Clyde.

Creditors knew that the consortium was operating on borrowings and, following Davies's remarks, began to panic. As they sought payment of sums due, the UCS was embarking on a course for bankruptcy. In June 1971, the UCS management approached the Department of Trade and Industry again and requested a loan of £5 or £6 million for working capital to see them through until they could become profitable, given the orders they had. The Board of UCS was meeting frequently and urgently. The need for both preventive and preparatory actions were now reaching a critical stage. They had met with the Secretary of State on Thursday 10 June and made their request. He had declined to give a specific answer but said he would consider their requests, although he indicated it was unlikely.

They met again on Saturday 12 June and the chairman advised board members that he had spoken to the minister at midnight and had been asked to delay any formal decision until the Monday. He indicated that he had advised that actions such as a composition of creditors and deferred payments were possible but an injection of capital would still be needed. Another offer to meet with the minister urgently was made wherever and whenever he could manage time.

On Monday 14 June, the board met again and the chairman advised that he'd travelled to meet the minister in his constituency in Knutsford, Cheshire, the day before. Nothing specific had been agreed but no indemnities were on offer for directors, even though reductions in staffing were offered. During the board meeting the chairman took a call from the minister. The call was relayed to the directors and was formally noted in the minute book.

The Secretary of State said that Her Majesty's Government had now reached the firm conclusion that they cannot put in large sums of money to save UCS, but that they were seeking to enlist the cooperation of the Provisional Liquidator so that they could explore what parts of the company might be saved and that they will be prepared to give him funds to that end.

As a result of the call, the board agreed to petition for liquidation. The die was cast and the company was going under.

That same day, 14 June, Davies told the House of Commons that he'd been approached by the UCS chairman the week before about the likelihood of being unable to meet the wage bill for the following week. The projected deficit for the consortium by the end of August was to be £4 or £5 million and they'd require the appointment of a provisional liquidator unless steps were taken to assist. The chairman had asked for £5 or £6 million in grant or equity to see them through that period and beyond. Davies said the government had reflected on the position, but that £20 million had been lent over recent years and the company was saddled with debt. On that basis, no new funds would be provided and a provisional liquidator would be appointed. A committee would be established to consider all options thereafter. Rolls Royce had been nationalised and Yarrow's hived off and effectively privatised, albeit with government credit provided, both ostensibly due to their strategic defence interests. However, there was to be no salvation for the four other yards and their primarily mercantile marine base.

The committee that was set up became known as the three wise men, though they were soon to become four. They were Alexander MacDonald from Distillers, the shipping magnate Sir Alexander Glen and David MacDonald of Hill Samuel merchant bankers. They were joined later by a fourth, Lord Robens. He had been a Labour MP but subsequently had become chairman of the National Coal Board, where he had presided over a significant period of closures in the industry. Needless to say, the workforce and many others feared a far from sympathetic hearing or outcome.

Their proposals were announced by John Davies in a parliamentary statement on 29 July. It was brutal and indicated that the continuation of the current UCS venture was unviable. They stated it had been a faulty concept all along and they also criticised the management of it. Their view was that it could not continue with the structure as it was, given the orders that were outstanding. They therefore suggested liquidation but also the reduction to just two yards at Govan and Linthouse. That would retain possibly 2,500 jobs which they felt was adequate for the remaining contracts. But still, it would mean the closure of two yards in Connell's and Clydebank, as well as the loss of 6,000 jobs.

However, by then both the workforce and the entire community had started to mobilise. The financial difficulties were obvious to the workforce and the scale of the crisis was becoming clear to the shop stewards. Conscious that the consortium was in trouble and jobs were being threatened, the stewards from the yards had met at the Trade Union Centre at Glasgow Trades Council on Sunday 13 June, the day before Davies's announcement in Parliament. Direct action was discussed, but the imminence of the blow was unknown at the time. Plans were made for delegates to meet with the government, but the announcement when it came shocked both stewards and workers.

Union members met with Prime Minister Ted Heath on 15 June. They were followed in quick succession by an STUC delegation and then a civic one, including the Provost of Clydebank. All received a polite hearing but an unfavourable response. The campaign in Clydeside began to step up a gear. A meeting on 21 June brought 800 stewards from across the west of Scotland together, along with trade union officials and even some clergy. At very short notice they arranged a mass march and rally with a token industrial stoppage called for 24 June. The support proved to be massive. Almost 100,000 people stopped work in sympathy and 50,000, including stewards, politicians and the entire Clydebank Town Council, marched to Glasgow Green.

On 28 July, a deputation of stewards met with John Davies to plead their case for the shipyards on the Clyde. Other stewards met politicians viewed as having influence. However, the response was a firm rebuff. Davies gave them short shrift and was adamant that there would be substantial redundancies. There was no understanding or consideration for the effect mass redundancies could have, not just on individuals but on entire communities. Many of the stewards, like Jimmy, could remember the lean times they had grown up in when mass unemployment and poverty were daily scourges. Unlike them, Davies was from a privileged background and, as the following decade under Thatcher was to show, the Tories were prepared to countenance mass unemployment once again: a sentiment that was borne out in his parliamentary statement the following day.

Though the men and the community had been aware of the possible axe falling, it still sent shock waves along Clydeside. Newspapers described Clydebank as being like a town in mourning, but the mood was soon to move from dismay to determination. Mobilisation of the men and the community continued, and the occupation was about to begin.

CHAPTER EIGHT

THE OCCUPATION

It was fortunate that so many outstanding individuals were working at UCS when the crisis struck. Jimmy, Sammy Barr, Bob Dickie, Jimmy Airlie, Sammy Gilmore and many more rose to the occasion when the occupation came to the fore. All were equally vital to the success of the campaign and their energy encouraged and sparked off each other throughout it. They and many more came together to contribute their skills and determination to what became a titanic struggle. It was a collective effort, even if Jimmy was in the spotlight more often than others, and Jimmy was always at pains both during and afterwards to make that clear.

The campaign was well structured and the strategy was clear. The stewards set out with a clear intention to have a solid base underpinning their campaign. The platform for it was the shop stewards' committee, which represented the trade unions in each individual shipyard. A coordinating committee was also established to bring representatives from all of the yards together. It had approximately forty members and it included not just delegates from the individual shop stewards' committees but representatives of management staff involved, and trade union officials. Others were brought in to deal with issues that arose such as press and campaigns. Moreover, given the effect of the occupation on the wider community, local groups and organisations, including local ministers, were invited along. Obviously, when it came to any issue that required a formal decision, only the delegates from the yards or staff associations could vote, but others in attendance were also able to contribute, thereby creating a bond with the community that would prove vital as the campaign dragged on.

They met once a week and the delegates then reported back to their individual shipyard shop stewards' committee. If needed, there could be departmental meetings within each shipyard amongst different trade unions. Mass meetings also took place on a regular basis to allow the entire workforce to be involved and to hear from their representatives. Bringing them together served as a morale booster and it was a vital part of the democratic process. Buses ferried people to and from the meetings which varied between Govan and Clydebank. It was a sizeable movement of people and, given the numbers, the police were often called in to aid the direction of traffic.

Jimmy Airlie was the chairman of the coordinating committee, replacing an earlier incumbent who had stood down. He had been the lead shop steward at Fairfield's. Like Jimmy, Airlie was a communist and in the AEU and he was also a very able public speaker. Born in Renfrew just along the river from Clydebank in 1936, he went to work at Fairfield's after his national service, and became union convenor. He was overshadowed in some ways by Jimmy's profile, but his role should not be ignored or downplayed. He was every bit as pivotal in the organisation of the occupation as was Jimmy. In behind the scenes organisation and marshalling the tactics, he was at the forefront of the goings on and the occupation's ultimately successful conclusion.

During the UCS occupation and for some time thereafter Jimmy and Jimmy Airlie were not only close comrades but good friends. There would be a schism when Jimmy later left the Communist Party and Airlie remained a member. However, at that time and for quite a period thereafter, they were very close. On Friday nights, you could often see them together having a drink and a singalong, even if many felt Airlie's voice left a lot to be desired. He subsequently became a full-time union official with the AEU and won Gavin Laird's Scottish seat in 1983, which Jimmy had contested almost a decade before. He died in 1997.

Sammy Barr, born in 1931, was a Glaswegian welder and a member of the boilermakers' union. He was the shop stewards' convenor at Connell's yard where he had worked since the late 1950s. Like Reid and Airlie, he was also a communist and had served on the Scottish committee of the party and stood as a candidate in several elections both national and local in the late sixties and seventies. Another bright and intelligent man, he was to thrive on the challenge and rise to the occasion of the occupation. He died in 2012.

Sammy Gilmore represented the electricians' union on the co-ordinating committee. Born in the Calton in Glasgow's East End in 1939, he was sharp and articulate. Gilmore was viewed as vital in ensuring both public support and maintaining the morale of the workforce throughout the campaign. He died in Glasgow in 2011.

Bob Dickie was the shop stewards' convenor at John Brown's yard and a member of the Amalgamated Society of Woodworkers.

A left-wing activist though not a Communist Party member, he still lives in Clydebank and is now a stalwart figure in the Asbestos Action Group, an organisation that tackles the disease that has afflicted many in the shipyards and the community where he worked and lives.

These men came together on the coordinating committee to decide on a campaign to save their jobs and protect their community from the devastation that would surely follow with mass unemployment. Talk of action had been ongoing for a while, but a normal strike wouldn't work given the redundancies that had been announced. Something else was needed if there was to be more than just marches and demonstrations but ultimate defeat.

It was Jimmy who came up with the idea of a work-in. The shop stewards were discussing their options for action and they well knew that if they went out on strike then they'd simply be locked out. During the ongoing debate concerning the circumstances and challenges they faced, Jimmy suggested a work-in. It was a stroke of genius. It was then discussed and debated by the stewards and they all agreed it. Jimmy never sought to claim the credit, but that's where it lies.

It then had to be put into action. On Friday 30 July, the day after Davies had made his announcement, the men and their fellow stewards met and took control of the yards. Stewards manned the gates. The liquidator had refused media access to the yards but that was overruled by the stewards' committee. It was to prove a wise decision. The world's press descended and witnessed not just the start of this historic event but an outstanding speech from Jimmy, in which he narrated the basis of their actions.

With the giant cranes featuring as the backdrop, an improvised stage had been prepared at the yard. Jimmy's words were to echo around the country and garner support from across the globe. He started by saying they were 'fighting for the right to work. And what better way to do it than by continuing working'. He then went on to lay out the basis of what they were going to do and how it was going to be carried out, stating:

> We are not going to strike. We are not even going to have a sit-in strike. Nobody and nothing will come in and nothing will go out without our permission. And there will be no hooliganism, there will be no vandalism, there will be no bevvying because the world is watching us and it is our responsibility to conduct ourselves with responsibility and with dignity and with maturity.

The speech was largely unscripted but it resonated far and wide nonetheless, capturing the mood and the moment. It laid down the workers' determination to fight but also the requirement to be organised. It confronted the men with the trials that they were about to face and warned them of the absolute need for discipline. It inspired them to fight, yet tempered how they would go about it.

His message succeeded both within and beyond the yards. He created a sense of strong determination within the workforce under the leadership of the stewards, and he succeeded in calling to arms support from far and wide, including from John Lennon of the Beatles who saw the TV clip and responded with a supportive note and £1,000 donation. When the rock star's donation was announced at a mass meeting, it led one worker to shout that Lennon was 'deid', thinking they were referring to Lenin. It was to be one of many donations large and small received, though others weren't met with quite the same disbelief.

Things were moving apace. A meeting held in Glasgow on 10 August was attended by 1,200 shop stewards from across both Scotland and the north of England. Financial and more general support was offered and began to flow in. A special congress of the STUC was called that also sought to mobilise support. Jimmy spoke at that and received a standing ovation. A commitment was made to back the strike and a rally was planned for 18 August.

That day saw glorious sunshine across the west of Scotland that smiled on the workforce and their supporters. Around 200,000 workers put down their tools in support of the UCS occupation, almost a quarter of all Scottish workers. About 80,000 people gathered at George Square in Glasgow for another mass march and rally. Tony Benn, Vic Feather, the Trade Union Congress (TUC) General Secretary, and Hugh Scanlon, the AEU Leader, were in the forefront with the shop steward leaders. Other political and civic leaders from communist through to nationalist affiliations were also present and spoke from the platform at Glasgow Green, which saw Scotland united behind the occupation. The loudest cheers were reserved for Jimmy, who, in a stirring speech, said:[*]

Today Scotland speaks. Not the Scotland of Edward Heath, Gordon Campbell, Sir Alex Douglas Home – of the lairds and their lackeys.

They have never represented Scotland, the real Scotland, the Scotland of the working people.

---

[*] Jimmy Reid, *Reflections of a Clyde-built Man*, pp. 84–85.

No title, no rank, no establishment honour can compare with the privilege of belonging to the Scottish working class.

That is what I want to say on behalf of UCS workers to our brothers and sisters who have responded so magnificently to our call for help and solidarity.

Government action has projected us into the front rank of the battle against the policies of redundancies and closures.

They picked the wrong people. We stood firm and refused to retreat. We were prepared, of necessity, to stand on our own and fight alone. But we were not alone.

Confident in our belief in our fellow workers, we told Heath and his government that this was the breaking point for the Scottish working classes ... indeed the Scottish people.

There were those – and they were few – who counselled against a precipitate appeal to the workers. But the shop stewards believed that time was of the very essence. That for too long the fight against redundancies and closures had been confined to the morass of high level negotiations. Meanwhile, workers whose livelihoods were at stake stood waiting outside closed doors to be told second hand whether they might work or whether they would sign on at the Labour Exchange.

And the Answer, invariably, was the dole queue. This time the workers and the shop stewards of UCS were determined this would not happen.

This time we took appropriate action and appealed over the heads of government and institutions.

We appealed to the highest authority in this land: to the people.

Already there was pent up anger and frustration. Hopes had been dashed. There was despair at our apparent inability to influence and determine our own destiny. There were creeping redundancies.

It needed only a spark to ignite those feelings. To give them positive expression. We suggest that the workers of UCS have themselves provided that spark. We are witnessing an eruption not of lava but of labour.

The labour of working men and women.

Let Mr Heath take note. Unless he and his colleagues are prepared to meet the urgent social needs of the people then this eruption will engulf both him and his Government.

It is incredible but the Downing Street mentality seems to be: this government has lost confidence in the people – let's change the people.

Edward Heath, I tell you this. We are going to fight and we are not going to change. Either you will change or we will change the Government.

The rally energised both the workers and their growing supporters across the land. It also further raised the profile of Jimmy, who, along with Jimmy Airlie, was becoming the face and voice of the campaign. The campaign had launched and was getting a fair wind, but it required constant efforts from the stewards and officials. It meant long days and great distances to be travelled for many.

The coordinating committee met at 9 a.m. every Monday and the meetings could run for up to two hours. Discussions and negotiations with senior management and the liquidator were always conducted by the committee, but convenors and stewards could deal with local management at individual yards. Various sub-committees were also established to deal with particular issues. A publicity committee was set up to provide a variety of pamphlets and literature. A weekly notification, titled the 'UCS Shop Steward Bulletin', was printed for the workers' internal information and posters and leaflets prepared for outside use by supporters. Bob Starrett, a young painter with a remarkable talent for cartoons and drawings, oversaw the creation of these documents. They brought workers some much needed light relief and boosted morale, as well as garnering the public's support.

An administrative committee was formed to deal not only with the organisation of meetings within the yards but with requests for speakers to attend rallies and events around the country and abroad. A finance committee handled the administration of funds as well as payment of wages to those who had been made redundant. This committee also had to oversee the workers' financial commitment to the cause. Every worker was levied 50p whether they were on the liquidator's pay roll or the campaign in the yard, and it was paid willingly by all.

Money poured in via donations from both individuals and other union groups far and wide. The Irish Transport and General Workers' Union sent funds, as did Soviet shipyard workers. East German trade unionists were precluded from sending money, but offered free holidays to 100 shipyard workers instead.

Considerable efforts to raise funds were also made by the men themselves. The former boxing champion Peter Keenan arranged a night's entertainment in Clydebank and leading Scottish actors and musicians including Roddy McMillan and former shipyard workers, including Johnny Beattie, Glen Daly and Russell Hunter, put on a fundraising show at the Kings Theatre, Glasgow, with all proceeds going to support the work-in. These contributions were greatly appreciated. It was indicative of how hugely the work-in affected the soul of the people of Scotland. It was clear that even those who had left the workforce were not going to forget their former colleagues in their time of need.

Recognition of it being a collective effort and for the community was demonstrated when the miners went on strike in early 1972. Conscious of the support they themselves had received, UCS donated the equivalent of one week's levy to their colleagues in their struggle against the Tory government.

Funds were badly needed not just to support the campaign but to pay the wages of workers who had been made redundant by the liquidator. Having refused to accept their redundancy notices, they had no other income than the funds raised by the coordinating committee. The weekly running costs amounted to £8,500–9,000, which was not an inconsiderable sum in those days. They were not covered by insurance for any industrial injury, so those men were not exposed to the riskier parts of the trade. They were, however, still contributing to the work being carried out in the yard.

A parallel structure emerged in the yards during the occupation to deal with those who were still employed by the liquidator and those who were paid by the coordinating committee. The former still had management and administrative staff to check people in and out and to pay the retained workforce. The coordinating committee therefore employed clerks to administer who had been made redundant, which included themselves.

Everyone worked closely together. It was in everybody's interests that good order was maintained and the yards worked effectively and efficiently. The liquidator benefited from orders being completed and he left the government and unions to resolve the wider political issues. He simply accepted the occupation and worked around it, and even allowed the yard's office computers to be used for the payroll for those who had been made redundant but were involved in the work-in.

Even the police played their part. They had been liaising with the stewards and helping with traffic control from the outset. Many, no doubt, privately supported the occupation given where they and their families were from. Indeed, Jimmy later commented that senior police officers had expressed concern to the government about whether or not they'd be expected to remove the workforce, indicating that they felt some officers may decline to do so. They gave their assistance on many an occasion, not just with the movement of workers but also with machinery. The good order that had been demanded at the outset by Jimmy was maintained. It's said that even the coming and going from the yard was more orderly than it had been before the work-in.

The campaign continued on other fronts. The STUC sought to pursue the social consequences of closure and the coordinating committee endeavoured to broaden that out to include the causes that were driving it. By that they meant the decision to refuse to provide financial support for the industry. Moreover, even eminent economists such as Professor Kenneth Alexander from the University of Strathclyde, who had been a director at Fairfield's, commented that UCS was viable if given an opportunity and some capital support. The breadth of backing was considerable.

However, it wasn't all plain sailing for UCS. Though the publicity had been welcome, many of the comments in the press were unfavourable. The *Glasgow Herald*, though sympathetic to the plight of those about to lose their jobs, opposed the work-in and accepted the case for closures. The *Daily Express* and many others expressed similar remark. Both those papers were to become despised by the workers for the position they took and the comments they made throughout the occupation. It made the coordinating committee's internal bulletin more essential than ever when it came to tackling misleading information and allaying fears.

As the occupation continued and work progressed on ships in the yards, another issue arose. When orders were completed at Clydebank and Scotstoun, there were no new orders waiting, given the announced closure of the yard. This problem was compounded by the additional men made redundant but working with their still-employed colleagues. The increased workforce was simply accelerating the pace of completion of the order, which, in turn, would lead to the more imminent closure of the yard: an invidious and ironic position given that the work-in was meant to save the jobs. Accordingly, the coordinating committee directed that where a retained worker was doubled up with one who had been made redundant, they would not exceed the work expected from a single employee. A sensible and pragmatic decision that saved an individual's job but protected the wider wellbeing of the yard.

In the shipyards, the tension didn't interfere with the humour that abounded. The venues that had seen Billy Connolly amongst others emerge from within were energised. The mass meetings that took place invariably included warm-up acts to amuse and settle the men before the main speeches and proposals were put. The entertainment came from workers themselves, many of whom were naturally gifted comedians or entertainers. They cheered the crowd up on what often could be cold, damp days, and relaxed the tension hanging in the air. The attendant media were amazed at the discipline and good humour present in the vast crowds.

In early September, news of the Ridley Report broke. It came as a shock to the workforce and was headlined in the press and media. The news was followed up by the government's announcement that followed their template to divide the workforce. On 22 September, Davies announced a proposal to separate the Govan and Linthouse yards from the consortium and form them into Govan Shipbuilders in an attempt to break the unity of the workforce. The company was to be chaired by Hugh Stenhouse, an insurance broker and a former treasurer of the Conservative Party in Scotland. After Stenhouse was killed in a car crash a few months later, he was replaced by Lord Strathalmond, who had experience in the oil industry. Others appointed to the board were similarly limited in shipyard experience.

Both Jimmy Reid and Jimmy Airlie were at the forefront of the calls to refuse the terms of the Ridley Report. At a mass meeting on 24 September, Jimmy described the proposal as 'jobs for the boys', and by boys, he meant the directors on the board not the workers in the yards, and noted its similarities with the structure that had previously failed and led to the demise of UCS. Their calls were challenged and they had to argue the case before the workforce. They recommended rejecting the proposals when the floor was opened up for questions and comments. A voice shouted out asking if they wanted the men at Govan to become redundant along with everyone else. Despite some barbed comments from others assembled, the heckler continued with his challenge and asked why Govan should be dragged down by Scotstoun and

Clydebank. Jimmy retorted, 'I don't anticipate defeat, I anticipate victory'.* He added that while meaningful discussions would be held, he implied that this wasn't the time. His sharp rebuttal of any surrender enhanced the mood of defiance and curbed any wilting support. It was received with huge roars of approval and it was viewed as a pivotal moment by shop steward colleagues.

While the proposal was overwhelmingly rejected, it was indicative of the challenge the coordinating committee still faced. Maintaining morale was hard, but it was something the committee was determined to do, especially considering the government's and the media's attempts to undermine them.

The following month, Jimmy Airlie reported back on negotiations with government over their proposals to another mass meeting on 8 October. He showed himself to be an able orator, if not in possession of the same flair or panache of his colleague. He said:

> We will not bow before intimidation and blackmail. The Tories cannot allow ordinary people to express their hopes and aspirations. If UCS is defeated, then men and women everywhere will be afraid to say 'we have rights'. But we will not fail the labour movement. We will not fail the working class. Above all we will not fail ourselves. All four yards, the entire labour force, no redundancies.†

The tag-team effort of the two continued when, at a mass meeting in January 1972, Jimmy Reid stated in his rousing address:‡

---

* Willie Thompson and Finlay Hart, *The UCS Work-In*, p. 65.
† Willie Thompson and Finlay Hart, *The UCS Work-In*, p. 83.
‡ Jimmy Reid, *Reflections of a Clyde-built Man*, pp. 89–90.

We are reaching a crucial stage in this fight. This campaign can be successful but there is the need for optimism and confidence. It can be won.

But I tell you to win any fight you have to have the workers in the yard or the factory concerned resolved to fight to their end and win. In the absence of that you can get all the decisions you want but there can be no final victory. We have this in abundance at UCS. No movement, no fractures, no cracks in unity. Whatever is said and written in the future I've never seen a better bunch of fighters than the UCS workers have demonstrated themselves to be since the end of June of this year.

Victory is important not just for us. There is now a tremendous feeling of responsibility on our shoulders because we have become the symbol of the fight against policies of redundancies and closures.

Defeat, or a settlement tantamount to defeat, a compromise which means the selling out of jobs, will have a harmful effect on all those workers who have been inspired to fight redundancies and closures.

On the other hand, success in UCS will have a regenerating effect on the whole working class movement. We have to say that, and we have to fight along these lines because there is now little doubt that since the general election unemployment has been used as an instrument of government policy. They rejected an incomes policy, but the strategy obviously was to create such a pool of unemployment that would make an incomes policy unnecessary.

The workforce remained defiant and public support remained strong. As the end of the year approached, there were signs that the government was backing down. Talk of mass redundancies ceased and the plan of the three 'wise men' slipped into history. Lord Strathalmond embarked on a new plan. He suggested that an injection of some £25 or £30 million would be necessary for Govan Shipbuilders, which was a significant move away from the previous proposal to close two yards and making significant redundancies. Moreover, the funding to support the shipyards would be required to come from a government that had previously said that lame ducks would not be supported and had turned against granting public funds for such industries.

It was clear that there was some commercial interest in the yards and especially from some businesses in the United States. Senior union representatives flew out to Texas in January 1972 to meet Marathon Manufacturing, who were then the world's largest oil-rig builder and who had shown interest. The government was asked by the unions to send a similarly high-powered delegate to the US for discussions, but it refused. However, as events were to show, the interest was there.

In the meantime, issues were arising that the workforce needed to address. After all, work had been ongoing and three ships were now nearing completion. Initially, it was decided not to allow the vessels to be released, as it would reduce the workers' bargaining power in the ongoing negotiations. The liquidator, however, was anxious for the ships to be launched and, after reflection, it was agreed that the *New Westminster City* ship would be released as a gesture of good faith in the ongoing and increasingly frought negotiations.

Jimmy was again at the fore of these negotiations. After the stewards had all agreed that releasing the ship was the right strategy, they still had to win over the men who saw retention as necessary and release of the ship as a sell-out. Jimmy tempered the heated debate between the two sides and spoke passionately for compromise. He stated:

> I'm all for standing on my own feet even if we get beat, but, by Christ, I'd rather be standing on my feet and winning, and that's what we've got to try and do.
>
> Sammy Gilmore said that if we did anything to lose the US bid for Clydebank and the jobs there, the punters will strangle us, and they'd be right as well.
>
> We've got to make sure that the government get no pretext for saying that these obscurantist saboteurs the shop stewards and workers have blasted negotiations.[*]

Once again, his oratory worked and the vote for releasing the ship was overwhelming. They had managed to ease defiance at a time when the workforce was nervous about an occupation, and even encouraged calm amid anxieties about a concession. Jimmy inspired the men to be realistic as well as resilient.

Jimmy was the star of the campaign even if it was a communal team effort. Requests for him to address meetings of all sizes came from around the country. As such, he was often on the road. He had to endure long hours and little rest. The work-in almost consumed his entire life. Despite still being young and fit and being passionate about the cause, he began to feel the strain.

Suggestions had been made to move the leadership of the

---

[*] Willie Thompson and Finlay Hart, *The UCS Work-In*, p. 89.

dispute from the stewards to the STUC. Some say that the idea had come from Jimmy Milne, the General Secretary of the TUC, but the proposal was rejected by the shop stewards, so support continued to be channelled through the coordinating committee.

Jimmy's commitments didn't simply involve the coordinating committee or the various support groups; he was also still committed to the Communist Party. They realised that he was their star player, even if he was no longer a full-time official for them, and they were keen to maximise his impact for them. The party appreciated how important Jimmy's efforts for the occupation were for them, both in the community and politically for them as an organisation. Johnny Gollan had said that the party needed to put everything behind UCS. Jimmy toured the country speaking at public meetings and to party branches. Little wonder that in November 1971 he topped the poll in the election for positions in the Communist Party's Executive Committee, even polling ahead of Gollan.

Jimmy's schedule was relentless. Meetings, rallies and media calls continued throughout the work-in and beyond. In an interview with the *Clydebank Press* in the October, Jimmy said that his diary commitments involved speaking in East Anglia and then spending forty-eight hours in London before returning to Faifley at a time when travel was considerably more arduous than it is now. That week wasn't unusual: it was just the venues that varied. The yard meetings and organisation of the work-in with his colleagues needed to be maintained, as did some semblance of family life with Joan and their three young children.

Something was bound to give, and it eventually did. In March 1972, he was taken to the Western Infirmary in Glasgow after suffering from what was described as nervous exhaustion. He was discharged shortly afterwards and continued the same frenetic pace. June saw him collapse in the family home in Clydebank and this time he had to be taken to Knightswood Hospital. he was diagnosed with bronchitis, but in reality, it was just his body being put through too much and it was clear that he was putting himself under too much strain. He was discharged after a few days' rest and returned to the fray, only to be hospitalised again in October in the Southern General on this occasion. All those incidents related to the work-load he was shouldering and the pressure under which he was operating. Fortunately, there were to be no long-term health issues as a result but it was a frightening time for the family, especially when, on one occasion, he had been taken away from the house on a stretcher. It was doubtless also worrying for him, even if he didn't show it.

It was a stressful time for the Reids. The telephone never stopped ringing and journalists would arrive at the door with no warning. That isn't to say, however, that this period didn't have its lighter moments. Joan recalled a BBC camera crew visiting only to be met by a host of young Clydebank children demanding that their favourite cartoon character Scooby-Doo, which had been axed, be restored to the screens.

Thankfully, the possibility of a settlement was becoming more and more likely. Govan Shipbuilders would take responsibility for the three yards in Glasgow, not just the two in Govan. Meanwhile, Marathon Manufacturing in the US would acquire Clydebank. Any redundancies would be purely voluntary. On 28 February 1972, Davies made yet another speech in the House of Commons on UCS, in which he confirmed the new structure of

Govan Shipbuilders. There he pledged £17 million to clear inherited losses and a further £18 million for capital development, as Lord Strathalmond had alluded to a few months before. In addition, aid would also be given to Marathon Manufacturing in their acquirement of the Clydebank yard. It was a far cry from Davies's pronouncements the previous summer that no support or succour would be afforded and yard closures and redundancies were to be accepted. It was a clear turnaround from a previous refusal to bail out a so-called 'lame duck' industry.

Though there was an inkling that a settlement was coming, it was still somewhat of a shock for both stewards and workers when it was officially announced. The surprise concerning the details coming from Westminster took some time to register. Jimmy was interviewed on television and welcomed the government's announcement, still somewhat nonplussed at the scale of their success.

The jobs and the yards would be saved. The work-in had succeeded. Seven months of struggle both in the workplace and around the country had been vindicated. A government that had refused to consider a £6 million line of credit and were prepared to make closures and mass redundancies had been defeated. Now, over £30 million was going to be invested and the only redundancies would be voluntary. Men who faced the dole queue had retained their jobs and communities that had feared catastrophe were spared. The relief and delight along the banks of the River Clyde was palpable.

In interviews given and comments made at the time, Jimmy was magnanimous towards John Davies and didn't take the opportunity as others perhaps might have done to gloat or revel in the workers' success. He was fulsome in his praise of his colleagues and of Jimmy Airlie in particular. He was keen as ever to ensure it was recorded as a team effort. When asked about his own ambitions, he simply said he wanted to get back to the yard.

There were still some job losses, but they were limited. The numbers employed dropped from 8,500 to 6,000, but this figure represents some of those who had taken voluntary redundancy, opting for new careers and a different life. Others departed due to retiring and others had passed away. Otherwise, the core workforce in the yards was preserved and the devastation on the wider community avoided.

It was not all plain sailing from then on, though. Issues that later arose at John Brown's were understandable given the nature of the new owner. Marathon Manufacturing were concerned with oil rigs rather than building ships. Accordingly, many of the fitting-out skills that were needed on a ship were surplus to requirement for a rig. Some outfitters were transferred to the ship yards at Scotstoun or Govan where their skills were still needed. For the others, the solution was to retrain them as boilermakers, but that was to prove problematic. There were issues in the selection for training and it created too many boilermakers for the management's need or liking. The new American owners weren't prepared to countenance a job-sharing scheme as practised by the work-in, as they sought to maximise their investment. Accordingly, by autumn 1972, the new owners were seeking to make redundancies at their new Clydebank site and were even threatening to pull out of their deal.

However, the threat didn't materialise. Some redundancies did take place at Clydebank, but they were very limited. Accordingly, the weekly 50p levy stopped that month and the campaign was formally wound up in October 1972. The new American owners managed to absorb all the ex-Clydebank workers by November 1973 with the exception of a slight delay with the boilermakers. There were issues transferring skills across the yards given the different abilities required for shipbuilding and oil-rig construction, but they were duly resolved.

Even so, the future of the shipbuilding industry remained bleak. Famous names such as Henry Robb's in Leith and Hall Russell's in Aberdeen were to close in the coming decades. South of the border, the great shipbuilding centres on the Tyne, Wear and Mersey were also vastly diminished.

The Clyde was to be no different. The Labour government under Jim Callaghan nationalised many of the yards in 1977 and delivered what many had sought over the years. However, his government was soon to be replaced by Margaret Thatcher's in 1979 and the age of privatisation came upon that industry and many others. Unfortunately, neither nationalisation nor privatisation was able to save many of the Clyde yards they had fought for so heroically. The interminable decline that had been ongoing for generations continued and many yards shut for ever.

John Brown's continued as Marathon Oil and built oil-rig installations until they sold their site to a French company in 1980. It finally closed in 2001. Now, the titan crane stands as a testimony to Clydebank's history as a shipbuilding community and the site itself is now the campus for a new college and other regeneration efforts.

Connell's in Scotstoun became part of Scotstoun Marine Ltd, which was a subsidiary of Govan Shipbuilders Ltd that had been established during the work-in. It continued to operate until 1980 when it finally closed. That brought the site's use as a yard to an end, concluding 119 years of use of the site for shipbuilding.

The site is now used by other industries, but far fewer people are employed there and the absence of the yards has dramatically changed the community.

Govan fared better, though not without considerable loss of employment over the years and regular threats about its closure. The Linthouse yard closed in 1972 as the Govan yards were merged. Fairfield's became part of Govan Shipbuilders which, when shipbuilding was nationalised in 1977, became known as British Shipbuilding. In 1988, as privatisation continued under Thatcher, British Shipbuilding was sold to a Norwegian company, Kvaerner. They, in turn, sold the company to Clydeport and the site is now operated by BAE Systems Ltd.

Yarrow's, which had cut free from UCS at the beginning of the difficulties, was also nationalised by Callaghan. A profitable venture, they were accordingly one of the first privatised by the new Thatcher regime. In the mid-1980s, it was sold to GEC-Marconi which, in turn, at the turn of the millennium sold it to BAE. Both Yarrow and Govan now form part of BAE Systems Surface Ships Ltd.

Closures were suffered all along the banks of the Clyde, not just on the Upper Clyde but also along its lower reaches. Scott Lithgow's in Greenock, which had come about through the amalgamation of two famous old Clyde firms, was nationalised and became part of British Shipbuilding in 1977. It was reorganised in 1981 and sought unsuccessfully to pursue offshore technology. It was subsequently sold on, but closed thereafter.

Now only Ferguson's in Port Glasgow stands today, though it was also regularly threatened with closure until very recently. Some diversification and input from a wealthy Scottish business man seems to have turned it around for the good of the workforce and the community forged by it. The great days of being Clyde-built, however, have sadly passed into history despite the historic efforts of the UCS workers.

Despite that, what the work-in achieved should neither be underestimated nor its significance underplayed. It wasn't simply the jobs and the wider communities that were saved, although they were important enough in an area that would have been devastated by the original planned closures and redundancies, as it would be when the full extent of Thatcherism hit home a decade later. Their fight fired the convictions of many across the land. Their victory energised others as the struggle between unions and the Heath government continued to be waged. Ultimately, it would help lead to Heath's election defeat in February 1974 when he went to battle with the miners on a subtext of a debate over who exactly ran the country. Heath would have faced challenges anyway, but the impetus given by UCS should not be underestimated.

Moreover, these modern Red Clydesiders laid the foundation for workplace and community action in years to come. It showed people that redundancies need not be accepted with equanimity and that radical action could bring success. Other workplace occupations would later take both heart and their lead from UCS. It was to become the stuff of legend and its legacy serves as a remaining beacon of hope in Scotland and elsewhere.

Just as how the great ships the workers on the Clyde built attest to their craftsmanship, the UCS's work-in testifies to their radicalism. Jimmy and his colleagues have gone down in history as an inspiration to fight for the right to work. But Jimmy wasn't one for sitting back on his laurels. Other struggles remained for him to undertake and he was on track for a rectorial victory.

CHAPTER NINE

RECTORIAL VICTORY

Jimmy's profile had never been higher than it was during the UCS work-in. He was a media celebrity and synonymous with the work-in. His comments were widely reported and he was eagerly sought after to speak at events. Both the UCS campaign and the Communist Party sought to capitalise on Jimmy's popularity. When the opportunity arose to stand for election as the Rector of Glasgow University, which occurred while the work-in was still taking place, Jimmy's candidacy was to prove an instant success.

Established in 1451, Glasgow University is the second oldest university in Scotland and the fourth oldest in the UK. Originally located in the city's high street, it moved to its current main site and campus at Gilmorehill in 1870. In Glasgow's west end, many of its principal buildings look down upon the Clyde. It stands today as it did when Jimmy first ventured there, though it has expanded hugely in scale and size as have all such institutions. The university boasts many distinguished alumni, including the philosopher Francis Hutcheson and the economist Adam Smith, as well as famous engineers and scientists such as James Watt and Lord Kelvin.

The role of Rector itself was a historic one, going back over the centuries to the university's very foundation. It was an honorary post and therefore without remuneration for its tenure of three years. Though largely symbolic, it was still a prestigious role and involved chairing the University Court.

The retiring Rector was Lord George MacLeod of Fuinary, who had founded the Iona community in Govan. Previous holders of the office had included Viscount Hailsham, then serving in Heath's government as Lord Chancellor, and Stanley Baldwin, the former Tory Prime Minister. It was normally a post held by an establishment figure, although MacLeod, John MacCormick, the Home Rule campaigner, and Albert Luthuli, the African National Congress leader, had all been elected despite their more radical bent. But never before had a working-class communist occupied the position.

Universities have grown in number, and the students attending them have increased substantially since Jimmy's days. In 1971, Glasgow was viewed as very middle class and rather conservative in nature, akin to many such ancient and grand institutions. It wasn't even a member of the National Union of Students, which was perceived as being too left wing. So Jimmy's running in the campaign was part of an ongoing dispute. He was asked to stand as he was viewed by many as a candidate who could win the support of a broad base across the left. Jimmy hadn't considered going to university and had no prior involvement with such academic institutions. Moreover, he was extremely busy given the ongoing work-in and the campaign surrounding it.

Both the election itself and any victory would be another commitment that would fall upon Jimmy's already weighed-down shoulders. However, given its location in Glasgow and the publicity it would attract, there were also opportunities that would arise from it. He and his colleagues on the coordinating committee thought it through and came to a collective decision. His colleagues consented as they could see the high profile he could gain for the cause. It was finally concluded that the pros outweighed the cons and he agreed to be nominated – although it must have been with mixed emotions that he consented.

Though nominated by the socialist society, he drew support from across the political spectrum. Communists, Liberals, Labour and the SNP, as well as the socialist society, backed him. Others in organisations as diverse as the International Club, the Catholic Society and Student Social Action also supported him. His campaign energised many seeking change within the university, as well as supporting the UCS campaign.

His opponents included former Labour minister Margaret Herbison and sitting Conservative MP Teddy Taylor. Margaret Herbison had been Labour MP for North Lanarkshire from 1945 until 1970 when she'd stood down. She'd served as a minister of social security in Harold Wilson's government between 1964 and 1967 and was an economics graduate of the university. She had the support of the Labour Club.

Teddy Taylor was the Tory MP for Cathcart, a constituency on the south side of the city. He was a right-wing populist making his name by calling for the restoration of the birch and capital punishment. Elected in 1964, he had held the seat against the odds. Eventually defeated in 1979, he thereafter won a seat in Southend which he held until he retired in 1997. Not only was he a local MP, but he had been a councillor in the city before that. He'd also been a minister in the Scottish office from the election of the Tory government in June 1970 until late July 1971 when he resigned over Ted Heath's support for the EEC. It was on the back of stepping down from ministerial office that he possessed the time and had been given the encouragement to stand.

Two other candidates – the poet Roger McGough and the media personality Michael Parkinson – were also nominated to stand. However, their papers weren't submitted appropriately and they were excluded from the contest, so it was to be a straight race between Herbison, Taylor and Jimmy. There was no firm favourite and there were no opinion polls and evidence was anecdotal; though it was generally accepted that Jimmy had a good chance of being elected.

Taylor, however, seemed to have an edge since he had the financial resource to produce glossy leaflets. Despite this, Jimmy had many young and energetic supporters keen to rally together for the cause. He went to a few campus meetings, though the campaign was largely carried out by young socialists in his absence due to his commitments both at the work-in and around the country in support of it.

It was a short campaign, with the election due at the end of October. Jimmy's manifesto of sorts sought to encourage greater student participation in the running of the institution. Jimmy called for a student assessor to be appointed, a role that would require assisting the Rector and also allow students direct voice in matters concerning the university. Lord MacLeod had sought to do that, but had been unsuccessful in his efforts.

Many of the Glasgow University students were from Greater Glasgow and lived at home. Most of them had probably not even been aware of Jimmy who, though he lived amongst them, operated in a different orbit as a leading communist and local councillor. All that had changed after the work-in. His speech at the first meeting had captured the attention not just of the media but of many young minds. He had since regularly been on TV, on the radio and splashed across the papers. In many ways, he was the man of the moment, even overshadowing Teddy Taylor's resignation from ministerial office that captured some attention in late July.

It was still no easy contest. Herbison and Taylor both had considerable support as well as resources, and would be no push-overs. Jimmy's core campaign group was made up of an alliance of young left supporters and radical spirits, but what they lacked in experience and resources they made up for in enthusiasm. These supporters canvassed for him and distributed leaflets and the campaign fed off Jimmy's public profile.

Something was afoot in Scotland and passions were being stirred beyond the university campus. Public support for the demonstrations and sympathy for the actions of the UCS work-ers straddled all social classes and age groups. Even middle-class students' families in leafier Clydeside suburbs were sympathetic to the plight of the workforce. Their student sons and daughters couldn't have avoided being caught up in it. Jimmy was the public image of the work-in and a vote for him was a vote for workers' rights. Moreover, he was showing himself to be a formidable talent, as well as a charming individual. The campaign began to gain momentum, even if the candidate was rarely present.

Despite Jimmy's limited direct involvement, he won a stunning victory, polling not far off 50 per cent of the vote to become the university's youngest, as well as most radical, Rector. The final result was:

Reid: 1,458
Taylor: 891
Herbison: 810

His victory made the headlines both near and far. Pictures of a jubilant Jimmy being carried by his student supporters appeared in many newspapers. Both his young student supporters and colleagues in UCS revelled in the result. Though unexpected, it was a welcome boost for him individually and the workers collectively. He was flooded with letters congratulating him and requests for him to speak at engagements, adding to the already heavy workload.

Jimmy's rectorial victory came when the work-in had been ongoing for three months and the attempts to divide the workforce had been made. It was hard going for all despite the support they were receiving from near and far. His success boosted morale as the dark nights and winter approached. It was a clear indication that support for the work-in was not simply in working class households but across a much broader range of society. Backing for the workforce was being shown to be widespread.

It was expected that the new Rector would give an address to the gathered congregation. Some previous office holders would have had their speech written for them, but not Jimmy. He was going to craft a speech by himself. He realised that this was another golden opportunity to promote his belief in the communist cause. His inauguration wasn't to be until April of 1972, due to the routine university procedures for the handover of the post and the other formalities that arose. This delay allowed him to concentrate on the successful outcome of the UCS work-in.

Jimmy picked up on some very pertinent issues faced by students. He supported the outcry of five undergraduates who had been unfairly evicted from a student hall of residence in February 1972 and he joined with students in opposing proposals for changes that would have given the university control over students' own funds. His support for students wasn't restricted to the university he represented as Rector, as he showed when joining national demonstrations against cuts to student grants in 1974.

However, notwithstanding his other efforts, it was to be his inaugural address that cemented Jimmy's legacy as Rector. It was delivered on the evening of Friday 28 April in the august setting of Bute Hall, sited in the gothic university buildings on Gilmorehill that look down upon the River Clyde. The topic of the lecture was for the newly installed Rector to select and Jimmy chose to speak about alienation.

He crafted the speech the day before and had it typed up. Though limited in preparation time, it was a chance to speak to and engage with a new audience, though he wasn't to know just how large it would actually be. There was a lot riding on it and he knew it. If he performed well, then it could open many more doors for him and the causes he believed in. He read and reread it, pacing the floor at home and speaking out the lines. By the time he delivered it, he was almost word-perfect, though he still read it seamlessly from the script.

The inauguration was a grand affair, full of the pomp and ceremony that goes with such events. The University Principal and Court were there in their finery and academics were resplendent in their robes. Jimmy, too, had to wear a robe and sport a white bow tie as part of the ceremonial regalia. It was the first time he'd ever dressed that way and it wasn't something he was ever comfortable with. However, such fripperies were fine for him if they afforded an opportunity to put his message across. Students and former graduates also packed the hall, joining friends and family and others who simply wished to be present.

The university establishment sat facing him in the front rows in the hallowed halls. Many hadn't wanted him elected in the first place, principally because of his political views. Some were even angered by the result, feeling that he was neither right for the role, nor up to it. They were quickly to be proven wrong. The hall soon became spell-bound by his address. His eloquence and thoughtfulness stunned many into silence. The end of the speech was met with wild cheering as everyone rose from their seats to give him a two-minute standing ovation. Even the academics who had doubted him had been won over, and were clapping as enthusiastically as long-time comrades. Jimmy had made his mark.

It wasn't simply the passion with which he conveyed it but the reflection and thoughtfulness contained within it. This was no communist dogma delivered from a soapbox but a view of humanity articulated in a way that deftly challenged the orthodoxy of the time. Some may have anticipated a rabble-rousing speech but this was to be a powerful, yet tempered, lecture. Others may have expected a socialist rant and castigation of capitalism – and it most certainly was the latter, but in a way in which Christ was invoked and ideology eschewed.

It was hard to argue against both the logic and conviction of it. The immortal phrase that 'a rat race is for rats. We're not rats. We're human beings' struck a chord amongst many, irrespective of political allegiance. The conviction that 'from the very depth of my being, I challenge the right of any man or any group of men, in businesses or in government, to tell a fellow human being that he or she is expendable' is equally hard to refute. In many ways, it was sermon delivered from the depth of his soul. The reception was rapturous and the coverage was equally so. Jimmy had reached another level and had shown he was perfectly comfortable performing.

This is the address he gave:

Alienation is the precise and correctly applied word for describing the major social problem in Britain today. People feel alienated by society. In some intellectual circles it is treated almost as if it is a new phenomenon. It has, however, been with us for years. What I believe to be true is that today it is more widespread, more pervasive than ever before. Let me right at the outset define what I mean by alienation. It is the cry of the men who feel themselves the victims of blind economic forces beyond their control. It is the frustration of ordinary people excluded from the processes of decision making. The feeling of despair and hopelessness that pervades people who feel with justification that they have no say in shaping or determining their own destinies.

Many may not have rationalised it. May not even understand, may not be able to articulate it. But they feel it. It therefore conditions and colours their social attitudes. Alienation expresses itself in different ways in different people. It is to be found in what our courts often describe as the criminal antisocial behaviour of a section of the community. It is expressed by those young people who want to opt out of society, by drop-outs, the so-called maladjusted, those who seek to escape permanently from the reality of society through intoxicants and narcotics. Of course, it would be wrong to say it was the sole reason for these things. But it is a much greater factor in all of them than is generally recognised.

Society and its prevailing sense of values leads to another form of alienation. It alienates some from humanity. It partially de-humanises some people, makes them insensitive, ruthless in their handling of fellow human beings, self-centred and grasping. The irony is, they are often considered normal and well-adjusted. It is my sincere contention that anyone who can be totally adjusted to our society is in greater need of psychiatric analysis and treatment than anyone else. They remind me of the character in the novel, *Catch 22*, the father of Major Major. He was a farmer in the American Mid-West. He hated suggestions for things like medi-care, social services, unemployment benefits or civil rights. He was, however, an enthusiast for the agricultural policies that paid farmers for not bringing their fields under cultivation. From the money he got for not growing alfalfa he bought more land in order not to grow alfalfa. He became rich. Pilgrims came from all over the state to sit at his feet and learn how to be a successful non-grower of alfalfa. His philosophy was simple. The poor didn't work hard enough and so they were poor. He believed that the good Lord gave him two strong hands to grab as much as he could for himself. He is a comic figure. But think – have you not met his like here in Britain? Here in Scotland? I have.

It is easy and tempting to hate such people. However, it is wrong. They are as much products of society, and of a consequence of that society, human alienation, as the poor drop-out. They are losers. They have lost the essential elements of our common humanity. Man is a social being. Real fulfilment for any person lies in service to his fellow men and women. The big challenge to our civilisation is not Oz, a magazine I haven't seen, let alone read. Nor is it permissiveness, although I agree our society is too permissive. Any society which, for example, permits over one million people to be unemployed is far too permissive for my liking. Nor is it moral laxity in the narrow sense that this word is generally employed – although in a sense here we come nearer to the problem. It does involve morality, ethics and our concept of human values. The challenge we face is that of rooting out anything and everything that distorts and devalues human relations.

Let me give two examples from contemporary experience to illustrate the point.

Recently on television I saw an advert. The scene is a banquet. A gentleman is on his feet proposing a toast. His speech is full of phrases like 'this full-bodied specimen'. Sitting beside him is a young, buxom woman. The image she projects is not pompous but foolish. She is visibly preening herself, believing that she is the object of the bloke's eulogy. Then he concludes – 'and now I give...', then a brand name of what used to be described as Empire sherry. Then the laughter. Derisive and cruel laughter. The real point, of course, is this. In this charade, the viewers were obviously expected to identify not with the victim but with her tormentors.

The other illustration is the widespread, implicit acceptance of the concept and term 'the rat race'. The picture it conjures up is one where we are scurrying around scrambling for position, trampling on others, back-stabbing, all in pursuit of personal success. Even genuinely intended, friendly advice can some-times take the form of someone saying to you, 'Listen, you look after number one.' Or as they say in London, 'Bang the bell, Jack, I'm on the bus.'

To the students [of Glasgow University] I address this appeal. Reject these attitudes. Reject the values and false morality that underlie these attitudes. A rat race is for rats. We're not rats. We're human beings. Reject the insidious pressures in society that would blunt your critical faculties to all that is happening around you, that would caution silence in the face of injus-tice lest you jeopardise your chances of promotion and self-advancement. This is how it starts, and before you know where you are, you're a fully paid-up member of the rat-pack. The price is too high. It entails the loss of your dignity and human spirit. Or as Christ put it, 'What doth it profit a man if he gain the whole world and suffer the loss of his soul?'

Profit is the sole criterion used by the establishment to eval-uate economic activity. From the rat race to lame ducks. The vocabulary in vogue is a give-away. It's more reminiscent of a human menagerie than human society. The power structures that have inevitably emerged from this approach threaten and undermine our hard-won democratic rights. The whole process is towards the centralisation and concentration of power in fewer and fewer hands. The facts are there for all who want to see. Giant monopoly companies and consortia dominate almost every branch of our economy. The men who wield effective control within these giants exercise a power over their fellow men which is frightening and is a negation of democracy.

Government by the people for the people becomes meaningless unless it includes major economic decision-making by the people for the people. This is not simply an economic matter. In essence it is an ethical and moral question, for whoever takes the important economic decisions in society ipso facto determines the social priorities of that society.

From the Olympian heights of an executive suite, in an atmosphere where your success is judged by the extent to which you can maximise profits, the overwhelming tendency must be to see people as units of production, as indices in your accountants' books. To appreciate fully the inhumanity of this situation, you have to see the hurt and despair in the eyes of a man suddenly told he is redundant, without provision made for suitable alternative employment, with the prospect in the West of Scotland, if he is in his late forties or fifties, of spending the rest of his life in the Labour Exchange. Someone, somewhere has decided he is unwanted, unneeded, and is to be thrown on the industrial scrap heap. From the very depth of my being, I challenge the right of any man or any group of men, in business or in government, to tell a fellow human being that he or she is expendable.

The concentration of power in the economic field is matched by the centralisation of decision-making in the political institutions of society. The power of Parliament has undoubtedly been eroded over past decades, with more and more authority being invested in the Executive. The power of local authorities has been and is being systematically undermined. The only justification I can see for local government is as a counterbalance to the centralised character of national government.

Local government is to be restructured. What an opportunity, one would think, for de-centralising as much power as possible back to the local communities. Instead, the proposals are for centralising local government. It's once again a blueprint for bureaucracy, not democracy. If these proposals are implemented, in a few years when asked 'Where do you come from?' I can reply: 'The Western Region.' It even sounds like a hospital board.

It stretches from Oban to Girvan and eastwards to include most of the Glasgow conurbation. As in other matters, I must ask the politicians who favour these proposals – where and how in your calculations did you quantify the value of a community? Of community life? Of a sense of belonging? Of the feeling of identification? These are rhetorical questions. I know the answer. Such human considerations do not feature in their thought processes.

Everything that is proposed from the establishment seems almost calculated to minimise the role of the people, to miniaturise man. I can understand how attractive this prospect must be to those at the top. Those of us who refuse to be pawns in their power game can be picked up by their bureaucratic tweezers and dropped in a filing cabinet under 'M' for malcontent or maladjusted. When you think of some of the high flats around us, it can hardly be an accident that they are as near as one could get to an architectural representation of a filing cabinet.

If modern technology requires greater and larger productive units, let's make our wealth-producing resources and potential subject to public control and to social accountability. Let's gear our society to social need, not personal greed. Given such creative re-orientation of society, there is no doubt in my mind that in a few years we could eradicate in our country the scourge of poverty, the underprivileged, slums, and insecurity.

Even this is not enough. To measure social progress purely by material advance is not enough. Our aim must be the enrichment of the whole quality of life. It requires a social and cultural, or if you wish, a spiritual transformation of our country. A necessary part of this must be the restructuring of the institutions of government and, where necessary, the evolution of additional structures so as to involve the people in the decision-making processes of our society. The so-called experts will tell you that this would be cumbersome or marginally inefficient. I am prepared to sacrifice a margin of efficiency for the value of the people's participation. Anyway, in the longer term, I reject this argument.

To unleash the latent potential of our people requires that we give them responsibility. The untapped resources of the North Sea are as nothing compared to the untapped resources of our people. I am convinced that the great mass of our people go through life without even a glimmer of what they could have contributed to their fellow human beings. This is a personal tragedy. It's a social crime. The flowering of each individual's personality and talents is the pre-condition for everyone's development.

In this context education has a vital role to play. If automation and technology is accompanied as it must be with a full employment, then the leisure time available to man will be enormously increased. If that is so, then our whole concept of education must change. The whole object must be to equip and educate people for life, not solely for work or a profession. The creative use of leisure, in communion with and in service to our fellow human beings, can and must become an important element in self-fulfilment.

Universities must be in the forefront of development, must meet social needs and not lag behind them. It is my earnest desire that this great University of Glasgow should be in the vanguard, initiating changes and setting the example for others to follow. Part of our educational process must be the involvement of all sections of the university on the governing bodies. The case for student representation is unanswerable. It is inevitable.

My conclusion is to re-affirm what I hope and certainly intend to be the spirit permeating this address. It's an affirmation of faith in humanity. All that is good in man's heritage involves recognition of our common humanity, an unashamed acknowledgement that man is good by nature. Burns expressed it in a poem that technically was not his best, yet captured the spirit. In 'Why should we idly waste our prime...'

The golden age, we'll then revive, each man shall be a brother,
In harmony we all shall live and till the earth together,

> In virtue trained, enlightened youth shall move each
> fellow creature,
> And time shall surely prove the truth that man is good
> by nature.

It's my belief that all the factors to make a practical reality of such a world are maturing now. I would like to think that our generation took mankind some way along the road towards this goal. It's a goal worth fighting for.

It wasn't just covered by the Scottish media, but by the world at large. While appreciative reporting might have been expected from some Scottish papers, the coverage in the *New York Times* could never have been anticipated. It reprinted Jimmy's speech in full, describing it as the most important speech since Abraham Lincoln's Gettysburg Address. Praise, indeed, and from an unexpected but authoritative source.

A few months later when Jimmy was at the university on rectorial business, a knock on the door revealed the world-famous Glasgow-born psychiatrist R. D. Laing, who was holding a copy of the speech. He asked Jimmy what kind of books he had read and studies he had carried out to reach his conclusions about alienation in contemporary society. Jimmy answered that his observations from working at John Brown's and living in Clydebank was enough material for him. The learned academic had obviously anticipated Jimmy to have undertaken a mountain of academic research.

Jimmy's speech resonated so widely at the time because he had encapsulated the feelings of many towards monopoly capitalism.

In Scotland, old traditional Scottish firms were being bought up by larger firms from south of the border or even multinational ones. It was shown in the shipyards but was occurring all across the manufacturing sector as well as impacting on the service industries. Headquarters and jobs that they both contained and sustained were being lost. Individuals who previously knew their employer were finding executives in their place who came from afar and knew little of the history of the company and cared even less for the needs of the community. It was the same in England where larger firms acquired smaller ones and headquarters drifted to London or even across the Atlantic. Even in the USA, combines were growing and small firms were reducing. Scale was everything and centralisation was happening apace. Society and politicians were struggling to adapt and hence the feeling of alienation as people lost control. Many saw their work and livelihood being bought and sold before their very eyes with little care for the consequences for them or effects on the wider community. The ability of individuals to act or react was limited and a sense of powerlessness was growing. That frustration, as well as the fear it invoked, was encapsulated in Jimmy's short speech. But what also mattered was that he said it needn't be. He challenged and stood up to what had simply been taken for granted. He gave hope and belief that there was a better way. No wonder it resonated on the Hudson as well as on the Clyde. Given the success of the UCS work-in, there was also some ground for optimism.

It was to project Jimmy to a new level of popularity. He was no longer merely a very articulate shop steward, but a figure who could eloquently argue for a cause disdained by most. Opportunities came to raise his own individual profile which he took to like a duck to water. Jimmy was a natural in front of the camera as well as on the political platform. He was not just articulate and erudite but charming and thoughtful with it. The Communist Party remained keen to keep his profile high and pushed Jimmy relentlessly.

In October 1971, he appeared on the ITV programme *Face the Press* and performed remarkably well, sustaining an argument for the workers and socialism in a manner that was passionate but unthreatening. It most certainly wasn't the monologue of a communist apparatchik or the loud-mouth ranting of an angry shop steward that many might have expected. People from all across the country wrote to the programme and to him personally. Those who were supportive of the socialist case were delighted to have such an appealing advocate and even those who disagreed respected his reasoning and logic.

Further appearances were to come on major programmes hosted by the likes of Robin Day, a formidable interviewer, where Jimmy again performed with aplomb. In May 1972, he appeared on BBC Scotland's *Open to Question* show with Lord George MacLeod of Fuinary, in whose Iona community's premises he'd first begun his political activism and whom he'd succeeded as Rector of Glasgow University. MacLeod had become minister of Govan Old Parish Church and had gone on to found the Iona community both in Govan and on the isle. He was committed to socialism and pacifism, as well as to his Christian faith.

It was followed that November by an appearance on the peak time BBC programme *A Chance to Meet* hosted by Cliff Michelmore, another celebrity interviewer of the time. The programme included a wider discussion on more philosophical matters. The synopsis for the show trailed 'I'd like to see the word "work" with "service" – service to your fellow human beings.' Had Jimmy Reid sacrificed these early high ideals? Can you be both a Christian and a Marxist in practice? Jimmy often quoted from Christ or the Bible; in his rectorial address, he had asked 'what doth it profit a man if he gains the whole world and suffer the loss of his soul?' He was knowledgeable about ecclesiastical affairs and biblical tracts and his socialism, while not a Christian socialism as advocated by some, was certainly based on the core tenets of Christian morality. He greatly admired Jesus Christ the man, though he never accepted either the existence or worship of a god.

Once again, following the programme, letters flooded in to him and the BBC. Many old communists and die-hard socialists took inspiration from someone articulating the moral basis for their beliefs beyond the economic arguments for a better or fairer world. He also inspired many theologians and clergy. Letters abounded from vicars in the south of England and clergy throughout the UK, saying how much they had enjoyed listening to him and recognised the shared values that they held. Many sought to engage in theological discussions which Jimmy may have had the inclination for but most certainly didn't have the time to respond to. The emphasis of many was on his articulation of humanity and Christian brotherhood having shared values. All of which had deeply resonated with many faithful. Moreover, they seemed to respond well to the way Jimmy had challenged them in a non-threatening way to consider the social and economic aspects of the world as much as their general theological doctrine. In many ways, it was an early articulation of 'liberation theology' that was to rise in Central and Latin America where socialism and Catholicism started to march hand in hand. It showed another side to Jimmy, as someone who was a politician but also an armchair philosopher, and Jimmy had both the intellectual hinterland to sustain it and the skilled TV persona to display it.

In 1973 he received an invitation to appear on the chat show hosted by Michael Parkinson. It was on at a prime-time slot on a Saturday night when television had far fewer channels. He was beamed directly into people's living rooms and the viewing figures were huge.

Several weeks before, the comedian Kenneth Williams had been on the show and, having strident right-wing views, he'd sneered at strikers and was scathing about socialism. Condemnatory of trade unions, he had even accused them of 'jeopardising their fellow man'. Michael Parkinson interjected at one stage to challenge Williams on some of his more outlandish claims, particularly when he contrasted his own actions as an aspiring actor with those working men.

It was thought appropriate to get Williams back on to the show along with an articulate trade unionist, no doubt to see what sparks might fly. With Jimmy's stock being high, what better contrast could there be than the plummy voiced English actor and the Clydeside communist. Many, and certainly the haughty actor, thought there would be no contest between the two. Parkinson later related how prior to the show, Williams had sought to belittle Jimmy. Williams quoted lines of classical poetry and arrogantly asked Jimmy if he knew who had written them. He was gobsmacked when Jimmy quickly and accurately named the poet. Jimmy in turn went on to quote other lines and asked Williams if he knew who had written them. Williams had to confess that he didn't and was astonished when Jimmy replied that he had.

The TV appearance was to be a surprise for the viewers who might have expected the shipyard worker to be pounded by the actor. As it was, Jimmy wiped the floor with the supercilious and snide Williams. His breadth of knowledge along with his calm demeanour and general humility was a welcome contrast with the overbearing and conceited manner of his much more media-experienced opponent. Jimmy was making his mark yet again. His profile was higher than ever.

However, while he enjoyed a rectorial victory, there was to be both political and union electoral defeat to come.

CHAPTER TEN

ELECTORAL DEFEAT

The pace remained intense for Jimmy even if the publicity dipped slightly. Union work, Communist Party duties, council duties and a young family were all in the balance. The focus politically was to move from the workplace to the community and the issue changed from job losses to rent rises. The UCS dispute was resolved in 1972 but rent rises come to the fore. It was to be as fraught as the work-in but, unfortunately, less successful.

Local authority elections had taken place in Scotland in May 1972 and Jimmy was comfortably re-elected to Clydebank Town Council. In a straight race with Labour, he polled 1,817, to the Labour candidate's 1,245: a majority of 572. Two other communist councillors were returned in Clydebank along with him, though Labour was the dominant party.

Arguments had been simmering between the government and councils over rent increases for a while. Tory plans both north and south of the border would see councils obliged to impose substantial rent rises upon tenants. The Housing Finance Act was implemented in 1972 in England and Wales and similar provisions provided for in Scotland. The Tory government's intention was to phase out direct Exchequer subsidies for council housing and make councils ensure a profit was made on their housing account.

Some councils had subsidised housing from other revenue prior to that. Rents would need to rise, not be kept low and affordable. North of the border and in many places south of it, council housing was meant to be available for all who wanted it, not just the poor. The effect would be to make better off tenants pay increased rent to subsidise poorer ones and the people paying the price would be moderately well-off workers. In Scotland at that time, when home ownership was low and council tenancies the norm, it would affect many and, in some cases, substantially so.

The driver for the Tory ideology was their view that poorer home owners were subsidising council housing, ignoring the fact that tax and rates were paid by council tenants, and home owners also qualified for tax relief on their mortgage interest. Moreover, council housing had been paid for many times over through rents paid. Some of the deficit in places was also in maintaining interest payments for land purchases made.

In reality, it was an attempt to attack council housing and to undermine local government, especially Labour councils. The Tories had lost heavily in local council elections and their political base there was limited. They saw many parts of the country as a Labour fiefdom and considered low rents as a tool used by Labour councils to maintain popularity. Anything that undermined Labour and could lead to a switch in housing tenure would suit them. The next Tory government under Thatcher would see that taken much further with the 'right to buy' and the wholesale sell off of huge swathes of council housing stock. In effect, it marked the beginning the start of moving council housing from being tenure of choice for all to welfare housing for the poorest in society. The Heath administration, however, simply decided to target rent increases.

Anger grew both in council chambers and in the community. The north of England, south Wales and the west of Scotland were again to the fore. In the face of growing opposition and to force delivery of the Act, the Tories legislated for draconian sanctions for councils and councillors who failed to invoke the required rent increases. Councils could be taken over and forced to implement it and councillors could be surcharged leading ultimately to disqualification from office.

The consequences of severe rent rises allied to a growing mood of militancy saw many keen to challenge the government in spite of the legal threats. The political temperature was rising, with the miners' strike and other industrial disputes still ongoing. The 1972 Labour conference saw overwhelming commitment given to councils and councillors seeking to oppose it. As so often happened, however, what was decided by the Labour conference and rank and file delegates was not matched by action by their MPs or even their NEC. In particular, the Labour shadow minister for the environment Tony Crosland wasn't supportive of councils refusing to implement the rise and advocated setting a rent increase, albeit seeking to mitigate it.

Some councils were still willing to oppose it and stood their ground. The ability to do so was limited, since their only options were either rent strikes or refusing to implement a rise. Most councils, despite their opposition, had agreed to implement the increases by the end of the year. Those that continued to refuse to included Clay Cross and Camden in England and Merthyr in

Wales. North of the border, where the increases would be significant, Clydebank, Cumbernauld, Denny, Saltcoats, Whitburn, Alloa, Barrhead, Midlothian and Cowdenbeath held out until 1973.

The pressure was mounting. The mood of the wider labour movement was not matched by support from the parliamentary party or leadership. As the months passed by, many councils buckled under the threats to themselves and their elected members. Some waited to be found in default and then implemented the rise, taking the view they'd held out as long as possible and had at least frozen rents for a while.

Soon, few were left standing other than Clay Cross and Clydebank. Clydebank Council then had fifteen Labour councillors, three Communist, two SNP and an independent. Jimmy was at the forefront of advocating both no rent increase and the need for the council to be prepared to confront the government, notwithstanding the risks. The Labour spokesman on the council was equally strident. The politicisation of the community that had come about through UCS was finding expression in the council chamber. There was also support within the wider community from tenants' groups and trade unions. Jimmy and others felt that, in light of the success of the work-in, mass action could overcome the threat of administration or disqualification.

The Tory government, though, was intent on enforcing it. They started to apply the powers they had legislated to drive home the message and enforce the increases. In January 1973, Clydebank Council was fined £5,000 for its failure to impose a rent increase. Any appeal looked forlorn. The Tories, after all, had crafted the law to suit themselves and the courts were simply implementing

Jimmy and Joan on their
wedding day

Joan and Jimmy at home

The Reids at home in Clydebank

On holiday in Russia in the
early 1970s

Jimmy and Joan at the Chinese
Embassy when he was a
full-time official with the YCL

Jimmy speaking during the apprentices' strike

Jimmy speaking to crowds of Upper Clyde Shipbuilders

Jimmy Airlie and Sammy Barr with Jimmy © THE HERALD

Jimmy, Sammy Barr, Sammy Gilmore and another official at the DTI © THE HERALD

ABOVE Jimmy at a yard with Harold Wilson, the Labour leader © THE HERALD

ABOVE RIGHT With Jimmy Airlie, Tony Benn, Sammy Barr and Bob Dickie on another march in Glasgow © THE HERALD

RIGHT Jimmy and Bob Dickie giving an impromptu press conference outside the Marathon yard in Clydebank © THE HERALD

Jimmy and Joan with their youngest daughter, Julie, in Clydebank during the February 1974 election.
Peter Kerrigan in the background © THE HERALD

ABOVE Jimmy speaking at a UCS event
© THE HERALD

LEFT Jimmy giving a speech
in the yard © THE HERALD

Jimmy speaking at a mass meeting in Govan © THE HERALD

Jimmy marching with Jimmy Airlie, Tony Benn and Willie Ross in June 1971. Far left is Sammy Gilmore, Vic Feather, Danny McGarvey and Hugh Scanlon © THE HERALD

In John Brown's yard in Clydebank after news of the workers' success © THE HERALD

Jimmy celebrating at a demonstration in June 1972 © THE HERALD

Jimmy celebrating with a beer after his rectorial address at Glasgow University © THE HERALD

ABOVE Jimmy and his mother

LEFT Jimmy in the 1980s as he was embarking on his media career

Jimmy Reid
A Celebration of his Life

'A Rat Race is for rats. We're not rats, we're human beings. Reject the insidious pressures in society that would blunt your critical faculties to all that is happening around you, that would caution silence in the face of injustice lest you jeopardise your chances of promotion and self advancement.'

James Reid 1932–2010

Page one of the order of service at Jimmy's funeral

Break, break, break,
On thy cold gray stones, O Sea!
And I would that my tongue could utter
The thoughts that arise in me.

And the stately ships go on
To their haven under the hill;
But O for the touch of a vanished hand,
And the sound of a voice that is still!

Break, break, break,
At the foot of thy crags, O Sea!
But the tender grace of a day that is dead
Will never come back to me.

Alfred Lord Tennyson

Page two of the order of service at Jimmy's funeral

Order of Celebration

Speakers
David Scott
Sir Alex Ferguson
Bob Thomson
Jimmy Cloughley
Billy Connolly CBE
Rt. Hon. Alex Salmond MSP,
First Minister of Scotland

Music
Ode To Joy
Paul Robeson – Bass
Symphony No. 9 in D minor, Op. 125 'Choral'
Ludwig van Beethoven

Widor's Toccata
Symphony No. 5 Op. 42 No. 1 for Organ
Charles-Marie Widor

Musicians
Bobby Wishart
Gino Ciancio
Pipe Major Iain MacDonald

' Man is a social being. Real fulfilment for any person lies in service to his fellow men and women.'
James Reid, Rectorial Address April 28th 1972

The family requests that during this celebration of Jimmy's life there will be no bevvying...

Page three of the order of service at Jimmy's funeral

Joan and the family wish to thank you for joining them today, and thank everyone who sent flowers, letters and cards. We would like to make special acknowledgement to David & Liz Scott and Dan & Nikki Edgar whose support has been truly invaluable.

Joan and Jimmy celebrating his 70th birthday outside their home in Rothesay

Why should we idly waste our prime
The golden age, we'll then revive,
Each man shall be a brother,
In harmony we all shall live and till the earth together,
In virtue trained, enlightened youth shall move each fellow creature,
And time shall surely prove the truth that man is good by nature.

Robert Burns

The back page of the order of service at Jimmy's funeral

it. Others had fallen by the wayside as the lack of support from the Labour leadership became clear.

Moreover, although there was a mood of militancy in a few areas and some tenants' groups, it was never transformed into the same level of support that existed during UCS. Many trade unions, no doubt taking their lead from the Labour leadership, were muted in their support and major public demonstrations were few. However, the fine imposed for failing to set a rent increase was paid not from council coffers but from some supportive left wing union donations and funds provided by other affiliated bodies.

Jimmy and the local council recognised they were staring defeat in the face and support was not going to be forthcoming nor could victory be achieved. An even larger fine loomed for the council if they continued, and action was threatened against individual councillors. They accordingly decided that further refusal was doomed. The fine was paid reluctantly and the first stage of rent increases agreed. Their struggle didn't end there, however, as they delayed the next stage of the rent increases the following winter, an act of defiance that resulted in a further fine of £20,000 being imposed.

The decision to implement the increased rents wasn't done quickly or easily. There was a lot of soul searching done by Jimmy and colleagues across parties. Unfortunately, the stakes were too high and defeat was certain. Jimmy and the council were heavily criticised by some on the far-left who felt that he'd let them down. While Jimmy was loath to accept increased rents, his view was that a glorious defeat might flatter some egos but it wouldn't serve the community or the cause well. He and others had sought to build a mass campaign against the rent rises, but neither the wider labour movement nor the general public were rallying to the cause. Sympathy might have abounded but direct action there wasn't.

In these circumstances, continuing the struggle would simply see the rents enforced by administrators brought in to take over the council and the possible bankruptcy of individual council-lors. That wouldn't serve the community well, nor would having leading left figures disenfranchised from political office be of assistance to the wider cause, whereas a strategic withdrawal at least kept a sympathetic council in office and could attempt to limit the extent of the damage. He realised that there came a time when all that could be done had been done, and living to fight another day was a wiser course of action.

As it was, Clay Cross continued to hold out and refused to im-plement the rises. Their councillors were ultimately bankrupted, disqualified from office and the increases imposed. When Heath was defeated in 1974, action was taken to change the legislation though increases by then had already come in. However, despite a Labour conference resolution in 1973 to support the Clay Cross councillors and for a future Labour government to retrospective-ly remove any sanctions imposed, no such action was ever taken. Clay Cross and its councillors were left to their fate and were required to serve their punishments.

In the absence of a mass campaign, individual actions, whether by one council or even a group of councillors, was never going to be successful, no matter how heroic. In a newspaper inter-view, Jimmy was critical of the Labour leadership and made it clear that if all the non-Tory councils had stood firm, then the Tory government would have been powerless. As it was, UCS had shown Jimmy what was needed for a successful campaign and it just wasn't there in this case. It had also shown that not everything could be won or opposed and futile gestures ill served everyone. Jimmy and his colleagues had done all they could at the time, but had correctly stayed in office to mitigate and campaign rather than engage in a glorious but futile failure.

There had been by-elections in Scotland that tested the political waters throughout the Heath administration. The death of the sitting Labour MP led to a by-election in September 1971 in Stirling and Falkirk. The Labour candidate Harry Ewing won with a comfortable majority, though there was a significant swing to the SNP. March 1973 saw a further by-election take place in Dundee East, a seat that Jimmy would himself later contest for Labour. It came about as a result of George Thomson, the Labour MP, becoming a European Commissioner. It was won by Labour but only narrowly, with a majority of just over 1,100 following a large swing to the SNP.

Then in November 1973, there was a by-election in Jimmy's home patch of Govan when the Labour MP, John Rankin, died. In the 1970 election, Labour had won with over 60 per cent of the poll, with the SNP trailing in third place with 10.3 per cent. However, in 1973 there was again a massive swing from Labour to SNP which was enough to see Margo MacDonald win the seat with a majority of just over 500. She polled 6,360 votes (41.5 per cent) to the Labour candidate Harry Selby's 5,789 (38.3 per cent). However, it was clear that the fallout from UCS and disgruntlement with both the Tory government and Labour opposition meant that votes weren't going to the Communists but to the Nationalists.

Labour would narrowly regain the seat by just 543 votes in the general election soon to follow in February 1974, when Selby polled 10,326 votes (43.17 per cent) to MacDonald's 9,783 (40.9 per cent). That would be increased further to a majority of 1,952 in the October election of that year. However, though she lost the by-election, the glamorous and popular Margo MacDonald was to boost the nationalist cause as elections drew near. She afforded publicity and offered some credibility for a party then with just one seat.

However, it was clear that the confrontation between Prime Minister Ted Heath and the unions was growing and an electoral test was not far off. Disputes had been ongoing throughout his tenure, and not just at UCS. To tackle high inflation, the Tory government had sought to impose pay restraints on the public sector. This had led to disputes with many workforces but especially with the NUM. There had been a miners' strike in 1972, the first since 1926, although there had been an unofficial one in 1969. During that seven-week strike running from January into February, there was a violent confrontation at Saltley Gate in Birmingham when flying pickets, as mobile union activists were called, surrounded a coke plant to restrict delivery. It was an extremely cold February and power supplies were threatened, which resulted in a state of emergency being declared. The miners subsequently returned to work, accepting a significantly improved pay deal.

Despite their success, high inflation quickly eroded the miners' gains and by the following autumn their salary had again fallen below recommended levels of pay. The mood turned more militant and the summer of 1972 saw Mick McGahey, a Scottish communist, elected National Vice-President of the NUM. McGahey was a contemporary of Jimmy's in the CPGB, where his father had been a founding member. Born in Lanarkshire in 1925, he had followed his father down the pits at the age of fourteen. A union and communist activist, he was always more aligned with the hard-line 'tankie' wing. The gravel-voiced and often stony-faced McGahey remained a member of the Communist Party until its dissolution. He became president of the Scottish Area NUM in 1967 and stood unsuccessfully against Joe Gormley for the leadership in 1971. There was always antipathy between the two men, particularly as McGahey sought to pursue a more militant line in the '72 and '74 disputes. Ironically, it is suggested that the ill will led to Gormley postponing his retirement until 1981, by which time McGahey was over fifty-five and ineligible to stand for the presidency. The result was to hand the post to Scargill.

In November 1973, the miners rejected the National Coal Board pay offer and imposed an overtime ban. With winter commencing, it soon began to have a significant effect on coal supplies. Coal in those days was a hugely critical part of the national energy supply. Coal was still king and the NUM was a powerful prince.

In response to the overtime ban, Heath's government announced a three-day week that was implemented on 31 December. Other restrictions to try and reduce power demands included all television channels closing down at 10.30 p.m. The relationship between the miners and the Tory government continued to deteriorate and, on 24 January 1974, the miners voted to strike. It began on 5 February and two days later Heath called a general election. Citing the dispute, he went to the county with the question of 'Who governs Britain?', believing that the public would side with him against the unions.

Initially, it seemed Heath might be proven right with pundits predicting a Tory victory. However, the miners ensured that there was no disorder that might have given succour to the Tories and boosted their support. In addition, two published reports upheld the miners' argument. Firstly, the Retail Price Index published on 15 February showed a 20 per cent inflation figure, thus confirming that the miners' previous pay rise had been eroded. Secondly, a Government Pay Board report, published on 21 February, showed the miners to be earning less in comparison to other workers, which contradicted the National Coal Board's claims. Both those reports, along with the debilitating effect of the ongoing three-day week, harmed the government.

On 28 February, the country went to the polls. All bar one opinion poll had the Tories winning. As it was, they narrowly outpolled Labour in terms of popular votes but lost in seats by 301 to 297. In Scotland, seven SNP members were returned, which marked the start of an SNP surge in Scotland. Meanwhile, a Labour minority government was formed in the UK.

Jimmy had been selected to contest the seat of Dunbartonshire Central for the Communist Party. The seat was one of three new constituencies formed from the old East and West Dunbartonshire seats. It was centred on Clydebank but also included Milngavie and Old Kilpatrick. He lived there, he was a councillor in the town and he had a huge profile following the UCS work-in. It was a campaign high in hopes and endeavour, but all involved were aware that no Communist had been elected to parliament since Willie Gallacher a generation before. While Clydebank did have a strong Communist Party presence and elected communist town councillors, it was still significantly smaller than the large and powerful local Labour Party machine.

Moreover, in 1970, Jimmy had stood in the old East Dunbarton seat but had come fifth, polling just 1,656 votes (2.3 per cent). He had also contested that seat in the 1964 and 1966 elections polling 1,171 votes (2 per cent) and 1,548 (2.5 per cent) respectively. Experienced though he may have been, he was still a long way behind. However, his profile and prestige after UCS resulted in many young students and other activists flooding in to campaign for him, some coming from Glasgow University where they'd worked on his rectorial election. Others were simply enthused by what they'd seen and heard during the work-in and wanted to help with his election. A political energy and buzz was soon established about the campaign rooms.

Though he ran under the Communist Party, most of the campaign was focused on Jimmy as an individual. He was popular even amongst those who would never have dreamt of voting Communist. It was the name more than the party that resonated with the public and it was Jimmy Reid that activists were asking people to vote for. In election literature, he was called the 'Man for the Job' and it said he wouldn't be answerable to any party whip. Leaflets were emblazoned with the phrase, 'People need Jimmy', and the party tag was in very small print.

Moreover, due to an error by his campaign team, he didn't even appear on the ballot paper as a Communist. A misunderstanding of the question on the form had seen him described as an engineer. It caused much mirth in the press but everyone knew his affiliations, even if they were downplayed.

Even so, the Communist Party still gave Jimmy great support. If the individual was popular, then pragmatic politics dictated that the support be garnered through them, as had been the case with Willie Gallacher and Harry Pollitt before. Peter Kerrigan, the party's national organiser, came up from London to assist in the coordination of the campaign, and other people and resources piled in.

With Jimmy as a candidate, Dunbartonshire Central was a constituency that both the pundits and the country watched closely. Though the campaign period didn't have the bitterness that Gallacher's defeat to Willie Hamilton had generated in 1950, it was certainly turbulent. The Labour candidate, Hugh McCartney, had been the MP for the old East Dunbarton constituency since 1970 when he had comfortably defeated Jimmy. He was also an engineer by trade and had been a councillor until his election victory in 1970. He had been fully supportive of the UCS work-in and was by all accounts a decent man, though he didn't possess the star material of Jimmy Reid. However, he was to retain the seat through the boundary changes until his retiring in 1987.

Even though McCartney had a high local profile, Labour were still nervous about Jimmy's candidature for the Communists. There was even some talk of Labour activists working for Jimmy, which caused great concern in Labour HQ and led to warnings being given by them to party activists. Though no doubt quietly confident, there was still the possibility for an upset given Jimmy's almost celebrity status. Labour therefore decided to take no chances either and backed their local candidate with help and resources. The Conservative candidate was Michael Hirst, later to become a

Tory MP for Strathkelvin and Bearsden and a Scottish office minister. The SNP candidate was Andrew Welsh, who became the MP for Angus South in the election in October that year and subsequently its MSP (Member of the Scottish Parliament).

The interest in the seat was incredible. The media and the public loved it. Crowds flocked to hear Jimmy speak and halls were packed out for hustings and meetings. One rally in Clydebank Town Hall drew a crowd of 1,200. Jimmy was in his element, his oratory in full flow. At that meeting, according to news reports, the crowd was in tears when Jimmy drew parallels between the New Testament and hope for the working class.

On the streets of Clydebank, activists and the other communities' campaign workers pounded the streets for their respective candidates. Public meetings were held outside the former John Brown's yard at lunchtime and as workers were leaving. Danny McGarvey, a senior AEU official and the shipbuilding representative on the TUC General Council, came up to campaign for McCartney. A sign, no doubt, of Labour's nervousness regarding Jimmy's candidature. McGarvey, though also from Clydebank, was part of the right-wing leadership within the AEU. However, notwithstanding his local roots and his prestigious office, it was Jimmy who drew the crowds when speakers appeared. Those standing around to listen to Jimmy Reid, and Jimmy Airlie who came to add his support, were always greater than the turn out for the Labour campaign team.

Labour played on the red scare and accused Jimmy of using UCS for his own ends. The Communist Party faced significant opposition and not just from the Labour Party or the right of the trade union movement. The Catholic Church's hostility to godless atheism, as communism was seen, was at its height. There was even a denunciation from the pulpit as priests read out a notice in the nine Catholic Churches across the constituency. It was clearly focused on Jimmy, even if he wasn't specifically named. It read 'a Catholic must not vote communist. The Church has always condemned Communism because Communism by its very nature, no matter how it may be disguised or presented, rejects God and religion and depresses human freedom.' There was also a suggestion that young seminarians were sent to the constituency to campaign against him, knocking the doors of the faithful to get the message home.

The campaign became nasty and bitter as Labour and Communist campaigners went toe to toe. Some Labour activists focused heavily on Jimmy's atheism and, while it was a factor in his ultimate defeat, it wasn't the defining aspect. It did leave a bitter taste with Jimmy all the same.

Despite the energy of the campaign activists, it wasn't to be. By the eve of poll, it was clear that Labour were going to win and that, although Jimmy would poll a good vote, it wouldn't be sufficient. His eldest daughter, Eileen, who, along with many other young people, was out campaigning earnestly, recalls being pulled aside by an older Communist member and told that defeat was looming. That came as a great surprise to many eager young activists who had been enthused by the size of the rallies and the warm response on the doorstep.

However, more experienced Communist campaigners knew that people could like and admire Jimmy, they could flock to hear him and love his oratory, but they still wouldn't vote for him. It wasn't simply due to the Communist label. In an area where hatred and fear of the Tories ran deep, as other parties were to discover in later elections, keeping them out was what mattered most. The final result was:

McCartney (Labour): 16,439 (40.4 per cent)
Hirst (Conservative): 9,775 (24 per cent)
Reid (Communist): 5,928 (14.6 per cent)
Welsh (SNP): 5,906 (14.5 per cent)
Harvey (Liberal): 2,583 (6.4 per cent)
Hammond (Workers Revolutionary Party): 52 (0.1 per cent)
Turnout: 83 per cent

Though Jimmy realised that defeat was coming, it was still a blow. Hopes had been high, artificially so as it was shown, though the packed meetings and large campaign rallies had felt convincing. He had put his heart and soul into the campaign. By far the most articulate and charismatic candidate, he'd been boosted by the applause and adulation received at packed meetings. These hopes must have made defeat all the harder to bear.

That was evidenced in his outburst at the declaration of the result. Shattered hopes and rage at some of the accusations had gotten to him, no doubt compounded by physical exhaustion. He vented his anger from the platform when addressing those present in the hall and in front of the watching TV cameras. He cried that he had been:

the victim of the most scurrilous, unprincipled attack on any candidate in Britain. I have not reacted. I have turned the other cheek as the Good Book says as I don't want to create social divisions such as exist across a stretch of water across from this island here of Britain.

He went on to add that there were 'elements within the Scottish Labour Party and Clydebank Labour Party who, if living in Spain, would be supporters of Franco and members of the Falangist Party'.

The attack was uncharacteristic for Jimmy and came as a surprise to many in the hall. He usually tried to be non-tribal politically and sought to forge alliances rather than fracture them. Moreover, although he was often criticised, he had developed a very thick skin and tried to appreciate that it was not about him personally but the cause that he represented. This rather venomous speech was out of character for him and one that he was to instantly regret. He rued it till his dying days and it was to come back to haunt him when he sought to join the Labour Party a few years later.

Though a defeat, it was still a remarkable result for a Communist candidate and testimony to his personal standing. It was the highest vote polled by the party in a general election since Willie Gallacher had been defeated in West Fife in 1950 when he'd polled 9,301 votes (21.6 per cent). The party had stood forty-four candidates across Britain that February election and only Jimmy saved his deposit. Most attracted derisory votes and the next highest to him was the 2,019 votes (4.4 per cent) polled in Central Fife. That was achieved by Alex Maxwell, another popular local Communist councillor, in the mining town Cowdenbeath, a seat that contained much of Willie Gallacher's old West Fife constituency. Those other results put Jimmy's vote in context and show the extent of his personal appeal. No Communist candidate would ever achieve an election result like it again.

There was to be little respite for political campaigners that year. The precarious position of the minority Labour government made that certain. An early election was in the offing, and by mid-September the new Prime Minister Harold Wilson had called one for 10 October. This election was more subdued than the earlier winter poll. The wounded Tories campaigned on the grounds of national unity whereas Labour sought a mandate to build on their early government actions.

The outcome saw Labour gain an overall majority, though only by three seats, which was to prove problematic in the coming years. They did, however, outpoll the Conservatives by 39.25 per cent to 35.8 per cent, as well as win more comfortably in seats by 319 to 277. The Liberals returned thirteen and others, including Northern Irish parties and the SNP, twenty-six. It was a big success for the SNP as they returned eleven MPs, polling over 30 per cent of the vote.

Unfortunately, Jimmy and the Communists did not achieve the same success. Having failed to win in February, the likelihood of success in the autumn was non-existent. The novelty factor no-longer applied and, in many ways, the election was simply a test to be got through. Moreover, with the backdrop of a minority Labour government and the prevailing fear of a return to Tory rule, Jimmy's vote was only going to be further squeezed. He stood again as the Communist candidate, but with no expectation of winning. Not to stand would have been a blow to the credibility of both him and the party, so Jimmy took the hit for the cause. The outcome, though not surprising, must still have been a blow when the final figures came. His vote dropped sharply and he trailed in fourth. The result was:

McCartney (Labour): 15,837 (40.2 per cent)
Aitken (SNP): 11,452 (29.1 per cent)

Hirst (Conservative): 6,792 (17.2 per cent)
Reid (Communist): 3,417 (8.7 per cent)
Cameron (Liberal): 1,895 (4.8 per cent)
Turnout: 79.8 per cent

A disappointing, if anticipated, result. Again, however, although his vote had dropped significantly, it was still by far the best result had by the Communist Party. He remained their star performer. Only twenty-nine candidates were stood by the party that election and Jimmy significantly outpolled them all. None came anywhere near his total, with the next highest being 1,404 (2.8 per cent) in Rhondda, a seat with a strong Communist history. That was to be as good as it got for the Communist Party. No Communist candidate in an election thereafter has ever polled above 2,000 votes.

Between the two parliamentary elections in 1974 were polls for the reorganised local authorities coming in to being the following year. After considerable debate, local government reorganisation was finally taking place in Scotland. Regional and district councils were being set up and the old burgh and county councils being abolished. Clydebank would have its own district council, as well as becoming part of the huge Strathclyde Regional Council. The old authorities would remain in place for a year while parallel institutions were established.

Elections for the new regional and district councils took place in May 1974 with those elected forming a shadow council until power was officially vested in them the following year. Jimmy sought election for the regional council and contested the forty-sixth or Clydebank/Kilpatrick North ward. It was another unsuccessful election, making it three losses suffered that year. The Labour machine rolled over him again, as it would in the subsequent October poll. He lost to Tony Worthington, who was later to become the Labour MP for Clydebank and Milngavie when boundaries were redrawn in 1987. Worthington retained the seat until it disappeared with the further boundary reviews in 2005.

The council result was:

Worthington (Labour): 5,820 (49.2 per cent)
Lawson (Independent Progressive): 3,302 (27.9 per cent)
Reid (Communist): 2,700 (22.8 per cent)

While a clear loss, Jimmy gained a higher percentage of the poll than he had in the February election. It was still considerably more than the 5.8 per cent the Communist candidate polled in the other ward, which proves Jimmy's local popularity. His Communist colleagues standing for election in the district council polls were also defeated and even experienced and highly respected town councillors like Jock Smith and Arnold Henderson were unsuccessful. Though, like Jimmy, they polled highly creditable votes of 25.9 per cent in the Faifley and 24.2 per cent in the Parkhall/Mountblow wards respectively.

It was a Labour tide in the council polls as it was in the general elections. The results were:

REGIONAL ELECTIONS
Labour: 38.5%
Conservative: 28.6%
SNP: 12.6%
Others: 15.3%

DISTRICT ELECTIONS
Labour: 38.4%
Conservative: 26.8%
SNP: 12.4%
Other: 17.5%

A scattering of individuals were returned for the Communist Party across the country, but an already very limited council base was almost obliterated by the local government restructuring. It must have been another portend for him when high-profile individuals and long-serving and hardworking councillors were defeated. As Jimmy said in a newspaper interview when asked about the result in Clydebank, 'they don't count labour votes, they weigh them'. All the same, his personal stock remained high across the country and he received an invite to address the Welsh miners' rally.

He was still a sitting town councillor for the old Clydebank Burgh and would remain one until the council ceased to be in April 1975, although his role was nearly brought to a premature end when he failed to attend the final six months of council meetings. Jimmy hadn't realised that his attendance was necessary, and numerous political and trade union commitments had seen his time taken away from his council responsibilities. Labour backed off from a motion to remove him and he departed gracefully with colleagues when the old council was wound up, deciding that his time and energy was best placed elsewhere.

Though he was defeated in local elections, there were still union contests for Jimmy to fight. The size of the union movement was bigger then and influence considerably more so than now. These were prestigious and high-profile positions that Jimmy contested and he again campaigned under the Communist banner. In many ways, the Communists would have more influence with him there, than as a lone MP in the House of Commons.

In the summer of 1975, a vacancy arose for the Scottish Executive member when the incumbent John Boyd stood down from the Scottish position to become General Secretary of the Engineering section of the AUEW. The AUEW, as the AEU had become, was no different to many other unions and a battle was being waged between right and left. Moreover, a victory for either candidate in the union leadership contest would tilt power in their political direction. The union president was Hugh Scanlon, one of the leading left-wing union leaders. He had been a Communist briefly, having joined at the time of the Spanish Civil War, but had left in 1954. He remained at the forefront of the broad left in the union movement.

Jimmy was to be the Communist and left candidate and Scanlon publicly backed him. His opponent was Gavin Laird, another Scot from Clydebank who had been the union leader at Singer's in the town. Laird had been a Communist but left after the Hungary crisis. In this election, he stated he identified with the policies of Michael Foot, then the Labour left-wing doyen. Though the Communists and many on the left disagreed with Laird's political views, they respected him as a negotiator. Laird was to go on to become General Secretary of the AEEU when there was a further union amalgamation, and was later knighted at the request of Blair.

As in the political elections the year previously, there was a great deal of activism carried out and enthusiasm felt amongst left-wing stewards and union members. Hopes were high amongst the left due to Jimmy's standing in the union movement and public profile after UCS. He had also served on the AUEW national committee for some years. However, despite that, Laird won the election quite comfortably by 24,838 votes to 12,115.

As with the general election the year before, a second union election came along quickly thereafter. This time, it was for the post of Scottish Regional Officer in the union, the post Laird had held until his election victory over Jimmy. That election in September 1976 saw three candidates contest it. The other candidates were Tom Dougan, who was a leading steward at Honeywells, and Ron Brown from Edinburgh, who would go on to become a Labour MP for Leith of some notoriety from 1979 until his deselection in 1992.

In the first poll Jimmy won quite convincingly.

Reid: 13,389
Dougan: 9,662
Brown: 5,704

However, as he didn't get an overall majority, there had to be a run off. Brown dropped out and in November there was a second ballot. This time Jimmy lost, but only by the very narrowest of margins of eighty-one votes.

Dougan: 15,913
Reid: 15,832

Jimmy believed that skulduggery had a lot to do with his defeat, since some of his supporters hadn't received their polling papers while others who had voted against him had ceased to be members of the union some time before. Family friends from the north-east and elsewhere who were all members of the union stated that they and many others hadn't received papers. It was more than just a few individuals here or there. The extent of it was significant and the margin of defeat had been slim. Jimmy sensed a stitch-up.

He called for an inquiry into its conduct, but it was ruled out by Gavin Laird, who was in charge of its supervision and conduct. Jimmy then launched a 'right to vote' protest and sought a second poll. That, too, was rejected. Infuriated, Jimmy approached lawyers and threatened possible legal action, but that ultimately didn't proceed.

At that time, monitoring of many internal union elections wasn't done with the same scrutiny as in later years. Often the votes were counted within the union itself and external monitoring was limited. There had previously been interference with ballots in some unions, sometimes even by Communists, which was one of the reasons that increased scrutiny and legislation was brought in. Ballot rigging was not unknown and the dislike between the left and the right in the union was venomous. Whether that happened here can never be proven, but Jimmy certainly believed he had been cheated out of victory.

He'd stand for election once more but this time with the Labour Party. Moreover, though he remained on the AEU executive board and was the shop stewards' convenor at Marathon Manufacturing, there would be no more union contests. Jimmy's political party membership was changing and so would his career. A new life in the media was beckoning and Jimmy was leaving the Communist Party.

CHAPTER ELEVEN

LEAVING THE COMMUNIST PARTY

The decision to leave the Communist Party was a long time coming. Jimmy had always had doubts, though he'd largely kept them to himself. While he abided by the party's doctrine, he had remained a free thinker in many ways. Even so, his resignation came about only after a lot of soul searching and private heartache; after all, the Communist Party had been his life for thirty years. The party had provided not just a political cause and employment but also a social life. Family and close friends were also members. Leaving would mean both criticism and no doubt the loss of some friendships.

He had been disengaging from the party bit by bit over past years. His activism in both UCS and the elections had masked a slow, and perhaps subconscious, withdrawal the party. Slowly but surely through the 1970s he was loosening the ties that bound him to the party, a move that was made easier after leaving his full-time position within the party in 1969.

It was probably undetectable to colleagues at the time, but, looking back, it's possible to detect Jimmy's gradual withdrawal. He hadn't attended a congress of the party in Scotland since 1970, which wasn't due to other commitments but a deliberate decision to remain away. The interest and desire simply wasn't there. The stifling debates and sectarian views of some were dispiriting for him. The internal battles being waged between those wishing to pursue a more progressive Eurocommunist line and those seeking to adhere to the soviet orthodoxy were causing him to both despair about the party's prospects and question its very purpose. In 1972, he resigned from the Scottish Committee, citing tensions as the reason.

The following year he declined to accept a nomination for the National Executive Committee. However, after leading members argued that his absence would be interpreted as a public disagreement with the party, he relented. Jimmy didn't want to cause any problems, particularly with his old mentor John Gollan, as his loyalty to his old comrade ran deep. Thus, his participation was born more out of loyalty to the party generally and a desire to avoid harmful publicity than a desire to stay involved in the inner circle of the party.

In 1972, after the UCS work-in had concluded, he and his family went on a holiday to the Soviet Union. The visit seemed to bring home to him the flaws and failings within the communist system and led him to seriously challenge and question his beliefs on his return. While away, they sojourned to Sochi, a popular destination by the Black Sea, and were treated as communist dignitaries with all the trappings that went with it. However, Jimmy was angered by the car lanes and limousines reserved for the *nomenklatura*. Loud arguments between Jimmy and Soviet officials accompanying them were overheard by family members. He didn't like what he saw and was prepared to tell them so. All in all, it was an uncomfortable trip with many arguments between hosts and guest. Jimmy believed in communism, but not as it was being practised there. It was yet another nail in the coffin for his faith in communism.

Jimmy was also tiring of some the new leadership developing within the party. Acrimony had been growing as a result of the disputes between Bert Ramelson and others. Ramelson was born in the Ukraine in 1910 and went to university in Canada where his parents had emigrated. He later worked in a *kibbutz* in Palestine and, afterwards, he undertook military service in the Spanish Civil War with the International Brigade and then with the British Army in the Second World War. Following the war, he became a full-time worker for the CPGB and occupied the role as the National Industrial Organiser from 1965 to 1977. Despite this colourful past, Jimmy felt that Ramelson had little, if any, knowledge neither of the shipbuilding industry nor indeed of the shop stewards' movement within it. Allied to that was Ramelson's limited grasp of the situation outside London, and Jimmy was concerned about the leadership becoming very London-centric.

In March 1975, as his sixty-fifth birthday approached, John Gollan announced his intention to stand down the following year as General Secretary. His replacement was to be Gordon McLennan, who, like Jimmy, started life as an engineer and who Jimmy succeeded as Scottish District Organiser in 1966. McLennan was a worthy and decent, if far from dynamic, individual who had worked for the party since the age of twenty-five. He had little profile or experience beyond the party and its cadre, and his nomination appeared to have more to do with the party's wish to reward dutiful loyalty, rather than any desire to enhance its external profile. A replication of what was to happen in the Soviet Union

until the appointment of Mikhail Gorbachev heralded a genera-
tional and policy change. There, the septuagenarian Brezhnev had
been succeeded by the equally aged Andropov and Chernenko
before a younger leader was appointed in Gorbachev, confirming
a changing of the guard in power and political direction.

On his succession, only a few months before Jimmy resigned,
McLennan made it clear there would be no change in direction
from the policies that were being pursued, despite their being
politically unsuccessful and increasingly anachronistic in the
fast-changing world. As Jimmy rather acidly commented later,
'the political parties of the labour movement cannot go on as in
the past ... Plagued by little men consumed by career ambitions
and leaders without vision.'* Later, Jimmy contrasted the Communist leaders of his youth with the stature they held and the
political lives they'd led, which made their modern successors
seem staid and rigid. Some of his disparagement was clearly
aimed at the King Street headquarters. He said the old guard had
been 'leaders in their own right' and authentic products of 'the
struggle of the British people', as their record of activism in the
community showed. That contrasted sharply with McLennan's
role as an apparatchik as opposed to a campaigner, working
within the party rather than in the community.

While Jimmy had been groomed for party leadership, there
was no suggestion that he was to succeed Gollan or that he left
the party in light of McLennan's appointment. Had he stayed,
he may very well have inherited the General Secretary post in
due course, since the nature of the Communist Party in the UK,

---

* Kevin Morgan, Gidon Cohen and Andrew Flinn, *Communist and British Society*, p. 142.

as in the Soviet Union, was hierarchical despite its egalitarian principles. McLennan was older, had been in the party longer and therefore was above him in authority and status. While it was the general direction of the party that grieved him most, McLennan's new post was still another nail in the coffin of Jimmy's party membership.

His time as an elected councillor had come to an end on Clydebank Burgh Council and he hadn't been elected to the new authorities that replaced it. His focus had moved elsewhere and the Communist Party was losing its hold on him. Moreover, though the party was declining, his stock was still high and it was natural to question whether the party not only no longer represented his political views but was an impediment to him being able to achieve them.

Jimmy always condemned and eschewed careerism. He stood up for the causes he believed in and the principles he sought to live by. But, the fact of the matter was that the Communist Party was dying and he had things to offer to the socialist cause. The time for the parting of the ways had come. His commitment to socialism and Home Rule remained, but the Communist Party was no longer the political vehicle for him. Despite his popularity and ability, he had often been defeated by people who had neither his talents nor his intellect and his political and trade union election defeats must have been a bitter blow to him. He knew he could contribute more and with greater sincerity than many others who were simply placemen, but those results confirmed that he was stuck on the margins. His commitment to socialism was unwavering, but he must have begun to wonder whether continued membership of a party that was going nowhere was worth it. However, despite his gradual withdrawal from the leadership, the party was still all-consuming. Leaving the party meant not just a change of party affiliation but a complete lifestyle overhaul. While Jimmy didn't rush into it, the decision still came as a shock to many. It was to cause a little acrimony and a great deal more sorrow. Friends and colleagues over the years were devastated. Those who were the most bitter were the Stalinists who had created the atmosphere that Jimmy could no longer endure. As well as harbouring personal animosity towards him, they were conscious that they were losing their most prominent and popular member. He had been their great communicator and, following his departure, the party's fortunes were to plummet even further and faster.

Looking back, it was the logical moment for Jimmy to leave the party. He was in his early forties and he was to leave the shipyards for good for a beckoning career in broadcasting. He and his family had moved to a house in Dalmuir and it wouldn't be long before the Reids bought their first flat in Kelvingrove Street, Glasgow, and departed Clydebank. Although a new life outside the Communist Party was within reach, Jimmy still had to tender his resignation and explain his actions to erstwhile comrades. After agonising for months, in February 1976 he wrote to Jack Ashton, the Scottish District Secretary, stating:

> This is my formal intimation to you that, as from your receipt of this letter, I consider myself no longer a member of the Communist party of Great Britain. It has been a heart-wrenching decision in spite of what some secretarians in the party may say. But, as you know, their opinions have never really caused me much concern.

The factors which made this the most difficult decision of my life are in the host of wonderful men and women I met, had the privilege of associating with, in the Communist party. To break with the party that you have been a member of during almost all your adult life is no easy matter.

During the past years, all my close associates in the party have known of my disenchantment with certain lines of action and decisions. As someone who has argued that no party can or should be a monolith, this may be surprising coming from me. But disagreements or differences in the party should in the 1970s have been within the parameters of 'The British Road to Socialism', that is the democratic path to Socialism.

The truth is that the ideological concepts of the 'British Road' have never permeated the lifestyle of working patterns of the party.

The result has been that the old styles of work, bureaucratic and formalistic, have persisted. This has meant that the democratic credentials of Communists, and to some extent the left, have not been established in the minds of the people.

This has created a dangerous situation. There is threat to democracy in Britain today from the extreme right in British politics and the left is partially disarmed in meeting this challenge because our credentials are somewhat suspect.

My total commitment in politics has been and always will be to the working class and to the people. I have argued honestly that membership of the Communist party did not conflict with this commitment.

Unfortunately, in the past years there have been instances where this has been shown to be untrue. Members of the party in my opinion have acted contrary to the interest of the working class. Their actions were condoned.

The people existed before any political party as we them today. They will exist in a developed, free socialist culture after political have departed from the scene. If there is a conflict of loyalty, then my loyalty is to the working class and the people.

I understand that this decision could place me in a sort of limbo, assailed from the right-wing establishment for my socialist convictions and attacked by at least some on the left who fail to comprehend my dilemma. If this is the price that has to be paid, so be it.

The letter was written in the language used within the party and with nuances often only understood by those intimately involved. There was never going to be an easy way to explain his reasons for leaving, but this letter was an attempt to justify himself in their terms. As with a marriage breakdown, it was complex and hard, if not impossible, to properly articulate and explain everything. While Jimmy's reasons for leaving were largely due a culmination of weariness and doubts that had grown over the years, he specifically took issue with an industrial dispute where communist members had been involved in a decision that was harmful to workers, and he felt it had been covered up by the party. He also believed that criticism of his comments on the party's position on the EEC ignored his rights within democratic centralism to speak out. In addition, the policy line to a seek a boycott of EEC institutions, despite the referendum vote having been to confirm joining, irritated him and seemed politically unrealistic. Though he had campaigned along with the party against membership and was sceptical of its benefits, he cited the need to accept democracy. In truth, the rigidity of the party was becoming stultifying for him. His later praise for the diversity of the debate at his first Labour conference was indicative of his frustration with the Communist Party.

The party's response was equally formulaic. There appears to have been some anger that others in the labour movement had been told about Jimmy's departure before the party leadership had been told. In a very structured and orthodox party, such procedures mattered but it was a matter of minor protocol which was overshadowed by deeper sadness and regret.

Both Jimmy's letter and Gordon McLennan's formal response were printed as a front-page story in the *Morning Star* in February 1976. McLennan stated:

I very much regret Jimmy Reid's decision, which I think is profoundly mistaken, as I have said to him in a discussion I have had with him about it. It came as a surprise to me, since I had no indication from him that he was considering such a course of action.

Only last November, Jimmy accepted nomination for the executive committee and recently expressed warm appreciation of the article on Socialist democracy by John Gollan in the January issue of *Marxism Today*.

Jimmy in his letter expresses support for 'the British Road to Socialism', the programme of our party. It is only our party which has such a programme.

Even if there are differences about the style of work of the party, or its tactics in connection with particular day to day problems, these surely do not outweigh in importance the agreement which exists on the basic questions of the aim of socialism, the democratic strategy for achieving it in Britain and the need for an organised party basing itself on the scientific principles of Marxism and seeking to unite the working class and its allies in the struggle for Socialism.

As Jimmy says, he has argued against the idea that the party should be a monolith and he does not say in his letter that it is.

In fact, there is constant and lively discussion of different views within the party and in the most important question of all, our programme 'The British Road to Socialism', our last congress decided to initiate a full-scale discussion on it to prepare for the adoption of a revised edition at our next congress.

But, Jimmy has also always recognised that in a political party finally decisions have to be arrived at and carried out.

We could indeed be a monolith if every decision was agreed 100 per cent by every member, but, as in other democratic organisations, those who disagree accept the majority decision after democratic discussion.

The question of resignation normally only arises if there is fundamental disagreement on basic policy and strategy and this does not appear to be the case as far as Jimmy is concerned.

As for his statement that the Communist party has condoned actions by members which in his opinion were contrary to the interests of the working class, he has never raised such questions with the leadership. We would not condone any anti working-class actions by members of the party.

In 1978, when he was selected as a Labour candidate, Jimmy was at pains to make it clear that the parliamentary candidature had not been the reason for leaving the Communist Party. In interviews he made it clear that he believed that the way to make social and economic progress in Britain was through democratic socialism and it was the British Labour Party that stood for that.

A more illuminating insight into Jimmy's ideological reasons for departing the Communist Party was given in an interview a few years after he left. In February 1979, Jimmy appeared on a television programme hosted by the right-wing American commentator William F. Buckley. He had been interviewed on the same programme some four years earlier on the theme of the Communist Party and British Policy. This time, he was back to argue his position, as well as to explain his reasons for leaving.

He indicated that, for ten years before he'd finally resigned, he had been 'in considerable disagreement with the party'. However, given the party's monolithic structure, 'fierce disagreements', as he put it, took place without it being discernible to those outside. He added that there was 'an air of inevitability' about his leaving. Asked to explain further, Jimmy indicated that he'd come to the conclusion that the structure of communist parties in Britain and in Western Europe were no longer relevant for the times they lived in. They'd been formed in pre-revolutionary Russia, when Lenin had designed a party based on 'professional revolutionaries' and where socialism was common as a result of the seizure of power by the working class. That had resulted in the party being formed almost on militaristic lines for the Russia situation as it was then. That couldn't be exported, and certainly not to Western Europe.

Jimmy believed that Eurocommunism was possible, but in order for it to be successful, it would have to embrace democratic socialism – but, in doing so, they would cease to be communist parties. He had been impressed by the Italian Communist Party, with its ideology based upon the thinking of esteemed theoreticians such as Togliatti and Gramsci, and even added that it was perhaps the one party which could make the transition. He believed that their commitment to democracy was genuine. He was sceptical of the French Communist Party's sincerity in their supposed conversion to democracy, and indicated that he just didn't know when asked about the Spanish party.

The questioning saw Jimmy expand on the reasons for his decision to leave. He said that he'd always felt committed to the democratic principle. Pushed on whether his distancing himself from the party was due to the inability to progress politically in the UK or the actions in the Soviet Union, Jimmy responded that it was an accumulation of many factors. Socialism he explained was not simply economic but about social, cultural and moral values. A rigid adherence to Marxism, he felt, was outdated given the changes that had taken place in Western society. He condemned Stalin but accepted that he'd joined the party when he'd been in power, explaining that it was as a result of his anger at the poverty he had seen all around him and his belief in a better society rather than a true affiliation with Stalinist methods.

The discussion continued with Jimmy once more impressing with his theological knowledge, as a debate again took place on Christianity and socialism. However, no further light was cast on the decision to leave though his explanation for joining and his continued commitment to socialism were further amplified. He had joined the Communist Party despite some doubts and even disagreements, he explained. In many ways, it had been a moral, as much as an ideological, choice and came about through multiple factors; though primarily his indignation at the poverty he saw around him and his belief in a better society. Likewise, when he chose to leave it was for a mixture of reasons. His frustration at the rigidity of the party and its failure to communicate with working people. A belief that the Communist Party in Great Britain was simply being told by a translator from the Communist Party of the Soviet Union what to say. Indeed, he felt the CPGB was being destroyed by the CPSU. The situations in the countries were radically different, as had been their histories. Simply seeking to impose it on a society that was hugely different was never going to succeed. As a result, he felt himself becoming much more distant from the party he had joined all those years ago.

Jimmy though still had a burning desire to tackle poverty and build a better society that couldn't be achieved through the Communist Party. Fundamentally its structure based on democratic centralism he now believed to be flawed and counterproductive, producing conformity when vibrancy was required. Moreover, there was an adherence as a result to historic dogma that again reduced the ability for change that was badly required. Others supportive of modernisation and democratisation had been leaving, as a consequence of which the necessary change became even less likely. It all became too much. Perhaps, even some personal ambition to try and achieve his full potential. It was after all something that had been instilled in him throughout his time in the party. There was much more for him to do and contribute. He knew he could achieve more and perform far better than many others.

Joan remained in the party for a while longer. Not because she disagreed with him but because they thought it would be easier.

She did, however, leave not long after. Eileen his eldest daughter had already left the YCL frustrated by its bureaucracy and centralism a while before her father. He had respected her decision but it must also have been another sign to him that the future of the party was looking bleak.

Jimmy still had a burning desire to tackle poverty and build a better society, but he remained committed to socialism and Scottish Home Rule and remained a political activist with energy and exceptional talent. He couldn't be idle for long and he would be joining the Labour Party.

CHAPTER TWELVE

JOINING LABOUR

Jimmy didn't rush to join another party. There were other things to enjoy as more free time became available to him. The pace of life slowed and there was an opportunity to engage with friends and family, which was particularly important as the children were growing up. He didn't entirely retire from politics, instead maintaining his interest and his passionate views but for a time as more of an observer than a participant.

However, his lack of direct participation could not last for ever. He remained an activist at heart and sitting on the side-lines soon became frustrating. He wanted to contribute and he knew he had a lot still to offer. Others knew that too, and he wasn't without opportunities to join other parties. Jimmy felt the need for restructure in politics on the left. Both the Communist Party and the Labour Party were, in his opinion, in need of reform. Change and evolution were occurring across the political spectrum. While politics was shifting in Scotland with the rise of nationalism and the setting up of the Scottish Labour Party (SLP) by Jim Sillars, that wasn't the radical realignment Jimmy was seeking, especially since the new party was lacking in both a union base and popular support.

The SNP, meanwhile, were riding high in the polls. Their breakthrough in the elections of 1974 had seen their profile and membership rise. However, while Jimmy's commitment to a Scottish Parliament remained undiminished, he didn't agree with their then centrist position. A party that failed to identify itself on the left was an anathema to him, despite his support for a Scottish Parliament, so it was never likely that he would consider joining them. Jimmy was still steeped in the trade unions and believed passionately in the power of the labour movement.

The SLP had been established in January 1976, the month before Jimmy left the Communist Party, by Jim Sillars, the Labour MP for South Ayrshire, John Robertson, the Labour MP for Paisley, and Alex Neil, Labour's senior researcher in Scotland. Although many flocked to join it, there were accusations of entryism by the International Marxist Group, and their Congress in October of that year was scarred by expulsions. This tarnished the party and it never really took off thereafter, crushed between the SNP and Labour monoliths. In 1977, they won only three council seats in the local authority elections. By 1979 they were wiped out after Jim Sillars narrowly failed to hold his seat that he had represented for years. John Robertson had not sought re-election and both his successor and the candidate in another seat were heavily defeated. The party was to be wound up within a few years.

Before its demise, Jimmy had never given any serious thought to joining the SLP. Some suggested that it had something to do with a clash between him and Jim Sillars, since both were outstanding orators with forceful personalities. However, the reasons for their not coalescing in the same party were much more practical than personal. Jimmy had only just left the Communist Party and felt it was too soon to join another party in any event, and, by the time he was interested and considering becoming active again, the SLP was deeply divided and going nowhere. Given his experiences in the Communist Party, it was never likely that he would seek to replicate that in another party, especially one which lacked the union base and popular support that he knew was needed.

Accordingly, the only real political home for Jimmy was the Labour Party. After all, he had been in the Labour League of Youth, albeit only briefly and a generation before. Scotland still possessed a manufacturing base and a strong labour movement within it, and Labour was still seen as the party of the Scottish working class. In the Scotland where Jimmy lived, it was the Labour Party that dominated. It was also ostensibly a socialist party and it had many left wingers within it who he knew well. It had also given its commitment to Home Rule, though Jimmy knew that the party was divided. However, exactly as he had fought with the Communist Party through the STUC, he knew he could fight within the Labour Party for it.

So, moving to Labour was the inevitable course of action, but joining was not without more soul searching. It wouldn't be easy for Jimmy given the criticism he'd made of Labour and some individuals in the past. Not least the vicious statement he had made at the election count in February 1974, never mind other comments made through the years. Despite these setbacks, join he did in 1977. The left-wing faction the Tribune Group within the Labour Party had announced his likely membership in their own newspaper as early as January 1977. They were to be very supportive and active in seeking to have him both join and ultimately stand as a candidate for parliament.

In September 1977, he applied to join the Central Dunbartonshire Labour Party. His application was passed to the local

Dalmuir branch, where memories were no doubt raw after the comments he had made during the February 1974 election. They delayed Jimmy's application by putting it on the agenda for the next meeting before ultimately rejecting it. However, it was then passed back to the constituency and Jimmy appealed against the refusal, with the Tribune Group supporting him. Richard Clements, editor of the Tribune Paper, urged Labour members around the country to write to the CLP requesting he be allowed to join. Eventually, in November 1977, he was finally confirmed by the constituency party as a Labour Party member.

From there, things moved rather quickly for Jimmy in the Labour Party. His profile was huge and, in January 1978, there was even some speculation in the papers that he might be a possible successor to Jimmy Milne as General Secretary of the STUC, although nothing came of it.

He was feted at the UK Labour conference that year by the Tribune Group and he received many other invitations to speak from branches and constituencies across the country. However, it was clear that not all were happy with his membership and many at Party HQ in Scotland were muted in their support. Some viewed his conversion with scepticism and saw it as a desire to get elected, while others simply held longstanding antipathy towards him. All the same, they did seek to use him when he could be advantageous electorally.

In January 1978, William Small, the Labour MP for Garscadden, died and a by-election was to be held in April of that year. The year before, the SNP had done well in council elections and hopes were high that they might win the by-election, as they had in Hamilton in 1967 and Govan in 1974. Labour were worried about the consequences, given the fragility of the government, and a battle royal was about to ensue.

Labour selected Donald Dewar, a lawyer from Glasgow who had previously been the MP for Aberdeen South until defeated in 1970, as their candidate. He would go on to become Secretary of State for Scotland in Blair's first government in 1997 and the First Minister of Scotland when the Scottish Parliament was re-established in 1999. The SNP selected another Glasgow lawyer, Keith Bovey, who was a leading figure in CND. The Communist Party candidate was Jimmy's old comrade from UCS, Sammy Barr.

At one stage, it seemed that the SNP were poised to win, but the shipyards played a pivotal role in their ultimate defeat and Jimmy was to contribute to that. The old Scotstoun yards, still major employers in the area, were part of the constituency. Issues arose in the by-election over military contracts and nuclear weapons and the SNP candidate was pilloried and portrayed as seeking the yards' closure. His unilateralism being accused of costing jobs, if not shutting a shipyard, dependent on Royal Navy contracts. It seemed to turn the election. Jimmy had been brought in to speak to the workers in support of the Labour Party and their candidate. Whether it made any difference isn't known, but it was indicative of his importance to them and the use they wished to make of him. Come the poll in April, Labour held the seat reasonably comfortably, albeit with a lower majority and a slight swing to the SNP. Given the success of the SNP in council elections the year before and the difficulties the Labour government were experiencing, it was one that many had felt they should have won. It would subsequently be seen as the turning of the tide against them.

The next task was to get Jimmy elected to Parliament. He was keen to seek a nomination for a constituency and many supporters were eager to see him elected to Westminster. His willingness to support the party was repaid by their being willing to allow his selection, despite a rule that a candidate had to have been a member for two years prior to an election. It didn't come about without a struggle, however, as many sought to block his possible nomination.

There had been some talk about seats in England becoming available, but Jimmy had ruled out a move south. Many constituencies in the west of Scotland already had sitting Labour MPs or had already selected candidates for the election. Then, in May 1978, he was nominated as MP for the Dundee East constituency. The Labour candidate for Dundee East had been killed in a car crash and the nomination procedure was required to be opened up once again. This again wasn't going to be without its difficulties within the party, both locally and nationally.

Though not on his home turf of Clydeside, there were good reasons to consider running for the position. Firstly, it was a seat where the AEU held sway and it was still an area of heavily unionised industry with shipyards and other large manufacturing works employing many local people. Despite Jimmy's previous unsuccessful efforts for posts within the union, he was still popular and the union would assist in his selection. Within the party, it was viewed as an AEU seat and where the union was critical to nomination.

Secondly, the seat was held by Gordon Wilson of the SNP. He had first contested it in a by-election in 1973 called after the sitting Labour MP left to take up a post in Europe. In that by-election,

Wilson had run the victorious Labour candidate George Machin close, reducing the majority to just over 1,000 votes. Machin had come up from Sheffield where he had been an active trade unionist and had got the seat through the AEU, but he never really gelled with either the city or the Scottish Labour Party. When in Westminster, he tended to sit with Yorkshire colleagues rather than with the Scottish contingent. Accordingly, when the February 1974 election came and the SNP vote was rising, Wilson won with a majority of nearly 3,000 votes. In the October election that year, he had increased the majority to nearly 7,000. Labour wanted to win it back and needed a strong candidate to do so.

There was some opposition to Jimmy being brought in as a potential candidate. There were already some local favourites from all sections of the party. Charlotte Haddow, a former chairwoman of the Scottish Council of the Labour Party, had support both locally and from many in party HQ. For the far-left within the party, Willie McKelvey, who had been Secretary and Organiser of the Dundee City Labour Party, was the favoured one. However, his nomination was precluded as he'd resigned from those posts less than two years before and that was contrary to the rules. He would go on to be the MP for Kilmarnock that year and retained the seat until he stood down in 1997. Jimmy's candidature therefore caused some unrest, since the rules had been abrogated for his nomination but maintained for McKelvey. Accordingly, he won the selection battle only with the support of the centre-right, and the constituency party was divided as a consequence.

Having won the nomination for the constituency, he still had to have it endorsed by the party nationally; the organisation subcommittee decided by nine votes to four to allow him to stand. The left representatives, including both Eric Heffer and Tony Benn, supported him, as did Alex Kitson of the STUC. After that, it still had to be formally approved by the NEC. That wasn't going to be either easy or unanimous. The right-wing Manifesto Group, some of whom would later desert to the Social Democratic Party a few years later, opposed him. They formally wrote to the party's General Secretary, stating that Jimmy's adoption was offensive to the vast majority of members and supporters. Shirley Williams, one of the original Gang of Four, along with David Owen, Bill Rodgers and Roy Jenkins, led the opposition to the NEC. However, Jimmy ultimately prevailed by fourteen votes to six.

Jim Callaghan had declined to call an election in 1978 when Jimmy may have unable to contest it. However, an election had to be called by October 1979 at the latest. The government was in trouble on many fronts. The economy was faltering and inflation was fuelling wage disputes, industrial unrest was leading to public frustration and, moreover, Labour's commitment to Home Rule was to be put to the test.

After great internal debate throughout the 1960s and 1970s, the Labour Party had finally come around to supporting Home Rule. Some were genuinely committed to it and saw it as the delivery of the party's founding principles. Others were driven by fear of the SNP, which sat second in most Labour seats. A section, however, remained implacably opposed to it. In 1978, the Labour government passed the Scotland Act that provided for a Scottish Assembly so long as it was supported by the electorate in a referendum.

It was a far weaker proposal for Home Rule than many in the SNP and others, including Jimmy, had sought. However, it still provided for a distinctive Scottish voice and there would be an opportunity to build upon it in later years. For that reason, Jimmy supported it. However, during its parliamentary passage in Westminster, Labour opponents, supported by the Tories, had added a 40 per cent rule to the bill. That meant that the threshold for victory was not 50 per cent plus one, but over 40 per cent of the total electorate. That significantly raised the bar to be crossed as abstentions and even those who had died but remained on the electoral roll would count against. It had not been invoked before nor has been required since in any subsequent referendum in the UK. It caused anger and resentment.

With the backdrop of a failing Labour government and a dissipating nationalist vote, the campaign was fraught with difficulties. The resentment between Labour and SNP saw separate and sometimes half-hearted campaigning in support of it. However, they faced a united opposition with Tories such as Sir Alec Douglas Home, who had supported devolution seeking a vote against it, ostensibly arguing for a better proposal to come in future.

As it was, the referendum held on 1 March 1979 was won by those supporting Scottish devolution, but not by a sufficient majority to clear the added 40 per cent hurdle. The result was:

Yes: 51.62 per cent
No: 48.38 per cent

The vote in Strathclyde had been 53.98 per cent, reflecting the fact that votes in favour were cast in more industrial parts of the country. But there was little time for the recriminations and fall out over the Assembly. The Conservatives, led by Margaret Thatcher, forced a vote of no confidence in Callaghan's government on

28 March, which was won by a single vote. The SNP group, mandated by their party and bitter about the outcome of the referendum, supported the Conservatives. It was to herald the charge of Tartan Tories that was to haunt them for many years to come. However, it's clear that the Labour government was faltering from its internal divisions and external failings, and was doomed anyway.

Jimmy was disappointed and aggrieved at the outcome of the referendum, believing it had been mishandled. But the spectre of Margaret Thatcher leading the Tory opposition galvanised him, as it did many others. She had taken the Conservative Party further to the right, and it was clear that she would be pursuing policies harmful to the working class and labour movement. Opposing her and her policies was the priority for Jimmy, rather than dwelling on recriminations over the Assembly.

So, it was into the cut and thrust of an election campaign for Jimmy as a Labour candidate. Although the local party was divided, he hoped that the campaign would unify the factions. Jimmy, like others, viewed Dundee East as a natural Labour seat that had gone to the SNP by mistake. Moreover, the SNP were in deep trouble. Their support was falling and public opprobrium was being heaped upon them for having voted with the Tories. Dundee was a working-class city with a greater percentage of council housing than even Glasgow.

The SNP, however, still had significant support in many areas that would have one time been viewed as Labour fiefdoms, despite the travails of the party nationally. It was a significant majority to try and overcome but hopes were still high at the start of the campaign. George Galloway, who later became a Labour and a Respect Party MP, was the city organiser. The campaign was largely fought in the industrial areas and council schemes of which there were many, although there were no candidate hustings that would have allowed Jimmy to excel on the platform. However, some public meetings organised by the Labour Party did take place, in which Jimmy went on stage adorned with a medallion given to him by Wendy Wood, the founder of the Scottish Patriots, to show his commitment to devolution and also no doubt to rile the SNP members in the audience.

The election closely followed the debates in Parliament over the nationalisation of shipbuilding, a topic which had been brought in belatedly by the Labour government, but had been opposed by the SNP. Labour strategists, and no doubt Jimmy himself, would have viewed it as an opportunity to win votes. However, when he had realised who his Labour opponent was going to be, Wilson had taken steps to try to cover himself in discussions about the shipyard. Though the yard shop stewards were hostile, the workforce was much less so. Yard meetings were attended assiduously by Wilson and he made sure he was on the committee dealing with the bill to nationalise the industry. As a result, he had an in with the workforce and often information and action that he could take for the unions. He also gave support to the Labour government on some aspects of the bill whether timetabling or other procedural matters that were helpful and which he ensured were known to the workforce. In addition, he made it clear that he opposed nationalisation, not on the principle of public ownership, but because he believed centralisation would harm smaller yards such as Robb Caledon. There was some sympathy for that amongst members of the workforce who had similar fears, if not amongst the stewards and union leaders.

Wilson's first attendances at the yard had been marked by hostility, but that lessened as further information came out. Wilson sought some concessions that stood him in good favour with the workforce. Accordingly, while Labour may have hoped to have won the shipyard workers' vote, it was not to be. Wilson polled a lot higher than Labour had predicted, doubtless amongst many of those who had shared Wilson's doubts about the benefits of nationalisation. As it was, the yard was to close in 1981, despite nationalisation.

The other large employers where Labour would also have hoped to have swayed votes were equally problematic. NCR, another major employer though in a different manufacturing sector than shipbuilding, was beginning to experience problems as technology changed. Wilson, again, was at the fore seeking to liaise between the unions and management in the USA. Timex was another plant where there was a great deal of sympathy for the sitting MP and his party. The SNP vote back then was considerably stronger in the city than in the west of Scotland.

It was therefore a much tougher seat to fight than might have been thought by many at the outset. A resilient SNP and a divided Labour Party didn't help. Whether Jimmy was fully supported by the Labour HQ in Scotland is also open to some speculation. Press releases and speeches sent in by him were invariably binned, the suggestion being that his intellectual analyses were not what was needed in the campaign where populism was sought. Given Jimmy's handling of UCS, that is surprising, and it's more likely that some individuals' longstanding antipathy was at the root of it. It was clear that in the Labour Party in Scotland, as on the NEC, there was some suspicion and dislike for this ex-communist.

The SNP was as relentless in its attacks on Jimmy and his

communist background as Labour had formally been. The antipathy between the two parties was as great then as it still is in many areas. The SNP campaign, however, was in trouble, and in the election their seats reduced from eleven to just two. One of the ones they kept was to be Dundee East, where Wilson hung on. Despairing of the national campaign, Wilson had cut loose in the final weeks and campaigned independently. Jimmy campaigned hard and increased the Labour vote and reduced the SNP majority to 2,519, but it was insufficient. The final result was:

Wilson (SNP): 20,497 (41.7%)
Reid (Labour): 17,078 (36%)
Townsend (Conservative): 9,072 (18.2%)
Brodie (Liberal): 2,317 (4.6%)
Battersby (Workers Revolutionary Party): 95 (0.2%)

Losing was another bitter blow to Jimmy, but he was to remain active in the left of the Labour Party for quite a while to come. His activity was more limited, however, contributing more through ideas and articles than direct involvement as his career in the media began to take off.

Michael Foot succeeded Jim Callaghan in the leadership election in November 1980. Both that vote and the reaction to the defeat to Thatcher saw Labour move further to the left. As a result, within months the Gang of Four, including Shirley Williams, who had vocally opposed Jimmy's candidature for Dundee East, had resigned from the Labour to set up the Social Democratic Party (SDP) in March 1981.

That same year, Tony Benn sought to stand as deputy leader

against the incumbent Denis Healey, who had been previously elected unopposed. Jimmy was very active in Benn's campaign for the deputy leadership, contributing and getting involved in the compilation of the radical manifesto upon which he stood. A third candidate, John Silkin, also entered the fray. It was to be the first vote under Labour's new Electoral College system which saw 40 per cent with the unions and societies and 30 per cent each with the Parliamentary Labour Party and the Constituency Labour parties. In the first poll, the result was Healey 45.4 per cent, Benn 36.6 per cent and Silkin 18 per cent. After Silkin dropped out, it became a straight race in which Healey defeated Benn by the narrowest of margins: 50.4 per cent to 49.6 per cent.

Although Benn was unsuccessful in his attempt, his platform provided much of the basis of the manifesto that was taken forward by Foot into the general election in 1983. It was an election in which Labour was trounced, losing over sixty seats and recording their worst election result since 1931. Much was made of the left-wing manifesto by the right-wing press. Though it's as likely that it was Thatcher basking in the aftermath of the Falklands War and Labour being split by its ongoing civil war that were the critical factors. The SDP had deserted but internal feuding continued.

Jimmy didn't stand in the 1983 election. He remained popular with many on the left not just in Scotland but across the entire UK, and was well connected within both the party and the union movement. No doubt he was still sore from defeats where the campaigns had been both exhausting and vicious. Moreover, it was also an inopportune time for him to stand. The Reids had moved to Glasgow and he was embarking on a new career in the media. He was fast developing a name and reputation but it was something he needed to work at, as it was still early days even if initial successes were coming. Enjoying it immensely, it was an enjoyable change from the bruising political battles he had been involved in.

Moreover, as many politicians find upon stepping off the political treadmill, the freedom allows them to rediscover family and life outside the frenzied atmosphere that politics generates. A life in politics requires being perpetually on the move and sacrificing many family and social events. There were others to consider as well as himself. In Glasgow, with a new career and more time with the family, a return to the frontline held much less allure.

So, he let that election pass him by, though he helped in the wider campaign. His opposition and contempt for the policies of Margaret Thatcher remained unbridled. Her willingness to sacrifice entire communities in the pursuit of private profit was an anathema to him. The pain suffered by many as mass unemployment returned to haunt the Clyde and elsewhere in the country both grieved and enraged him. The Scotland that he had grown up in of heavy industry and council housing was once again under attack. Gordon Brown had Jimmy speak at his adoption meeting when he was selected as the Labour candidate for Dunfermline East. Though he never had a close relationship with the man who would become Chancellor and later Prime Minister, it shows that Jimmy remained a major attraction for party meetings. Brown was viewed as the rising star, but having Jimmy's endorsement gave him added credibility.

Following Labour's calamitous election defeat, Michael Foot stood down as leader, thus opening up a contest for the leadership. After a great deal of speculation about possible candidates, including Denis Healey, who ultimately declined to stand, four candidates went forward: Roy Hattersley, Eric Heffer, Neil Kinnock and Peter Shore. Kinnock won the vote convincingly, polling over 70 per cent on the first ballot and avoiding the need for further counts. Roy Hattersley won the deputy leadership battle against Michael Meacher.

Some on the hard left were angered that Jimmy supported the moderate-left candidate, Kinnock, because the new leader hadn't supported Tony Benn in the deputy leadership contest a few years earlier. Kinnock had then backed John Silkin in the first ballot and called on his supporters to abstain in the next round when it was Benn versus Healey.

Jimmy was close to Kinnock and respected and supported his early efforts to modernise and galvanise the party. Issues such as the miners' strike found the two in agreement. It's even suggested that some of Jimmy's comments were urged by Kinnock who did not wish to court the controversy by saying them himself, but wished them to be said all the same.

He was approached in the mid-1980s about contesting a safe seat in the north of England for the election that would come in 1987. It was something that he had to think through long and hard. He had sought to be able to contribute politically, but his life was changing with his media commitments. He even went to the extent of seeking the advice of Kinnock personally. It was the Labour leader who encouraged him to stay in the media and refrain from entering Parliament, Kinnock arguing that Jimmy's contribution through columns, especially the one in *The Sun*, was more important for the party than having him in Westminster.

Jimmy supported Kinnock through Labour's internal problems

in dealing with the Militant Tendency. He had been frustrated by the ongoing bickering and the entryism that had been practised by the hard-left group. They were a Trotskyite group, which was a clique that he had always opposed, and who he saw as being unrepresentative of the working class in most instances and unrealistic in their understanding of political and trade union campaigning. Although the fight within the party was won by Kinnock, it had been wearing and the entryism remained in several areas of the party. Jimmy wrote about his party experiences endlessly but his opinion is perhaps best encapsulated in a piece he wrote regarding the miners' strike in *New Society* in January 1985.* Somewhat whimsically but cuttingly, he wrote:

> I remember some years ago speaking at a meeting in London when the Trotskyists' slogan was 'General Strike Now.' (When you think of it, that is their slogan for all seasons.) Anyway, this man was arguing that the TUC should call a general strike. I asked for his analysis of the likely alignment of forces, and what were the possibilities of victory or defeat for the workers in the event of a strike. He brushed these considerations aside. Eventually we got to the truth. He had never been on strike. In fact, he was an investment analyst for some stockbroking firm. But he was a militant, prepared to fight to the last drop of some worker's blood. Now this didn't surprise me, for ultra-leftism – which embraces all the fifty-seven varieties of Trotskyist and Leninist sects – has nothing to do with the working class. It is a middle-class phenomenon; a philosophy of political dilettantes.

* *New Society*, 17 January 1985.

That's why you will find more Trotskyists in Equity and the National Union of Journalists than in the Boilermakers'.

While Jimmy supported Kinnock, the reforms taken by the new Labour leader went far beyond his attacks on the Militant Tendency and included wholesale policy reviews that ran counter to Jimmy's beliefs. He began to despair of the party being stripped of its socialist ethos and traditions, and the distancing from the unions and a watering down of a commitment to socialism grieved him. By the time of the 1987 election, he was concerned that the party was moving to the right and losing its broader labour movement soul. In a piece he wrote after the election, he commented that 'it was easier to spot the ball than spot a trade union boss on a Labour Party platform'. In that election, Kinnock reduced the Tory majority but Labour still finished 10 per cent behind the Tories. Seats were won in Scotland, Wales and northern England but the votes were lost in the south.

That was the beginning of the end for Jimmy and the Labour Party. The modernising tendencies of Kinnock were to be supplanted and accelerated by Blair and New Labour, and that was to prove a mortal wound to his allegiance to the party, though his support for the wider labour movement remained undiminished. He always believed that it was Labour that had changed rather than his political views or values and, finally, in March 1998, Jimmy resigned from the party.

He retained a party card for years to come, but his activity lessened as his media and other activities increased. Away from Labour, he was to embark on a new career in journalism and broadcasting. It was the start of the early media years.

CHAPTER THIRTEEN

EARLY MEDIA YEARS

Following the 1979 election defeat, Jimmy was faced with challenges in the yard. The situation at Marathon had been deteriorating. Orders were nearing completion and new ones were urgently being sought and redundancies would follow if they weren't obtained. Support was sought from the government, this time a Labour administration that was still clinging on to power. Jimmy was vociferous in his demands that financial backing should be provided given the potential job losses and the consequences for the community. Unemployment in Scotland was fast approaching 200,000 people and alternative work was limited. Clydebank, along with many other industrial towns, was already suffering. Singer's had been laying off employees and would finally close the following June.

The Labour government, however, was reluctant to provide financial support or offer a 'bail out', as the energy minister Dr Dickson Mabon called it. Jimmy reacted angrily to the term 'bail out', condemning the insinuation that the workforce was absorbing public money without contributing anything and driving home the fact that unemployment was double what it had been at the time of UCS. Jimmy instead sought to have Marathon relocate work from yards elsewhere in the world, but that was something that the company rejected on the grounds that it was impractical for a variety of reasons, including distance. As the situation worsened, 900 redundancy notices were issued, threating the bulk of the workforce.

However, as it was, neither Jimmy nor his colleagues were going to be involved in any repetition of UCS. The following year saw Marathon sell the yard to a French company and, while there was a reduction in the workforce, there was not the total closure that had been feared. The new owners continued the operation on the site until it finally closed in in 2001. But it would operate without Jimmy. Just as when he left the Communist Party, it was a long time coming and there were many factors leading to the decision. He'd contributed all he could as the shop stewards' convenor and, although he was involved in the AEU, the posts he'd sought had eluded him.

Moreover, though he took his post seriously and was committed to it, he must have been yearning for something that might stimulate him both intellectually and creatively. There was a desire for a fresh challenge. He'd done all he could in that job but there was still more that he could contribute. He knew he had the ability to write well and many were telling him that he should try something else. He was worn out by the goings on at the yard, and it was to be an opportune time for Jimmy to start a new life and career in journalism.

Jimmy left the yards for the last time in early 1980. It was a sad farewell in many ways, but his colleagues, such as Bob Dickie, wished him well in his new career. The writer William McIlvanney even wrote a piece about it in a newspaper. It was, after all, a momentous moment in both the passing of the old trade and the start of a new career. There must have been a tear in his eye as he departed but a spring in his step at the thought of the new life ahead.

In the late 1970s, the Reids had moved into a slightly bigger council house in the Dalmuir area of Clydebank. Jimmy refused to consider buying his council house, remaining true to his opposition to the cheap sell off of public housing stock. The slightly larger accommodation allowed him to create a study where he could work undisturbed by the family. It was to be a new beginning and he was happy to be embarking on it.

In many ways, it was a brave and risky decision, as although he'd written for the *Morning Star* and *The Tribune* on a regular basis as well as other journals and periodicals, there was no guaranteed work awaiting him. However, Jimmy had become well versed in writing throughout his years. His semi-autobiographical book *Reflections of a Clyde-built Man* had been published in 1976 and he had written for many papers and journals. His intelligence and extensive vocabulary meant that he was able to craft words and articles every bit as evocatively as in his speeches. In addition, his natural humour and analytical skills added humanity and depth to what he wrote.

With no guaranteed income and limited deals lined up, it was still a slightly nervous time for him. However, he didn't have to wait long before a contract from a newspaper came his way. In the summer of 1980, he started his professional journalistic career with a weekly column about TV programmes in *The Herald* in Glasgow. Jimmy was wanted by the paper given the profile he had and the draw he would be for readers. For him, it was a start with a quality leading paper and a steady income.

He realised that he couldn't change the editorial line of the paper, but he could contribute in his own way, as he would with other papers in later years. He wasn't directed what to write and while pieces may have been written with the readership of the paper in mind, the thoughts expressed were always his own.

The Reids didn't stay long in Dalmuir and the steady income would see the family move from Clydebank to Glasgow. Jimmy and Joan tried to buy a place in Clydebank, but having missed out on the purchase, instead bought a flat in Kelvingrove Street, Glasgow. It was closer for his new work, as well as being larger for the family. Jimmy was also a Glaswegian at heart and returning there suited him, though he'd enjoyed his years in Clydebank.

The social scene was greater in Glasgow than in Clydebank and Jimmy, who was in his element when in company chatting and discussing anything and everything, lapped it up. Being close to the city centre also allowed Jimmy to socialise more and enjoy the venues that were, if not quite on his doorstep, certainly closer than they had been in Clydebank. Visits to jazz clubs with friends and family became a regular occurrence and the children were often taken on a Sunday afternoon to give them an introduction to music. He and Joan enjoyed Saturday nights there and at other venues. They also frequented the Musicians' Club in Berkeley Street, Glasgow, and trips through to the Edinburgh festival were also made each year. There were bars nearby where he could meet with pals and chat with regulars. It could be frustrating for Joan and other family members when out with him, however, as he was a celebrity and many people wanted to talk to him. Jimmy was always accommodating and good natured, listening and chatting even when those he was out with were privately fuming at the interruption.

His column in *The Herald* was called 'TV View by Jimmy Reid' and it enjoyed significant readership. There were fewer channels back then and without Twitter or Facebook, Jimmy's comments gained a large audience. Jimmy's column featured prominently within the paper, and although ostensibly it was a critique of programmes that had aired, Jimmy ranged far and wide, making comments related to the programmes being reviewed but interspersing them with current views and recollections from the past. Reviewing a production of Arthur Miller's play 'The Crucible', he reminded readers that Senator Joe McCarthy had sought to ban it.

He could be light-hearted and funny about some programmes and thoughtful and incisive about others. He enjoyed comedy and praised shows that he'd enjoyed, but on occasions, he could be excoriating as when Nationwide televised a Glamorous Grannies Competition. Needless to say, it was shredded it for its inanity.

While he wrote in an accessible way, his erudition always shone through. He could discuss programmes on high culture as well as more low-brow shows, enjoying both. Other articles on specific issues appeared in the paper and in other outlets. The growing unrest in the shipyards in Gdansk, Poland, and the rise of solidarity saw him pen pieces on the issue with insight from his own working life and former Communist Party membership. The summer of 1981 saw him interview Michael Foot, the new Labour leader, and a few months later he wrote scathingly about the policies of Thatcherism in response to the riots taking place in English cities.

In the autumn of that year, Jimmy started a regular column 'My View' in *The Herald*, which allowed him to go beyond TV critiques to expressing his personal opinions and thoughts. The content was balanced between some heavy pieces on major world affairs and lighter comments on sport or culture. One column in November 1981 started with praise for Dundee United FC, who had defeated a German team in a European football competition, only to move on to castigate General Alexander Haig who was President Ronald Reagan's Secretary of State. It was a remarkably insightful, if acerbic, piece, tempered with humorous references to Russian spies.

The year 1982 saw 'My View' continued as before. He commented prolifically on major events at home and abroad with many reflections from his own experiences. The crisis in Poland continued in Europe and the travails of the Labour Party mounted in the UK; as nuclear tensions grew, Jimmy called for all parties to pull back from the precipice; he was supportive of the Papal visit to Scotland, which he thought would promote religious harmony, and argued eloquently for justice for the Palestinian people; condemning the violence of the Provisional IRA, he said he was a supporter of James Connolly but explained that he'd have rejected their methods; the Hillhead by-election in 1982 saw him castigate all parties; and he questioned the Falklands War that broke out that year, especially since he questioned whether some Labour MPs would have handed the Falklands over to fascists.

Although he was still active in the Labour Party, Jimmy was willing to write frankly about both it and the wider labour movement. As the conference season came around and the focus fell upon the TUC and later Labour, he wrote openly about faults he saw and fears he had. He criticised the lack of democracy within parts of the TUC, arguing for the election of full-time officials.

In a later piece, he condemned the Redundancy Payments Act for the effect it had upon political and union actions and insisted that morality as well as money needed to be considered when it comes to job losses.

A few weeks later, he condemned the Trotskyite faction within the Labour Party and the effect it was having upon it, writing that the most 'devastating criticism of the Labour Party was that in the past three years of internal bickering it has failed to bring a ray of hope to our people that things might or could be different'. He was equally scathing of the right within the party, as internal bickering continued and Kinnock was blocked from becoming employment spokesman. In November, he wrote that time was running out for the Labour Party.

However, he could equally turn his hand to sport which he loved and did so with relish. That year saw him comment on the World Cup, laughing at the antics of the Scottish fans and condemning the hooliganism of some of the English ones. His love of sport and his talent as a writer saw him given a column in the back pages as well as in the front of the paper. Another column, 'Jimmy Reid: Side lines', started that year in which he wrote as thoughtfully and humorously about sport. Some sport journalists were resentful and queried Jimmy's credentials as an armchair enthusiast, but his talents soon overcame their doubts. Football was his first love, but, as with literature, Jimmy enjoyed and appreciated the skill and craftsmanship across all fields and arenas.

Nonpartisan at club level, he was as passionate about Scottish football as were most Scottish working men. In the days before a Scottish Parliament, it offered a channel for Scottish identity and latent Scottish nationalism to take its hold. Even so, he was a huge fan of the English cricket team and, like many Scots, saw no contradiction in supporting England at cricket while wishing their defeat in football. Radio 4 even broadcast a programme about Jimmy's affection for the Marylebone Cricket Club. In later years, he was treated by family in London to visits to Lords Cricket Ground.

Under the headline 'The Company I Keep', Jimmy wrote profiles of individuals such as Hugh Scanlon, the AEU President, and leading Glasgow bookmaker Tony Queen. Most interesting, though, was a piece on Scargill which appeared in October 1982. In it, Jimmy described how he had known him for twenty-five years since Arthur Scargill had been on the YCL National Executive Committee when Jimmy became National Secretary. Jimmy wrote that he was a throwback in time, though a member of no particular hard-left sect, and added that Mick McGahey should have been the miners' leader.

Jimmy soon became a columnist for the *Daily Record*. His column, in what was then Scotland's biggest selling paper, was similar in content to his pieces for *The Herald*, even if the style was slightly changed for a more working-class readership. Again, Jimmy proved popular for the paper. At one stage, a falling out with the editor saw him threaten to leave and the proprietor, Robert Maxwell, recognising his worth, persuaded him to stay by offering him an additional column in their sister paper, the *Daily Mirror*.

He had a further falling out with them in 1986, and left to write for their rival *The Sun*, who were then seeking to expand in Scotland. As these papers were part of the Murdoch media empire, this drew some criticism from the left, but the opportunity to contribute a different perspective was seen as important by many. Jimmy's decision was welcomed by Kinnock, with whom he was still in contact, and, as Jimmy said in his own defence, the paper was read then by some 12 million readers across the UK. Jimmy never hesitated to attack Thatcher in his columns and promoted the Labour Party in the campaign for the 1987 general election. In the run up to the election, he wrote that 'the choice is stark. There is a moral dimension. Kinnock exudes a sense of compassion. Mrs Thatcher doesn't.' However, despite his best endeavours the Tories were returned. These columns across the papers continued through 1983 and, the following year, another book of his was published. *As I Please* was a collection of articles that he'd written.

However, since Jimmy wrote about issues as he saw them, he could provoke controversy and cause issues with old friends on the left. The most controversial of all proved to be his comments on the miners' strike.

CHAPTER FOURTEEN

THE MINERS' STRIKE

The miners' strike of 1984 was to be the focus of a lot of Jimmy's writing. His criticism of Scargill in particular was biting and, as a consequence, Jimmy was attacked mercilessly by many on the left. A few former comrades were to be as scathing in their attacks on him as he was of Scargill, and a bitter taste remained.

The dispute was a long time coming. Even before Thatcher came to power, right-wingers within the Tories were devising a strategy to take on and defeat any strike within key nationalised industries. As with UCS, the architect of the strike defence plan was Sir Nicholas Ridley. In 1977, he prepared a report in which he detailed how a future Tory government should act and, in due course, it would be implemented by the Thatcher administration.

Ridley's report detailed that the government should choose the battleground as they were clearly preparing for a fight with the trade unions. It provided an assessment of industrial areas in Britain and the risks and possibilities within them of strike action taking place. The coal industry was considered reasonably likely to see strikes. The report directed that coal stocks ought to be built up at power stations and plans should be made to import foreign coal in the event of a strike. Non-union lorry drivers were to be recruited to drive the haulage fleet necessary and dual-fired coal and oil generators were to be installed. In the event of a dispute, steps were to be taken to target both strikers and union funds. Finally, a mobile squad of police trained in riot tactics were to be on hand to deal with violent picketing if it occurred.

Like the shipyards in the 1970s, coal mining was an industry in decline. From its heyday of a thousand pits in the first half of the twentieth century, it had fallen considerably below 200 by 1984. Many of the richest seams had been exhausted and mechanisation was reducing the need for the size of workforce that had previously existed. The coal industry itself was quite heavily subsidised and that was compounded by the availability of cheap foreign coal. It was an opportunity for Thatcher's government to sharpen their knives, as the Heath administration had done with shipbuilding a decade before. The desire to confront the unions was already there and the plans were already in place. Some in the leadership of the NUM seemed oblivious to the trap they were walking into.

In February 1982, some twenty-three pit closures had been planned in line with agreed procedures, but the Tory government backed off after realising that they weren't yet ready for the major confrontation which would have resulted. A few pits, such as Kinneil in Bo'ness, did shut but redundancies were reduced by transferring the workforce to other mines. Still, the distrust between the NUM and the Thatcher regime was evident and growing over issues such as closures and wages. The NUM balloted for strike action in June and October 1982 and March 1983 but didn't achieve the necessary support. In November 1983, however, the NUM imposed an overtime ban.

The Tories were preparing for it. In 1983, Ian MacGregor was put in charge of the National Coal Board (NCB). He had previously been at British Steel, where he'd earned a reputation for both taking on the unions and cutting jobs. The writing was on the wall for a major confrontation, and so it was to be. In March 1984, the NCB announced a change to former agreed procedures about pit closures. Twenty collieries were to close across Scotland, Wales and the north of England with the loss of 20,000 jobs. The miners' reaction was swift. Some unofficial strikes began, and on 12 March Scargill declared support for the strike action called in Scotland and Yorkshire. Some regional ballots took place, with areas such as the Midlands and North Wales voting against and Northumberland narrowly in favour, but below the required 55 per cent threshold.

However, crucially no national ballot was sought as Scargill argued that the strike was a series of local regional disputes and therefore no national ballot was required. That was in spite of the previous attempts to win a vote that had been made over the past few years, when national ballots had been sought but the required threshold not obtained. It was to hamper the cause greatly and be the source of much of Jimmy's criticism.

The absence of a ballot harmed the miners in public opinion where there was sympathy for their plight but much less for the methods being used by the union. It's been suggested that Scargill rejected a national ballot as he was afraid he would lose, although there's also evidence to suggest that a national ballot may well have been won given the strength of feeling amongst the miners. However, Thatcher used the lack of a democratic mandate to attack Scargill and invoke the actions already planned.

She viewed it almost as a war and even described the miners as the enemy within.

Despite the lack of a national ballot, the strike was overwhelmingly supported in many areas including Scotland, South Wales, Yorkshire, Kent and some parts of the north-east of England. In the Midlands and North Wales, however, picketing crowds tried to encourage or enforce a stoppage. The National Association of Colliery Overmen, Deputies and Shotfirers (NACODS), which represented the pit deputies and oversaw the safety of the workers, voted to strike in April 1984, but failed to obtain the required two-thirds majority.

However, when they voted again in September of that year, the result this time was overwhelmingly in favour of strike action. The NCB immediately reacted by conceding a change in the criteria for pit closures, which NACODS accepted. That was an opportunity for the NUM to end the dispute, which would have been accepted by MacGregor and the government, who were concerned about the strength of strike support. It was an offer which, while it still guaranteed some redundancies and pit closures, would have saved many more jobs that were ultimately lost. Scargill, however, rejected that and demanded that there be no closures whatsoever. He was intent to see the war to the finish, regardless of whether or not it could be won. As it was, men started to drift back to work as the pain and hunger endured after almost a year on strike became too great.

It was to be a bitter and venomous dispute. It was unlike anything the UK had seen since the general strike in 1926. The Ridley Report was implemented, coal stocks had been built up and foreign imports ordered. Non-unionised lorry drivers moved vital coal stocks about the country and action to restrict miners' benefits and orders attacking union funds were brought in. Hardship for the mining community grew and support for their plight intensified. Police and security services were mobilised to counteract the strike. Mass picketing took place seeing major confrontations between strikers and police culminating in the infamous Battle of Orgreave, which saw running fights with police brutally attacking strikers.

While the support for the strike remained strong in the NUM heartland areas in the north of England, Scotland and Wales, in Nottinghamshire and other Midland areas, support was beginning to fragment. Even the union broke down after an alternative organisation, the Union of Democratic Mineworkers, was set up. By June 1984, although the strike was still emphatically supported by many, over 50,000 miners were still working.

By 1985, the hardship for miners and their families had grown and the hostility on the picket lines intensified. Clashes between strikers and police increased, with over 11,000 people arrested and almost 200 imprisoned. Nearly 9,000 miners were dismissed from work for being arrested for picketing, even when no charges were brought. Though picketing at the pits may have worked, it was a much less successful strategy in other industries. Power companies maintained supplies and major industries, dependent of coal and energy, carried on largely unaffected. The strikers' antipathy towards those working or strikebreaking, whether in the pits or moving coal, intensified. David Wilkie, a taxi driver carrying a strikebreaking miner to work, was tragically killed in Wales when a concrete block was hurled at his car by two strikers.

Although public support for the miners' cause was significant, political support was much less so. Moreover, unity across the trade union movement hadn't been obtained. The steel workers continued working, fearful for their jobs and ignoring both the miners' pleas and pickets. Kinnock and the Labour leadership vacillated, condemning the Tory government while distancing themselves from Scargill.

With no prospect of victory, the strike ended in March 1985. The NCB postponed the closure of a few pits as a concession but, in reality, it was crushing defeat of the miners and their industry. In 1994, John Major's Tory government privatised the industry, creating UK Coal. Longannet power station, the last major deep mine in Scotland, closed in 2002 and the last mine in the UK shut in 2015, bringing to an end an industry that had been pivotal to British industrial success. As with the major shipyards, these closures meant that another part of Scotland's industrial heritage was lost for ever.

Jimmy's opposition to the strike wasn't to do with the miners or their struggle and fears. He was always sympathetic to their cause and he never underestimated Thatcher's attacks upon them. It was about Scargill's leadership and the lack of a ballot which undermined the strike action from the very start. As Jimmy had predicted, it would lead to chaos and disaster for the miners, their communities and the labour movement. As early as July 1983, almost nine months before the start of the strike, Jimmy used his column in the *Daily Record* to caution the miners about precipitous action. He pointed out that another defeat for the leadership on a ballot for industrial action would be a serious dent in their credibility. He said that in a democracy, 'you can only move at a speed or in the direction willed by the majority'.* As it was,

* The *Daily Record*, 4 July 1983.

Scargill decided to proceed without one, despite trying to obtain a democratic mandate in the years before.

Once the strike was called, Jimmy very early on reiterated the need for a democratic basis for the strike, which meant a national ballot. Writing in *The Times* in May 1984, he said 'the equivalent of what has been done in the NUM would be a majority vote in the House of Commons to cancel a general election on the grounds that Parliament is a higher body and doesn't need a mandate from the electorate'.*

Numerous pieces were to follow as he was a leading columnist and the strike was the major issue of the day. Jimmy was no longer a political leader – he was a commentator on political events; not an active participant but a former activist, albeit with an extensive history of industrial struggle. Failing to do so would have been remiss of him, and equally from his perceptive failing to speak out would have been a neglect of his duty to the wider cause he still believed in.

He denounced Scargill's leadership and described his supporters inside the Labour Party as 'zealots'. His criticism of the NUM leader was stark and harsh. On a Channel 4 opinion programme, he said that his criticism of him 'was not for being militant but for being a stupid militant', adding bitingly that 'if Kamikaze pilots were to form their own trade union, Arthur would be an ideal choice for leader'. Again, in his *Record* column in September 1984, Jimmy wrote that 'the decision not to have a ballot has split the miners and dragged the union back to the turmoil of the twenties'. Of those who extolled the miners' leader, he wrote

---

* *The Times*, 14 May 1984.

'Scargill has become the Ayatollah, the focal point for all the hard left, sectarian, leftist groupings within the labour movement. They now demand uncritical adulation of Scargill as proof of socialist purity. Anything less is deemed a betrayal of the working class. That isn't socialism – but Stalinism.'* He also dubbed Scargill as Britain's Lenin in an article in *The Spectator*.†

Jimmy's comments were quickly met with backlash from former comrades. In September, Mick McGahey attacked him in the miners' paper with the headline 'Broken Reid'. His former UCS colleague Jimmy Airlie also denounced him. Some of the attacks were personal and vitriolic. Accusations of doing so for monetary gain and failing to stand by the working class were made from many quarters.

However, Jimmy stood by his position, which he most clearly articulated in a piece he wrote for the *New Society* magazine in January 1985 just weeks before the collapse of the strike and the defeat of the miners. He started by pointing out that Scargill was benefiting Thatcher. 'Over three million unemployed, the pound at its lowest ever, our manufacturing industry in chronic decline and our welfare services close to collapse, and yet if the general election were tomorrow she would romp home with a greater majority.' He feared for the consequences for the labour movement.

It will destroy the National Union of Mineworkers as an effective fighting force for the rest of the century. It will damage trade unionism in general and alienate millions. It places in

---

* *Daily Record*, 16 September 1984.
† *The Spectator*, 13 October 1984.

jeopardy any chance of a revival of the electoral fortunes of the Labour Party. Only the extent of the damage is in question.

He lamented the trap the miners had walked into recalling the steps taken by the Tories to prepare for vengeance. He condemned what he saw as Scargill's abuse of democracy Scargillism, which he described as 'the politics of seizing power, not winning it'. He reiterated that the crux of the problem was the lack of a national ballot, pointing out the absurdity of seeking support for strike action from other unions when it had been ignored in the principal strike they were being asked to back. He castigated Scargill's methods, pointing out that seeking to bring down a democratically elected Tory government was as wrong as trying to do so to a Labour one. He also criticised Scargill's argument that there could be no pit closures, pointing out that some pits were exhausted and would have to close in the face of evolving technology, and, while government support for communities was laudable, it was not inexhaustible. Some pits he recognised would have to close as technology and society evolved. Finally, he took Scargill to task for his absolutism and failure to settle when the NCB had made overtures, stating that he had 'rejected this offer and thereby snatched defeat from the jaws of victory'.

While Jimmy was deeply shaken by the criticism his comments received, he always felt it was right and necessary to speak out, for the miners and their communities. His friend Sir Alex Ferguson invited him up to stay with him in Aberdeen and recalled how bruised Jimmy was by the vitriol against him. But he strongly believed that the case for the industry and their communities was lost in the disunity created by Scargill's tactics.

Divided within and without from the outset, and with the focus on the leader not the cause, Scargill's leadership played into Thatcher's hands and led the miners and their families into the trap laid for them by the Tory government. The consequences for mining communities were savage, and yet could have been mitigated. Scargill's 'victory or nothing' approach had resulted in total defeat of communities Jimmy had known and revered throughout his life. The outcome grieved him greatly. Moreover, the effects of the Tories' defeat on the wider labour movement were equally significant, with Thatcher strengthened and trade unions weakened. It resulted in further hardship and a further decade and more of Tory rule.

Jimmy was pilloried for his views and his reputation amongst many on the left was tarnished irrevocably as a result. However, his position was consistent and principled, and he said what others thought but lacked the courage to express. Indeed, both in the Labour Party and the NUM many felt that the lack of a ballot had undermined the strikes from the beginning and that both Scargill's tactics and his failure to take the settlement had been catastrophic. Some, like Kinnock, appeared keen for Jimmy to speak out but were reticent in his defence. Others simply condemned his comments despite not disagreeing with his assessment. Jimmy's crime for them was not what he said, but that he said it. Mick McGahey and others were known to have privately disagreed with Scargill although they publicly defended him.

Perhaps Jimmy's ire became too focused on Scargill's leadership, but it became the prominent issue for many throughout much of the dispute. Besides, from his previous experiences leading strike action, Jimmy knew how to win support but also when to retreat and salvage what you could. As it was, he was prescient in his dismal prediction of the consequences. The strike was brutally crushed, the NUM fatally wounded and the miners and their families suffered dreadfully. Both the Labour Party and the wider labour movement were damaged.

But Jimmy wasn't to let all of that criticism affect him. He had to focus on his growing reputation in journalism and upcoming breakthrough in broadcasting.

CHAPTER FIFTEEN

MOVING FROM JOURNALISM
TO BROADCASTING

Making the move from journalism into broadcasting, Jimmy was to prove to be as natural in front of the camera as he was in print. His friend, the playwright Peter McDougall, credited Jimmy for saying things as he saw them and speaking directly to the viewer. As with his columns, Jimmy wrote almost all of the scripts himself. While this was mostly a success, he once managed to lose 12,000 words in cyber space. As with many of his generation, he found the transition to technology challenging, especially as he had always used a manual typewriter.

In January 1984 it was announced that Jimmy would headline a Scottish Television (STV) show called *As I Please*. The promotional material for it described it as an opinion show shaped for a man 'who is not afraid to voice his own opinions but at the same time let others have their say'. It was scheduled to go out at the same time as Robin Day's *Question Time* on BBC1, showing the faith they had in Jimmy's drawing power given the competition it was facing from an established show and famous presenter. The very first show concerned the sentencing of criminals, and in it Jimmy interviewed a renowned retired police officer, a judge, a right-wing Tory councillor and a convicted bank robber. It was to be the start of a highly successful show that would be followed by many other appearances on programmes on STV and other channels.

In December 1985 that year, the BBC booked him in for a weekly programme titled *The Reid Report*, which saw Jimmy addressing specific issues and general current affairs. Then, in 1987, it was off to Channel 4 to front the show *Down the Line*, which was composed of a dozen half-hour shows on topical issues.

The success of those programmes didn't go unnoticed. Gus Macdonald had taken over as Director of Programmes at STV in 1986 and would later become Managing Director. Like Jimmy, he had a background in the shipyards, having done an apprenticeship at Alexander Stephens, and had been involved in an apprentices' strike in 1959 (the one after Jimmy's 1952 efforts). He was keen to bring Jimmy back to STV.

The two became quite close and conceived the idea for Jimmy to do a programme on Russia. The Soviet Union was undergoing significant change at the time. Gorbachev had come to power with his policy of *perestroika*, which seemed to trigger a shift from authoritarian communism to a more democratic socialism. However, the Soviet economy was in deep trouble and the regime was floundering, though few could have predicted the speed or extent of its collapse.

And so, in 1987, Jimmy returned to the Soviet Union for three weeks to research and then for a further ten weeks to film the programme *Reid about the USSR* which aired the following year. Jimmy was delighted to be there during the seventieth anniversary celebrations of the Revolution. He knew the country was on the cusp of change. Any illusions over the nature of the Soviet

Union itself had long since been lost, but Jimmy still embraced the ethos of what the revolution had intended. There was a sense of sadness at what might have been, as well as a modicum of guilt at having encouraged others to follow him in support of a system that had been abused.

The show allowed Jimmy to reflect on his past communist allegiances and cast a critical eye on modern Russia and its satellite states. He visited not just Moscow and Leningrad, as St Petersburg was then, but also Latvia, Georgia and Kazakhstan. The show involved interviewing both key players and ordinary people across the vast land. He was adept at engaging with people even where there was a language barrier, possessing an ability to relate to folk and draw them out in discussion. The show was very well received, winning a silver medal at the New York International Television and Film Awards, as well as two BAFTAs.

That success led to a commission to do a programme on the Polish Solidarity leader, Lech Wałęsa. Jimmy had written extensively over many years on the growing crisis in the Gdansk shipyards that had spread across the entire country. The strikes in the yard in 1980 had seen the launch of the trade union Solidarity that gathered millions of members across Polish society. The army under General Jaruzelski intervened in 1981 to impose martial law and avoid a possible repetition of the crises in Hungary and Czechoslovakia with a Soviet invasion. Wałęsa was initially imprisoned and, although he was subsequently released, he was unable to accept in person the Nobel Peace Prize due to the travel restrictions imposed on him. In the early eighties, his work had to be conducted clandestinely, but by the time Jimmy interviewed him, Solidarity was out in the open, talks of change were ongoing and the regime was about to fall. As it was, partially free elections took place in 1989 and a Solidarity-led government took over thereafter.

Jimmy had always been supportive of Solidarity and Wałęsa, but that wasn't a position uniformly held on the left or within the trade union movement. There were still some residual 'tankies' and union activists who preferred to fraternise with Soviet trade unions, whose legitimacy was highly questionable, and criticise the virulently anti-communist Polish leader and organisation. Solidarity was, after all, heavily influenced by the Catholic Church, which was a big part of people's lives across all Polish society. Financial support was given by the CIA which again raised suspicions on the left, but Jimmy took the democratic position and sided with the workers in their struggle. They, and not the cadre in charge with military support, were the legitimate voice of the Polish working class.

The ongoing stalemate between Solidarity and the regime of General Jaruzelski was highly topical. Meetings were being held to broker a peaceful settlement and avoid clashes between the people and the military. Within a very short space of time, Wałęsa was in government and was elected to the presidency in 1990, which he held until 1995. Although Jimmy was supportive of the workers' struggle, it is fair to say that he didn't warm to Wałęsa as an individual. Though both were radical and from the shipyards, their personalities and their backgrounds were different. The Polish leader was very rigid and Catholic in his outlook, and, in the midst of a titanic struggle, was less inclined to be forthcoming to Jimmy who had hoped for greater access to him. The programme did present Jimmy with another opportunity to reflect on the realities of communism and he successfully documented a land in turmoil and transition. The programme was very well received.

His televised portrayal of communism past and present didn't end there. In 1992, he was commissioned by STV to film a programme called *Moscow Gold* which aired in 1993. It exposed the Soviet funding of the Communist Party in Great Britain over the years, enabled by old Soviet files and archives being opened up for public scrutiny. Again, it was both enjoyed by viewers and cathartic in a way for Jimmy. Despite his having been at the heart of things in the party's HQ and knowing that financial support had been accepted, he appeared surprised by the extent of it. Similarly, he had always known about the block purchasing of papers by the Soviet Union whereby thousands of copies of the *Morning Star* had been bought as an additional way of channelling funds. But he had believed that more of the substantial funds to sustain it had been from subscriptions and trade union contributions. The support from Moscow was far more extensive than he had believed to be the case. Those with him at the time of the programme's creation recall that it was a perplexing time for him. By then, the Soviet Union had collapsed – something that was ruminated over by Jimmy. He saw a society that had established a framework to build a better world, but then created the evidence that it wasn't the way to achieve it.

It got him thinking. He told a close friend at the time that he had been rereading Eduard Bernstein, the German social democratic politician and theorist. Bernstein viewed socialism as evolving through capitalism rather than being a result of its collapse. Castigated by the likes of Rosa Luxemburg for being a revisionist, Bernstein pursued the parliamentary and trade union route for reform rather than revolution. Jimmy explained to his friend his belief that once capitalism could reform itself no further, it could progress to social democracy and then democratic socialism. That seemed to offer Jimmy some comfort at a time when Gorbachev's attempts to reform the regime towards a more social democratic basis were supplanted by Boris Yeltsin's unbridled acceptance of a neo-liberal agenda. While the Soviet Union had veered from the socialist path, Jimmy still believed in the socialist way, and how to achieve it continued to drive him.

Another incident entangled Jimmy in his communist past. Jimmy was hired to do some media work abroad and a first-class round-the-world air ticket was provided for him and Joan. Landing in Hawaii, they were required to complete the declaration that they weren't and hadn't been members of the Communist Party. They both answered truthfully, only to find themselves taken to the interview room and subsequently blocked from their sojourn there. They regretted missing out on the sights but had no regrets for past commitments.

Alongside his newspaper columns and TV shows, Jimmy recorded a radio programme with the news presenter Richard Baker on Jimmy's favourite jazz music. Ably to fondly articulate about jazz musicians and the evolution of the genre over the years, from Louis Armstrong through to his favourite Charlie Parker, it allowed Jimmy to indulge his passion away from politics.

There was never any suggestion of Jimmy seeking candidature in the general election of 1992. Jimmy realised his days of active involvement in politics were over. Although his focus was on his successful media career, he commented publicly and advised privately on political affairs. He continued to support Labour, though he began to despair of the party. He had drifted away from his previously close relationship with Kinnock but still contacted him to caution him on Labour's stance in Scotland. Jimmy felt that Kinnock was ignoring the growing frustrations felt by many in Scotland upon enduring a government that they didn't elect. There was a democratic deficit and Kinnock's antagonism to nationalism was ignoring increasing agitation for a Scottish Parliament.

As his political allegiance began to move, so did his residence. The family moved home once again, this time to his native Glasgow Southside. In 1990, he and Joan bought a flat in Newark Drive, Pollokshields, which offered more space and a shared back garden that the family could enjoy. Though not a gardener, the green space appealed to Jimmy and his children and grandchildren. Nearer to the Govan of his youth, he was able to meet up with his wide circle of friends. Not all were political animals; Ernie Walker, who had been the Chief Executive of the Scottish Football Association, was someone who accompanied him on his many trips to watch the Scottish international football and rugby teams.

In 1994, Jimmy along with friends launched a radical left-of-centre paper. It was something he had wanted to do for a considerable time, so, with some more time on his hands and greater financial security along with respect in the media, it seemed an opportune time. After all, he'd been an avid reader of socialist and left-leaning papers since he had been a boy. Although he enjoyed his columnist work and was happy that his copy was read widely, he still yearned to be at the forefront of a radical paper.

He believed such an outlet was needed for both intellectual and socialist debate to flourish.

Seven Days Scotland was to be a current affairs magazine jointly edited with his friend Bob Houston with contributions from other leading lights, such as Hugh McIlvanney and David Scott. Financial backing of almost £100,000 was amassed and the paper launched in the May. It would be available both sides of the border but was primarily aimed at a Scottish market. Jimmy believed not only that it could survive the challenges facing the print industry, but that it could prosper and be commercially successful. In his interview on STV at the time of its launch, Jimmy said:

> We want to see our magazine in there, as a forum of discussion and debate. Let me make this point. Everyone knows where my politics are. I'm left of centre; the magazine will be left of centre. In that, it will reflect the general mainstream of Scottish politics. But I also object to politicians of the left and the right trying to score points instead of making points. And therefore, I want people of the right to come in, they have arguments, they have legitimate arguments, and I think they've got to be addressed and not sneered at.

The 40,000 copies printed in the first run were met with a great deal of scepticism in the trade. Times were challenging in the print industry and launching a new paper – especially a left-leaning one – was a significant mountain to climb. Although Jimmy was hopeful, the sceptics who had scathingly said that they would give it seven days were sadly proven right. Initial purchases didn't turn into regular orders and advertising revenues were hard to come by in challenging economic times. While the quality of its content was enjoyed, hope and sympathy were insufficient to sustain its production. It lasted a short while but eventually had to close. It wasn't the first or last venture to find the obstacles too great and Jimmy had significantly fewer resources than many. In its failure, there was no disgrace and many plaudits were given for his efforts. Jimmy was disappointed, but retained the belief that there was a market for such a publication. It was something that he would return to a few years later.

Meanwhile, alongside his continuing media work, he was beginning to make another political move as his journey on a Scottish road to socialism began.

CHAPTER SIXTEEN

STEPS ON THE SCOTTISH ROAD

The election of Margaret Thatcher in 1979 was a bitter blow to Jimmy and much of Scotland. The imposition of her right-wing Tory policies caused unemployment to rise and immediate enormous hardship that continues to this day in many parts of the country. The election saw Labour defeated overall in the UK but still win convincingly in Scotland. The results were:

SCOTLAND
Labour: 41.5% (44 seats)
Conservative: 31.45% (22 seats)
SNP: 17.35% (2 seats)
Liberals: 9% (3 seats)

UK
Conservative: 43.9% (339 seats)
Labour: 36.9% (269 seats)
Liberal: 13.8% (11 seats)

Despite Labour's win in Scotland, the defeat was generally accepted with little reference to the constitutional dimension, other than within nationalist ranks. It was seen as one that had occurred across the entire UK and its resolution remained in that framework. The focus at the time was to take actions to oppose Thatcher and protect communities from the consequences of her policies, north and south of the border, rather than on a Scottish Parliament. Although a Campaign for a Scottish Assembly continued, the focus in the aftermath was on social and economic problems more than the constitutional issue. Unemployment and industrial closures were the major concerns. Moreover, other than to committed nationalists that seemed still best tackled through a British route. In that Jimmy was no different to most others and continued his political efforts within the Labour Party.

The election saw a catastrophic defeat for the SNP, which went from eleven to just two MPs. It commenced a period of internal division as members squabbled over the reasons for the loss and their political direction forward. It resulted in a lurch to a more fundamentalist nationalism and a move away from a gradual approach. These issues would see them remain on the margins of Scottish politics for some time to come.

Labour, meanwhile, became embroiled in a battle for the leadership of the party after Jim Callaghan stood down. It heralded a fight between left and right who were wrestling to govern the party's direction. Jimmy supported Tony Benn and a move to the left.

The next general election in 1983 occurred in the aftermath of the Falklands War. Despite crippling levels of unemployment across Britain, Thatcher enjoyed another convincing win. While Labour remained dominant in Scotland, it was once again crushed south of the border. Both the leadership of Michael Foot and the radical manifesto upon which he stood were castigated. The defection of the Gang of Four and internal divisions also led to Labour's crushing defeat in the polls.

The SNP were in an even worse position. Their vote was to plummet further from the loss sustained in 1979. They kept the flame of nationalism alive, but with little signs of any fire being lit in the country any time soon and with the threat of the SDP/Liberal alliance, their chances were not looking good. The results were:

SCOTLAND

Labour: 35.1% (41 seats)
Conservative: 28.4% (21 seats)
SDP/Liberal: 24.5% (8 seats)
SNP: 11.8% (2 seats)

UK

Conservative: 42.4% (397 seats)
Labour: 27.6% (209 seats)
SDP/Liberal: 25.4% (17 seats)

The re-election of Margaret Thatcher was a bitter blow for many in Scotland. Her policies were harming not just individuals but entire communities. Manufacturing industry was paying a heavy price for her monetarist policies and Scotland along with many areas in northern England and Wales was suffering greatly. Large employers were closing not just in the shipyards but across the entire manufacturing sector. Other industries felt threatened and the miners' strike would soon follow.

The SNP maintained their demand for Scottish independence

and Assembly campaigners their call for a Scottish Parliament, but the political solution still appeared to be through a British road not Scottish route. Nationalists referenced the Conservative victory south of the border but it had little resonance in a land where opposing Thatcher was the key priority. Little was made of the democratic deficit in Scotland where the party elected did not form the government. Indeed, Jimmy's views adhered to the general view that defeating Thatcherism was the most pressing issue and that the method to do so was through the UK Parliament. However, the divergent voting patterns north and south of the border were too great to ignore and the democratic deficit and the question of an electoral mandate had to be raised. That would come initially not through the SNP but through Labour. Jimmy declined to stand in the 1987 election but supported his campaign in the 1987 general election. Sadly, although Kinnock made modest progress, Thatcher was re-elected for a third term; but the Tories had once again been convincingly defeated north of the border. The Scottish dimension was to begin to come to the fore. The results were:

SCOTLAND
Labour: 42.4% (50 seats)
Conservative: 24% (10 seats)
SDP/Liberal: 19.3% (9 seats)
SNP 14.1% (3 seats)

UK
Conservative: 42.2% (376 seats)
Labour: 30.8% (229 seats)
SDP/Liberal: 22.5% (22 seats)

For the third consecutive election, Scotland had rejected Thatcher but she had won a record third term. Demonstrations followed in the wake of the election and although the attendances were not huge, they were indicative of the growing questioning of the legitimacy of the Tory government in Scotland. The mood was beginning to shift from despondency at another Tory victory to challenging their right to govern.

Though, just over a generation before, Scotland had voted Tory and had been dependent on Labour support from south of the border, the voting patterns were now clearly diverging. North of the border the decline in Tory support was more marked and was matched by a significantly greater increase in backing for Labour. The SDP/Liberal alliance loss was also greater in Scotland than in the rest of the UK. The SNP vote may have remained low but the constitutional issue was coming onto the political agenda despite that.

Labour was emboldened by their success in Scotland and frustrated by their political impotence. Returning fifty MPs was a remarkable feat but they were already facing taunts from the SNP of being the 'feeble fifty'. Many of their MPs began to speak out about the situation they confronted. Senior party representatives questioned the lack of a democratic mandate and questioned the Tories' legitimacy, as they faced another five years in opposition. They included senior figures such as Robin Cook, John Maxton and John Home Robertson. However, the priority still remained an electoral victory in the UK. Thatcher was beginning to falter as Kinnock started to make progress and, for many, it seemed that one more heave would see the Tories removed both sides of the border.

However, across huge swathes of Scotland many people began to feel that something was very wrong with a system that enabled the Tories to do as they wished despite an overwhelming rejection of them by the electorate. They wanted a solution to the constitutional issue that loomed so large. The resentment towards Thatcher and her policies was also compounded by the imposition of the poll tax, which they introduced in Scotland a year earlier than in the rest of the UK. Uproar followed given its impact on wider society as well as its longer-term effect on councils. Not only did Scotland have to endure a government that they hadn't elected, but now they were the first to be subject to its poll tax. Feelings ran high and many in Scotland began to mobilise. Non-payment campaigns were formed and public protest grew. The issue began to dominate Scottish politics and there was soon to be a political opportunity for the public mood to be tested.

In 1988, Bruce Millan MP was appointed as an EU Commissioner, a move which created a by-election in his Govan constituency. The SNP's Margo MacDonald had won a spectacular victory in November 1978 and, this time, the SNP candidate would be her husband, Jim Sillars. He had been a Labour MP before leaving to help form the Scottish Labour Party, and was now a senior SNP figure.

Millan had won the election in 1987 with a majority of 19,500 and almost 65 per cent of the poll. The SNP trailed in fourth with just over 10 per cent. However, in this election, poll tax was the major issue and the SNP was clear in its support for a non-payment campaign. The electorate was angry at the Tory poll tax, most especially in a deprived and radical area such as Govan. Labour, however, worried about the effect of non-payment upon council revenues and concerned about where the questioning of the Tories mandate might lead politically, were hesitant. They called for payment though they continued to oppose the tax, and that vacillation was to cost them support with activists and embolden the SNP's presence.

The defiance shown by the SNP and their charismatic candidate resonated. Jim Sillars won a spectacular victory with a 33 per cent swing and a majority of over 3,500. Although he was subsequently defeated in the general election of 1992, Sillars created a political storm and his ongoing poll tax campaign had a huge part to play in Thatcher's ultimate political demise.

The SNP's buoyed presence after Sillars's victory in the by-election resulted in the Claim of Right for Scotland being signed in 1989, not just by Labour and Liberal Democrat MPs, but also by local authorities, churches, trade unions and other civic organisations. Prepared by the Campaign for a Scottish Assembly, it declared the sovereignty of the Scottish people. It had no legal standing, but was symbolic of the growing frustration felt and was part of the process of the move towards Scottish devolution. There was a growing view that the Assembly, voted for in 1979 but refused under the 40 per cent rule, would have offered some protection against unmitigated Thatcherism. While Scottish independence was still a fringe view, the need for a Scottish Parliament was becoming mainstream thought. It was clear that the constitutional issue was coming to the fore in Scottish politics and life.

It also was to lead to the setting up of the Scottish Constitutional Convention, established to promote the case for self-government. It succeeded the Campaign for a Scottish Assembly and as with the Claim of Right had support across both political and civic Scotland. The SNP subsequently withdrew due to independence not being considered as an option and it was vehemently opposed by the Conservatives. It still though had widespread resonance across civic society.

Kinnock was stridently opposed to nationalism. He had, after all, been opposed to devolution for Wales in 1979. After the Govan by-election, Jimmy contacted Kinnock to take him to task on his views on nationalism, disagreeing with his analysis and saying how badly it would be perceived by the working class in Scotland. Jimmy recognised that the lack of an electoral mandate for the Tories and the democratic deficit in Scotland were issues that needed to be addressed by Labour. It was becoming evident that a Scottish Parliament was needed to protect Scottish society and its economy. Working people both hated and feared the Tories, and if Labour couldn't or wouldn't act, then there was the danger that voters would overwhelmingly turn against Labour and towards the SNP in despair and a desire for action.

Jimmy sought to explain to Kinnock the difference between nationalism and chauvinism and how nationalism didn't conflict with being an internationalist. In many ways, it replicated the arguments he had made within the CPGB during his time there when seeking to win support for a Scottish Parliament. However, it seemed he had little influence on Kinnock, and constitutional change was put into abeyance as all Labour's efforts were once again to simply be put into defeating the Tories in the forthcoming UK election.

However, the 1992 general election yet again saw a Tory government returned, albeit not under the premiership of Margaret

Thatcher. The poll tax had taken its toll and ultimately done for her. She was challenged within her own party and ultimately stood down to be replaced by John Major. The polls as the election approached predicted either a Labour victory or a hung parliament. Hopes were high both sides of the border that the Tories would be defeated. At a rally in Sheffield, Kinnock made his infamous victory address and sentiment in Scotland was similar, as a change in government was eagerly anticipated.

As it was, the Tories clung on to power. They almost held their vote in the UK and though Labour's increased it wasn't enough. In Scotland, Labour actually suffered a modest reversal losing a few percentage points and lost one seat while the Tories won an additional seat. Another Labour defeat brought home all the issues over the democratic deficit and lack of mandate. Scotland was again at a constitutional impasse, having voted against the Conservatives but facing another five years of Tory rule. The modest Tory increase didn't mask their continued unpopularity in the majority of the country. It was a Tory government that was continuing to move to the right, even though Thatcher had gone and the poll tax had been replaced by the community charge. The ideological attacks upon the working class and trade unions both sides of the border continued. The divergence in voting patterns north and south of the border remained clear and anger and frustration were continuing to rise.

The biggest winners in terms of increased votes, though, were the SNP, increasing their vote by 50 per cent despite retaining only the three seats they had and losing the by-election victor Jim Sillars. However, many saw it to be a good result for the SNP and it was to mark the start of many beginning to move to the SNP.

While the party didn't have enough votes to win, it had enough to threaten Labour and create fear of what might be. The results were:

SCOTLAND
Labour: 39% (49 seats)
Conservative: 25.6% (11 seats)
SNP: 21.5% (3 seats)
Lib Dem: 13.1% (9 seats)

UK
Conservative: 41.9% (336 seats)
Labour: 34.4% (271 seats)
Lib Dem: 17.8% (20 seats)

While John Major did not generate quite the same animosity as Thatcher had done north of the border, he was perceived by many as leading a government with doubtful legitimacy. The Tories had themselves changed in Scotland under Thatcher. Gone were the days of 'One Nation' conservatism and maintenance of the social consensus forged during and after the war. The party drifted to the right becoming ever more isolated from wider Scottish public opinion. Malcom Rifkind even referred to the post of Secretary of State being akin to that of 'A Governor General'. As he was replaced by Ian Lang and then Michael Forsyth the feeling of an alien regime being imposed on Scotland intensified. The days of patrician Tories having some 'noblesse oblige' and maintaining some element of the post-war consensus were long gone. When Sir George Younger was succeeded in 1986 by Malcolm Rifkind it had heralded the start of the period of the 'Governor Generals' when Tory government policy was foisted on a country that continued to vote heavily against them. The rightward drift continued when Rifkind was followed by Ian Lang in 1990 and in turn by the bete noir of the left and nationalists, Michael Forsyth, in 1995. The latter epitomised Thatcherism for many Scots and almost seemed to revel in the animus towards him.

The constitutional issue was now at the forefront of Scottish politics. John Smith, who took over as Labour leader from Kinnock in 1992, described devolution as unfinished business and the settled will of the Scottish people. It was clear that Labour was moving in support of a Scottish Parliament and one that would be more powerful than the previously proposed Assembly. While Smith, who was a committed devolutionist, took the lead, others less persuaded of the merits of devolution recognised that, as in the 1970s, with the SNP back as a credible force, failure to act could see the loss of Labour votes in favour of the nationalist party.

The nationalists had fought an overtly pro-independence campaign and polled well, despite the general pressure to vote strategically for Labour to remove the Tories. While the party had only three MPs, the SNP were now back as a political force to be reckoned with. Moreover, Alex Salmond was elected their new leader in 1990 and was beginning to make his mark. Though still a distant dream for a small minority, independence was once again on the political agenda.

But the issue was much larger than political parties and their activists. The people of Scotland were growing restless and angered by another five years of Tory rule that they had again voted against. A significant demonstration took place in Edinburgh where the turnout of people marching to show their desire for change surprised even the organisers. The mood was moving from despondency to a determination to take action.

The issue was not if there should be a Scottish Parliament but what powers should it have and how could it be achieved. The opposition parties began to work more cohesively together. The Constitutional Convention established in 1989 was given added impetus and began to prepare the blueprint for what would become the Scottish Parliament. It was published on St Andrew's Day in 1995 and laid the framework for what was to come in the following years.

While Jimmy was not directly involved, he was still an influential figure and a political weather vane for the mood in much of Scotland. His comments in his columns both articulated and were prescient of the views of the Scottish people. Prior to the 1992 election, Jimmy had called for self-determination for Scotland as well as cross-party unity and even extra parliamentary action. The Claim of Right and the establishment of the Constitutional Convention that followed were both steps he supported. He wrote extensively on the topic of the democratic deficit that existed with Scotland and the week after the result in July 1992, he wrote in his *Herald* column:

What I can't understand is how Westminster MPs, including Labour MPs, can support the right of self-determination for Croats and Bosnians but not for Scots; how some of them support a referendum on Maastricht but not for Scots to determine how they would like to be governed. If sovereignty is the name of the game, then what about our sovereignty?

The following year Jimmy wrote scathingly in his column about Labour as Rosyth Naval Dockyard lost out to Devonport in a review and jobs were lost accordingly. Labour in Scotland had been ramping up the rhetoric about a Tory government with no legitimacy in Scotland but didn't challenge the loss of jobs which went with the absence of sovereignty. In 1994, at the launch of his *Seven Days Scotland* magazine, Jimmy went even further, describing the Tory government as 'an alien political culture' being imposed on the Scots.

As 1997 approached, another election neared. John Major had pulled off a remarkable victory against the odds five years before, but the smell of political death around the Conservative Party was pervasive. The Tories were despised by the outside and divided within. Their defeat after eighteen long years seemed guaranteed; it was simply a matter of when the election would be called. Removing them became the principal method of delivering social and economic change, as well as being the key to unlock the impasse on a Scottish Parliament.

John Smith had died suddenly in 1994 and was succeeded by Blair. Blair was someone Jimmy never warmed to and New Labour was a brand he disliked intensely. Although he always tried to eschew personal animosities in politics, he just couldn't contain his contempt for the new Labour leader.

Though far from passionate about devolution, Blair did not seek to obstruct Labour's commitment to it. The demand for it within Scotland and much of the Labour Party was evident, as were the risks of a nationalist surge should there be any failure to deliver it. For most, a Labour government remained the key for a

Scottish Parliament. Indeed, even for nationalists it was a critical opportunity to pursue their dream of independence.

The 1997 general election saw a Labour landslide both sides of the border. Senior Tories such as Michael Portillo were defeated in England and every Tory seat was lost in Scotland, including those of Cabinet ministers Malcolm Rifkind and Michael Forsyth. The extent of the Tories' defeat, however, masked the continued divergence in votes north and south of the border: the Tories dropped to just 17.5 per cent in Scotland, but still polled 30.07 per cent in the UK. The result was:

SCOTLAND
Labour: 45.6% (56 seats)
SNP: 22.1% (6 seats)
Lib Dem: 13% (10 seats)
Conservative: 17.5% (0 seats)

UK
Labour: 43.2% (418 seats)
Conservative: 30.7% (165 seats)
Lib Dem: 16.8% (46 seats)

There was a strong expectation that a Scottish Parliament would be delivered this time around. Labour reigned supreme, but in Scotland they were conscious of the need for a Parliament. It had been eagerly anticipated by many and Blair quickly delivered on the commitment to a referendum. That wasn't without its controversy as Labour's initial position had been that a parliament would be established if a Labour government were elected, the electoral victory providing the mandate to deliver the proposal. However, Blair imposed the need for a referendum which was not without significant controversy itself given that it was a rolling back on the agreed position.

A bill to hold a referendum was lodged quickly and a vote was held in September 1997. The powers of the Parliament were fairly limited, although more than had been on offer in 1979 with the proposed Scottish Assembly, but less than had been sought by the Red Clydesiders generations before. However, for most it was simply the delivery of a long overdue Parliament and a base that could be built on in future years. Simply achieving it was the priority. The argument was between those who wanted it irrespective of however limited its powers may be and those who implacably opposed it in its entirety. As it was, the Tories were the only major party to do so and the result was overwhelming.

The referendum asked two questions: firstly, whether there should be a Scottish Parliament; and secondly, whether it should have tax-varying powers. The answer, as the vote showed, was a decisive Yes on both counts. With a turnout of 60.13 per cent, the results were:

Question 1:

I agree that there should be a Scottish Parliament: 74.29%

I disagree that there should be a Scottish Parliament: 25.71%

Question 2:

I agree that a Scottish Parliament should have tax-varying powers: 63.5%

I disagree that a Scottish Parliament should have tax-varying powers: 36.5%

The two areas which recorded the highest support for it were Jimmy's old stomping grounds of West Dunbartonshire (84.7 per cent) and the City of Glasgow (83.6 per cent). Those areas had remained loyal to Labour in the general election but the extent of the support for constitutional change was becoming clear. Some voted in the hope of independence, while others voted for a devolved Parliament but with the powers to mitigate Conservative rule. But, for whatever reason they voted for it and whatever powers they thought it had there was at least now a Scottish Parliament to allow the country to decide on many of its own affairs. It was symptomatic of the growing importance of the constitution and the voice of the working class in Scottish society.

CHAPTER SEVENTEEN

FINAL STEPS ON THE JOURNEY AND CLOSING CHAPTERS IN THE MEDIA

Although Jimmy's political involvement had ebbed throughout the late 1980s and 1990s, becoming more of a commentator than an activist, his interest remained strong. Specific contributions to party manifestos were replaced with wider assessments of politics more generally. He was, however, still a major figure in Scottish politics, not simply because of his influential and well-read columns, but because of the iconic image he still possessed. His commitments to socialism and a Scottish Parliament remained resolute though his loyalty to any particular party was wavering. He still held a card for Labour and, although it would be many years before he finally departed, doubts about the party had long since set in. He had been both angered and saddened by the rightward drift that had taken place in Labour under Kinnock's leadership, despite his initial support for him and some of his reforms. A mixture of contempt for the party's move to the right and other work commitments saw him gradually distance himself from Labour altogether.

When John Smith was elected leader after Kinnock stood down, Jimmy hoped for some change in the policy direction.

While Jimmy was further to the left than the new Labour leader, he still respected Smith's intellect and integrity. Smith was also a longstanding supporter of a Scottish Parliament, so things were looking up for many Scottish people. But all that was to change in May 1994 with Smith's tragic and untimely death and the installment of his successor, Blair.

As mentioned in the previous chapter, Blair was someone that Jimmy had never warmed to. He believed Blair and his vision of New Labour didn't share the values of the Labour Party or wider labour movement, and those doubts were only going to increase. Blair was bad enough but the New Labour project that he unleashed was an anathema to Jimmy. The modernisation that had started under Kinnock was modest in comparison to an almost full-scale revamp of the party that followed. For Jimmy, it wasn't just a name change from Labour to New Labour, but a selling out of the old values he believed in.

In his *Herald* column on 4 July 1996, Jimmy eloquently outlined the basis of his trenchant opposition to Blair and the New Labour project under the headline, 'Means may not end Tory rule'.

That the end justifies the means is a flawed concept. If the means are bad they debase the end, even if the end was originally well intentioned. History is littered with examples of how bad means corrupt good ends.

Labour Party members have accepted the abandonment of Labour principles and values, almost as electoral ploys, because they so desperately want to see an end to Tory rule. Blair has promised to deliver this. He could in the formal sense. The Conservative Party might be out of office. But will it be an end to Tory rule in an ideological sense, in terms of content. That is something else. Blair has got the Tories flummoxed for bizarre reasons. John Major, as leader of Britain's right-wing party, has to contend with a Labour leader who, in essence, is as far right as he is and, on some important issues further to the right. Last week Lady Thatcher opened an exhibition at the Imperial War Museum on 'Conflict since 1945'. She told a group of brass hats: 'I'm not a Tory anymore – I'm a Thatcherite'. She praised Blair for being in her mould. 'I'm sure he would press the button', she said, 'when he is in power'. Blair's economics differ not a jot from Thatcher's. His social nostrums are Thatcherite. There is abundant evidence to suggest that Labour is being re-made in the image of Tony Blair, who is fundamentally a Conservative. People keep telling me that he has no principles. He has Tory principles. He's in the wrong party.

Jimmy went on to lament that 'You can't seek to destroy a party's soul and leave the party as an organisational entity unchanged. Labour's democracy has been ravaged.'

It turns out that Jimmy was prescient in his prediction on Blair's ultimate fate, writing in that same column:

'Blair's arrogance might be his downfall. He sees himself as a man of destiny, and Lord protect us from men of destiny.'

The Labour leader's diktat on the Scottish Parliament, which Jimmy increasingly saw as the route out of the morass, also infuriated him. He continued in the article:

We in Scotland saw his imperious style of leadership at work last week. It was an eye-opener for some. Labour's policies for a Scottish Parliament with fund-raising powers had been settled.

Agreed by party conferences. The NEC. The Convention. A vote for Labour or the Liberal Democrats would be treated as a mandate for the implementation of this agreed policy. The Tories in Scotland had made no measurable impact by their tartan tax campaign. There was no negative factor operating in Scotland that required any change of direction. There were problems in England. Blair decided early last week to assuage the feelings in the south by leaving the Scots in the lurch. We got the referendum scam. There was a substantial inbuilt majority on the Scottish Executive against this policy somersault. The Blair cabal got to work. Union bosses in London were dragooned into line.

Despite his anger, Jimmy remained a Labour member – albeit a critical one. He sought the end of Tory governance on both sides of the border while he continued to express his concerns about New Labour both within the party and publicly through his columns. Moreover, he was driven by the desire to see a Scottish Parliament delivered that might offer new opportunities for the Scottish people, even if there was now the hurdle of a referendum to cross.

Jimmy believed that the defeat of the Tories was inevitable. Their internal divisions and the public antipathy towards them made a Labour victory certain. Any Labour leader would have won, as far as he was concerned, whether it was Blair or somebody else. As far as Jimmy was concerned, it was the Tories who had lost the election, not New Labour who had won it. Labour's abandonment of core policies and principles was therefore not just unnecessary but damaging, and he perceived Labour to simply enact an alternative Tory government. However, as it was in his final years in the Communist Party, his doubts were offset by old ties of loyalty, as well as the lack of an enticing alternative.

Accordingly, in the 1997 general election, Jimmy campaigned for Labour locally in the Govan constituency where he lived. The Labour candidate, Mohammad Sarwar, was to become the Labour MP for Govan and Scotland's first Asian MP. There had been internal ructions over the selection process that had spilled over into the wider public domain. Jimmy wrote sympathetically about the man who was to become Scotland's first Asian MP and castigated the political machinations that tried to defeat him. Jimmy's writing resulted in his being nominated for Best Campaigning Journalist in the Scottish Press Awards. It also resulted in him being courted by Sarwar to assist with his campaign.

Jimmy gave Sarwar public endorsements during the election campaign, spoke at a rally in Govan with Jack Jones, the former trade union leader, and even shouted out of a megaphone while being driven around the constituency by his friend Bob Thomson. He still loved campaigning and being actively involved; he enthusiastically joined in the local activity, if still dubious about the party more largely. Indeed, that same year, Jimmy had declined an invite to attend a Labour fundraising dinner where Kinnock was a principal speaker, denouncing him as the man who abandoned Clause IV.

As it was when Jimmy left the Communist Party, leaving Labour was a long time in coming. Like many others, he savoured the defeat of the Tories in the 1997 general election and was excited by the possibilities offered by the restoration of the Scottish Parliament. Achieving its successful establishment and ensuring it was headed in the correct direction became his political focus.

However, as the new Labour government came into office, Jimmy's shift away from the party accelerated. There were, of course, actions taken by them that he welcomed. After all, they were coming into power after eighteen years of Tory rule and progress was set in motion in terms of tackling poverty and in re-establishing a Scottish Parliament. But he viewed Blair's government as Labour in name only, as he had outlined in his *Herald* column the year before.

He also was concerned that in many ways the sins of the old institution of Westminster would be visited on the new Scottish Parliament. Protecting it from the ways of the old order was vital. Not just the pomp and ceremony, but the venality and centralisation of power were aspects he loathed. It wasn't simply the restoration of the Parliament that mattered, but what it could deliver and how it would do so.

He viewed New Labour as a threat to that and if it were to dominate there, as in Westminster, it might well negate the gains of its restoration. It had to be a fresh start not a continuation of the old regime. The Scottish Parliament couldn't just be a replication of it north of the border. It had to be different not just in policy but in style. For him, leaving Labour behind would not be long in coming once a Scottish Parliament was restored. That would offer a new road to be followed in pursuit of his political dreams.

Accordingly, after the election in May 1997, and with the overwhelming public support for a Scottish Parliament in the referendum that September, the break soon came. On 11 March 1998, Jimmy wrote about his departure from the Labour Party in *The Herald*. Similarly to his resignation from the Communist Party, he laid out his position, though this time with less political theory and more a heartfelt explanation. Headlined 'The dilettante who destroyed the people's party' and below that 'Why I quit – Jimmy

Reid', he detailed his personal and political motivations from his early years in Govan to his current distaste for New Labour.

About three months before the General Election I had decided to leave Blair's Labour Party, having become convinced that the man and those around him were essentially Thatcherites. His ideological commitment to her concept of economics became clearer as he tried to explain his position. She was for a deregulated market, which is simply another name for nineteenth-century laissez faire capitalism that more or less dominated the world until the start of the Second World War. It created vast wealth and mass poverty. The poor lived in wretched ghettos, often demoralised, sometimes desperate. Some sought escape from the hopelessness of their lives in cheap booze. Laissez faire capitalism created cyclical booms, catastrophic slumps and two horrific world wars. It was an unmitigated disaster.

The human toll was ghastly. My parents lost three daughters. The oldest was eighteen months. We lived in the disease-ridden tenements of the Gorbals when Britain was the richest country on earth. The very young died like flies. Those who survived were often physically marked for life in the form of rickets, stunted growth, etc. These cruel conditions were compounded by the massive slump of the 1930s. Life was hell. Relief came through another horror – the Second World War. My father could find no work in the thirties until war was declared, and then the men of the slums were needed to fight for Britain and work for the war effort.

I have my sisters' death certificates. They died, so it says, from various diseases of the lungs and chest. I don't believe it. In the space reserved for 'cause of death' should be written 'Laissez faire capitalism'. It was and is a cruel and evil system. It is no way for human beings to live. It contaminates even the very wealthy it spawns. Marx said it left 'no other nexus between man and man than callous cash payment'. He was at least right about that. The Scottish labour movement was foremost in the fight against this evil system. My family moved to a council house in Govan. It had two bedrooms, a living room, kitchen, and inside toilet. I remember the bare floors, furnishings that were minimal, but, compared with where we had lived, it was a paradise. The slum clearance plan had been put in place by John Wheatley, Minister of Housing in the 1924 Labour Government.

Our abode was called a Wheatley House. Is it any wonder I love the labour movement? In the labour movement we had socialists, left-wing social democrats, social democrats, right-wing social democrats, all legitimate elements that could rightly encamp under Labour's banner. We argued like hell, but within certain parameters. But we were all against laissez faire capitalism. We hated the beast. We never in our wildest dreams envisaged a Labour Party leader that would one day embrace the bloody beast.

The 1945 General Election was a turning point in British history. I was a schoolboy at the time and remember the joy and tears of happiness in our home and among all the neighbours as the election results came through and Labour had won. The two words I heard most were; 'Never again'. And I don't think they were talking specifically of the war, but of unemployment, bad housing, under-nourishment, depressions, impoverishment, the means test, the indignities that all this entailed. The 1945–1951 Labour Government delivered a welfare state that brought a bottom-line security to everyone, from the cradle to the grave. Those who haven't experienced it can't imagine the utter destructiveness of lifelong insecurity on the human psyche. Men and women lived their entire lives one pay packet from penury. All that changed in 1945. To be fair, it has to be said that Tories like Harold Macmillan, Rab Butler, and Ian MacLeod subscribed to that post-war consensus.

This consensus governed Britain from 1945 till 1979. Things were by no means perfect, but for the ordinary people these were the glory years in the recorded history of the UK. Killer diseases rampaging through communities were wiped out, and not just by new medicines but from vastly improved social conditions. Then in 1979 a zealous dogmatist of the hard right became Prime Minister. Her idea of progress was to mount a white charger and gallop back to the last century. The welfare state was referred to contemptuously as the nannie state. She claimed it was no responsibility of government to create jobs. Markets were deregulated. Public assets sold off at giveaway prices. Taxes on the rich were reduced to the lowest in Europe. Public spending became a dirty word. The health service began to fall apart. The welfare state was under attack. There was mass unemployment. A new chronic poor emerged that was to become known as the underclass. They lived in ghettos. They are dying much younger than the rest of us. The infant mortality rate is higher in the ghettos. Many are demoralised, some seek escape in drugs. Déjà vu.

Blair accepted Thatcherite economics. That means accepting Thatcherite social policies. Economic priorities determine social priorities. Blair did his deal with Rupert Murdoch. As his agenda emerged it was seen to be indistinguishable from Thatcherism in its fundamental handling of the economy. And that tells you everything you need to know about a potential government. I've known Harold Wilson, James Callaghan, Michael Foot, Neil

Kinnock and John Smith. That means every Labour leader over the past thirty-five years. All loved the labour movement. Blair doesn't. He has no feel for it. No background in it. To me, he's like a political dilettante. His obvious locus in politics was with the Tories. Cherie probably guided him towards Labour. I wish she hadn't. These were my feelings months before the election as any reading of this column will testify. I didn't want to be associated in any way with a government I was convinced would betray the cause of labour and in the process do great damage to the wider labour movement. I had urged others who shared my fears to speak out. They wouldn't. And gave me the usual crap about not wanting to rock the boat. I was convinced that the Tories couldn't win. People all over Britain were at last rejecting the cruelties and crudities of Thatcherism. The election was lost by the Tories, not won by New Labour, as any objective analysis of the result will show. And, anyway, the pursuit of power unrelated with what you want to do with it is completely unacceptable in a democracy.

I was going to pack it in but was persuaded by colleagues to wait until after the election when a fight to curtail might start. I've waited and my worst fears have been confirmed. The Blairites have destroyed Labour Party democracy. North of the border comrades scurrying for seats in a Scottish parliament have kept their noses clean. It is totally squalid, and has nothing to do with modernisation. It is an unholy mixture of reactionary and Tammany Hall politics. The last straw for me was New Labour's Scottish Conference in Perth. New Labour, it seems to me, is no place for a socialist or social democrat.*

---

* *The Herald*, 11 March 1998.

The response from New Labour was muted as they sought to avoid a fight and play down any significance of Jimmy's announcement. They tried to portray him as yesterday's man, someone who had both Old Labour and Communist skeletons in the cupboard. There must have been quite a few in the party hierarchy who were glad to be rid of somebody many of them hadn't welcomed in the first place. Within the wider membership, however, some were angered and others saddened, as letters that followed showed.

While it caused a bit of a press stir and many friends and colleagues privately agreed with Jimmy's analysis of Blair and New Labour, there was no mass exodus of Labour members at that stage. Some wished to stay and seek change from within or doubted the wisdom of leaving at that juncture; others perhaps merely lacked the courage to act or speak out as Jimmy had. New Labour was, after all, politically dominant. Most members were simply delighted to be rid of the Tories after eighteen long years. Hopes and expectations were rising for the opening of the new Parliament in Scotland and for a new direction across the UK. Concerns about the policies of New Labour still seemed to be the prerogative of the old left and individuals like Jimmy. Cool Britannia was coming into vogue and there was a general feeling that Blair could do no wrong.

However, Jimmy's anti-New Labour sentiments would resonate and be echoed by many in years to come. The feeling that New Labour had abandoned them rather than their principles or beliefs would become widespread amongst many and not just old time socialists and trade union activists like Jimmy. A perception that it wasn't the party it had been or the one that they had joined. It would be followed by the haemorrhaging of members from the one-time Scottish people's party.

However, that was to be a few years away yet, and in the interim Jimmy remained a voice in the political wilderness. But his was still an important voice, and one which had set many thinking. The political focus in Scotland remained the re-establishment of the Scottish Parliament. Its restoration almost 300 years since the Act of Union in 1707 was causing great political excitement amongst both politicians and the public. The election for the new devolved Parliament was scheduled for May 1999.

Jimmy believed that a new and radical start was needed. Scathing about Westminster, he viewed Scottish devolution as a chance to make real changes. However, he was convinced that this fresh start couldn't be provided by New Labour. When he had left the Labour Party, no other party as yet seemed to exist that could deliver his hopes and dreams. His ideas came together in a column he wrote some six months on from his resignation from the party.

In his column in *The Herald* on 4 November 1998 he set the scene, as he saw it, as powers prepared to transfer from London to Edinburgh.

As Thomas Carlyle opined: The hour is great and the honourable gentleman, I must say are small. That could be said of today's parliamentarians. Big issues abound, so do small minded MPs who effortlessly stoop to every occasion. In six months' time Scotland will have her Parliament back. It will be a historic landmark in the unfolding life of the Scottish nation. The restoration of Home Rule by Scots over important areas of everyday life within the framework of the United Kingdom as a whole. This relationship with the rest of Britain will remain until such time as the Scottish people decide otherwise.

He continued with a scathing denunciation of Westminster and New Labour.

A Scottish Parliament should represent a clean break from Westminster, its trappings and political culture. As a model, Westminster stinks. It reflects in structure, procedure, rituals and mores the shotgun marriage between English feudalism and emergent English Capitalism. Its working ethos was made for the English businessman/landowner/politician who spent mornings in his counting house and afternoons looking after the affairs of state. It was after all, his state. When the burdens of the state became too burdensome he delegated the running of it to his appointees who continued to guide the ship of state wherever he wanted it to go. And so, it continues to this day. The widening franchise caused some problems. Other classes particularly, the more numerous working class wanted in on the act. They sorted that out with New Labour who run the state in their interest when the Tories are out of office. Britain is now a two party, one party state.[*]

He then went on to make an assessment of the current political situation and made a plea for a new party or organisation to arise to represent his views, stating:

But, there is no way I could vote New Labour. Such a vote

---

[*] *The Herald*, 4 November 1998.

would be interpreted as endorsement of Blairism which I think is the most disgusting hydra headed monster ever to have infiltrated the body politic of the British labour movement. These sentiments are by and large shared by lots of Scots. They will be disenfranchised unless from the Scottish labour movement emerges a group which will give such people the possibility of voting Real Labour/Social Democrat/Democratic Socialist. Thousands have left New Labour over the past year or so. Others are on the verge of leaving. Many thousands of Labour voters have resolved not to vote New Labour, for they believe it has betrayed everything Labour has ever stood for. A new political grouping that gives expression to these sentiments and beliefs could poll well in the election and could win seats. People are fed up with the intellectual sterility, widespread cynicism, corruption and imposed conformism so evident in the mainstream political process in and around Westminster.*

Jimmy was wooed by the newly formed Scottish Socialist Party (SSP), and in the article he had written that if it were a choice between New Labour and them, he'd vote for the latter. However, there was little likelihood of that. There was always a spectre of Trotskyism about the SSP with many members having come in from the Militant Tendency, although Jimmy retained good links with many individuals within it. Jimmy was finished with the Labour Party but as yet there was to be no new political home for him to join.

When the elections for the newly restored Scottish Parliament came about in 1999, the campaign saw a substantial push forward

---

* *The Herald*, 4 November 1998.

by the SNP. Proportional representation and the hybrid constituency and list electoral system opened up electoral opportunities previously denied by the first-past-the-post system. Moreover, the restoration of the Parliament gave a specifically Scottish dimension to politics that had been precluded in Westminster elections, where the choice was simply between a Tory or Labour government. The Greens and the fledgling SSP also contested.

The possibility of nationalist victory was seen off by Labour but only after initial concerns and a considerable effort. The electoral system had been devised to try and ensure that there could never be an outright majority government for fear of a nationalist victory, and it forced Labour into a coalition with the Liberal Democrats. Donald Dewar, who Jimmy had supported in the Garscadden by-election in 1978, became First Minister.

The result in 1999 was:

SCOTTISH PARLIAMENT

Labour: 43% (56 seats)

SNP: 27% (35 seats)

Conservative: 14% (18 seats)

Lib Dem: 13% (17 seats)

Green: 1% (1 seat)

SSP: 1% (1 seat)

Independents: 1% (1 seat)

The establishment of the Parliament was to have profound implications for Scotland. It provided a platform for Scottish political debate and agenda previously restricted to council chambers or the odd debate at Westminster.

Donald Dewar died suddenly in 2000 and was succeeded as First Minister by Henry McLeish. McLeish's administration was to divert dramatically from Westminster on the issue of free personal care for the elderly, a measure that had been recommended by a substantive report carried out in Scotland by Lord Sutherland. It was opposed by the Labour government in Westminster on the grounds of cost, but the Scottish administration went its own way, ignoring the requests of their London colleagues. It turned out to be highly popular north of the border as well as being a hugely symbolic signifier that the new Parliament was pursuing its own distinct agenda. It wasn't an outright call for independence, but it was the start of independent action from Westminster.

Though the SNP had failed to win the election, the outcome had made them the main opposition party providing them with a profile never before available. It provided the party with a base from which it could expand, and the return of MSPs along with added support staff gave the party resources previously denied them. It was an opportunity they would seize, even if there was to be continued disappointment for a few years to come.

The expectations that followed the reopening of the Parliament had been huge. There was never any likelihood of them being met and certainly not with the limited powers it possessed. In some ways, it was only to be expected. No government, let alone one with very limited economic powers, could have satisfied the pent-up frustration of almost 300 years of absence. Similar disappointment had been experienced in the Baltic States and other former Soviet Republics where independence and capitalism failed to provide the immediate wealth and improvements that had been assumed would follow. The demand for social and economic progress in Scotland couldn't be delivered straight away and certainly not to the levels expected, with the limited powers available. Its progress was further hampered by rows over the construction of a Parliament building along with other petty issues, and so the legislature struggled to find its feet. In many ways, the row over the construction of the Holyrood building became the lightning rod. The spiralling costs saw endless criticism that contrasted the Scottish Parliament with failures perceived or otherwise in health or other areas of government. As a consequence, many felt disappointed, if not disillusioned, in the once-promising institution.

In many ways, Jimmy's views were reflective of those of many others in Scotland. He was aggrieved by the actions of New Labour in Westminster but equally disappointed at the failure of the Parliament to grasp the opportunity available in Scotland. While the SNP were not in power, they were the party most associated with the restored Scottish Parliament and, with the Parliament's troubled start, the party suffered electorally as a consequence.

That first election to the restored Scottish Parliament was soon followed by another UK election in what was to become almost a constant cycle of elections north of the border. Jimmy was inactive during that election which Labour won comfortably again across the UK. The outcome was reflected in Scotland, with only one seat changing hands from the SNP to the Tories.

Alex Salmond had stood down as leader of the SNP and this was the first major electoral challenge for his successor John Swinney. It was to be a difficult election with New Labour still in the ascendancy under Blair and the SNP under fire over Holyrood. It was to be a setback for John Swinney personally and the

SNP as a whole. However, the Tory vote in Scotland was still just half of what it was south of the border, showing the continued divergence of voting patterns with the rest of the UK.

The result was:

SCOTLAND
Labour: 43.3% (56 seats)
SNP: 20.1% (5 seats)
Lib Dem: 16.3% (10 seats)
Conservative: 15.6% (1 seats)

UK
Labour: 40.7% (413 seats)
Conservative: 31.7% (166 seats)
Lib Dem: 18.3% (52 seats)

As the millennium neared then passed, Jimmy had slowed down his pace of work. While this was to do with getting older and wanting to enjoy other aspects of life, the decision was partly made for him when his column in *The Herald* was cut. It appeared they advised him that his column was no more when Jimmy was abroad watching a Scottish international rugby match. He was disappointed about how it had ended given how long he had written for them and the service he had provided. He'd had good times there and had made many friends in the staff and amongst the readership, but he didn't dwell on it or let it upset him unduly.

He wasn't to be idle long as he was soon snapped up by *The Scotsman*, eager to have his name on the by-line. His first column appeared on 12 February 2001 and he continued in his usual style. The piece tackled the Old Firm of Rangers and Celtic football clubs and the sectarianism that stalked them. It was something he'd written about oft times before and an issue that he still cared deeply about. The ignorance and divisiveness amongst the working class concerned him. Although it had improved immeasurably since he'd been a boy in Govan and even since he'd penned pieces in *The Herald* a decade before, it still lingered and, in his view, harmed Scottish society.

In the piece, headlined 'Sick tribes that know only hatred – bigotry and sectarianism are alive and well among those huddling beneath the Old Firm banners', Jimmy wrote: 'Ask Celtic or Rangers supporters why they feel so strongly about transubstantiation and they won't know what the hell you are talking about. But the tribe gives a sense of belonging. Most of them don't go to church. You can't really call them Christian without defaming Christ.' Columns that followed were to be similarly challenging and sometimes confrontational. The column was considered lively and readable and the feeling at the paper was that he brought a different perspective to their opinion pages, as well as a welter of experience from a lifetime in Scottish politics. That offset any doubts about age or past communist allegiance.

However, Jimmy's stint at *The Scotsman* wasn't to be as happy as some of the others he'd enjoyed. The paper's liberal perspective changed when it was acquired in 1995 by the Barclay brothers. They installed Andrew Neil as Chief Executive of all the titles they operated and sweeping changes took place; not simply in their office accommodation, which moved from North Bridge to a new building on Holyrood Road opposite the Scottish Parliament, but also in its political stance, which moved undoubtedly to the right.

A paper that had championed devolution in the '70s became an ardent opponent of independence in the new millennium.

The column was to run for just under two years. Jimmy's departure seemed to be the result of an executive decision and a change in editor. As well as writing his column, he provided some political insight to Rebecca Hardy during her tenure as editor, accompanying her to some conferences and offering knowledge of individuals and issues. It was something he appeared to relish. However, on her departure, that role ended and the new editor soon sought to move him out, although he remained popular with colleagues. By then, Jimmy was seventy and slowing up even more. Although disappointed to be dropped by the paper, he remained stoic about it.

His final piece published on 30 December 2002 showed he had lost neither his spark nor his insight, ending it by writing:

> I wish you and yours a happy New Year. I fear, however, that we will be dragged, by Mr Bush and Mr Blair, into a senseless war against Iraq around about February or March.
>
> But it need not happen if we make our voices heard. Don't sit back; speak out.
>
> Alas, this is my last column for *The Scotsman*. It's been a pleasure knowing you, even if only extraneously.
>
> Goodbye and good luck.

As it was, a crowd of 100,000, including Jimmy, was to march in Glasgow against the war on 15 February. A million marched in London and millions more marched around the world, but it was all to be in vain as the US-led coalition including the UK launched their invasion of Iraq on 20 March. Both the folly and the fallout from it reverberate to this day. It would also have huge implications for Blair, New Labour as a brand and Labour support more generally. It appalled Jimmy and further increased his contempt for Blair.

TV work had also begun to dry up a few years before that. New programmes and young presenters were on the scene as well as new channels being on the go. Moreover, it was the age of New Labour, and the Old Labour that in some ways he epitomised had been jettisoned. That allied to his age meant that TV work had also come to an end.

However, his passion and intellect remained the same. Despite the failure of *Seven Days Scotland* the decade before, his desire to see a left-wing paper published and printed in Scotland still existed. It was something he still believed was necessary for debate and discussion on the left in Scotland. In 1999, he had set about with friends and kindred spirits to launch another left-wing journal and the result was the publication the following year of *Scottish Left Review*.

One of the people who joined Jimmy's *Scottish Left Review* endeavour included his long-time friend Bob Thomson, a former union official as well as a former chair of the Labour Party in Scotland. Jimmy had known Thomson for many years since they were both young union officials. They'd often journeyed back from London together on the overnight sleeper and had whiled away the hours drinking and chatting. Others involved included Henry McCubbin, a Labour MEP from 1989 to 1994, John McAllion, a Labour MP and MSP between 1992 and 2003, who later left for the SSP, and Roseanna Cunningham, the SNP MSP and Scottish government Cabinet Secretary.

The magazine was less ambitious than *Seven Days Scotland*, taking a more realistic appraisal of the commercial challenges faced and the readership that existed. It was an opportune time to launch the magazine, with the Scottish Parliament restored and a distinctive debate beginning in Scotland. Old political allegiances were breaking down and new thinking was taking place. It launched in 2000 and runs to this day with bi-monthly editions and an online version. Jimmy remained involved with it until age and incapacity forced him to give up. It was to be his last major media commitment.

By then, Jimmy and Joan had moved home again, this time from Glasgow to Rothesay on the Isle of Bute. They had holidayed there a few years before, Jimmy reminiscing about his childhood holidays there as he showed the island to Joan, who had never been, and both loved it. They decided to buy a house there in the future when work allowed it and the opportunity arose and, just a few years later in 1998, they finally achieved it. The move offered a more relaxing lifestyle than they'd enjoyed before and was part of Jimmy's slowing-down process in terms of his media and political commitments. He still was writing columns, and had a study that afforded stunning views across the bay. The island life also allowed for long walks with Joan and the dog, as well as relaxing lunches in pleasant pubs and hotels. The house with its own garden and the island with its micro climate were to provide a perfect distraction from writing. Access to Glasgow was still relatively easy, and Jimmy frequently returned. If he was going to miss the last ferry home, he'd contact his friend Bob Thomson and arrange to stay with him, with a chance to share a drink and reminisce.

It was from Rothesay that he watched the next vote in the

Scottish electoral cycle in 2003. This was the second election for the Scottish Parliament. The election was fought against the backdrop of the Iraq War, though neither the extent of the catastrophe nor the full duplicity for its launch was known. The SNP had been weakened by the setback in 2001 and were the biggest losers in votes and seats. The media's focus was accordingly on them, as they returned to Holyrood visibly depleted in numbers though still the largest opposition party. The result was:

Labour: 38.8% (50 seats)
SNP: 20.9% (27 seats)
Conservative: 14% (18 seats)
Lib Dem: 13.2% (17 seats)
Green: 5.4% (7 seats)
SSP: 4.7% (6 seats)
Independents: 3.1% (2 seats)

However, the focus on the SNP's losses masked a decline for Labour, whose vote dropped by almost 250,000 and fell below a 40 per cent share for the first time since 1992. The SNP vote dropped by 4.9 per cent but their votes didn't directly transfer to Labour. It was a bad night for the SNP, but Labour also lost votes, which transferred to the SSP, the Greens and other fringe parties, which should have been a concern for the party. The edifice was crumbling, though few realised just how quick or rapid the final decline would be. The march of Scottish working-class votes away from Labour was clearly underway.

Moreover, it wasn't just its Scottish parliamentary support but in its council base that the Labour edifice would soon begin to totter. Jack McConnell had succeeded Henry McLeish as First Minister in 2001, following an expenses scandal. As part of a continued coalition deal with the Liberal Democrats in 2003, he agreed to legislate for proportional representation in Scottish local elections from 2007.

Changes had been made to Scottish local government in 1996 by John Major who oversaw a move from regional and district councils to unitary authorities. That was done to undermine the huge profile and power base that Labour possessed in Scotland. The new authorities would be both smaller and less significant, limitations that were compounded by the new Parliament pressing from above. The Labour local government machine that had held huge sway over the huge Strathclyde region and many other parts of Scotland was in decline and proportional representation would reduce it significantly more.

Jimmy was again inactive in the 2003 election. Age and health were obvious restrictions but, in reality, no party appealed to him. Despite the plea in his column some five years before, no new party had sprung up from the Scottish labour movement. There was no going back to Labour with its shameful intervention in Iraq, and his contempt for Tony Blair remained unbridled. The SSP were a peripheral force and Jimmy despised their streak of Trotskyism. Meanwhile, the SNP were in disarray about both leadership and direction. However, all that was soon to change, though Jimmy's political activism would remain limited.

The SNP had suffered in the Scottish Parliament election in 2001 and the UK vote in 2003, losing both votes and seats. Their leader, John Swinney, resigned after the European elections in 2004. Alex Salmond, who had stepped down in 2000 and had left Holyrood to return to Westminster in 2001, entered the fray once again, despite previously having said that he wouldn't seek party leadership again.

In the 2004 SNP leadership contest, Salmond ran a campaign with Nicola Sturgeon standing as his deputy, with a view to Sturgeon leading the SNP parliamentary group in Holyrood until Salmond could win re-election in 2007. It was a high-risk strategy, but Salmond sensed that there was an opportunity. Though Labour had held their position comfortably at both Holyrood and Westminster, the underlying signs – vote loss and a change of public mood – suggested that Scotland was ripe for change. The Salmond/Sturgeon ticket duly won and they embarked on a strategy of preparing the SNP to take power in the Scottish Parliament.

A fondness and respect for Salmond's deputy, Nicola Sturgeon, developed. Jimmy knew her through her general political profile and more closely as she had been contesting the Govan seat since 1997, but their differing personalities and interests were to preclude the same camaraderie and bonhomie that he would share with Salmond.

Jimmy had been wooed by the charming and charismatic Salmond over many years, with whom he bonded over their shared love of politics and horse racing. They knew each other through reputation and met at many events, political gatherings and even social occasions. An acquaintance and huge mutual respect soon began to form into a friendship. At an STUC conference in Dundee early in the millennium, the erstwhile SNP leader had approached Jimmy at the *Scottish Left Review* stall and the pair went away for a long and amicable chat. Later, at Jimmy's seventieth birthday party at Haggs Castle Golf Club in 2002, the ever-audacious Salmond had sent him a note of congratulations along with a party membership card. It caused some mirth to Jimmy and provided laughter in the hall. That gesture and other meetings were to set Jimmy thinking, even if it would be a few more years before he'd actually take out his own SNP membership card. The gallusness of Salmond, as well as his intellect and ability, appealed to Jimmy, who was to become very fond of the future First Minister.

Another person who was to bring Jimmy closer to the SNP was John McFarlane, a longstanding friend who had lived nearby Jimmy in Glasgow. McFarlane had been an ILP activist, campaigning for Maxton up until his death and the demise of the party. Thereafter, despairing of the labour movement's commitment to Home Rule, he joined the SNP, remaining a member until his passing in 2006. He also worked in the betting industry and therefore shared the same passion for sports with Jimmy. As well as socialising in their homes, they often went on trips away to watch football and rugby matches. He was very keen to broker Jimmy's relationship with Alex Salmond, presumably partly as a means of persuading him to join the SNP, as well as being genuinely fond of both. Knowing the two intimately he played a pivotal part in forging the closer ties between them.

As the bond between the two grew, Salmond often sought Jimmy's counsel on political issues in particular on the trade union movement and the key individuals within it. Who to approach, who to beware of, where they stood on the national question and what they were like in general were all aspects touched upon by an SNP leader eager to increase his party's standing in the wider labour movement. Jimmy was happy to be asked and delighted to be of assistance. His advice and guidance would prove as important for the SNP, as his final membership of them.

Alex Salmond was able to partly repay his mentor's assistance when Jimmy's column in *The Herald* was summarily ended. Salmond had himself been writing a racing column for *The Herald* at the time but had been approached by *The Scotsman* about moving to write for them. He had delayed but was incandescent at the treatment of his old friend by the title they had both been writing for

Accordingly, unbeknown to Jimmy he approached *The Scotsman* and indicated that he would move if his friend would also be taken on. Salmond also suggested that Jimmy may be of great help in providing some Scottish political insight to the editor, as well as his incisive column. And so, the change from *The Herald* to *The Scotsman* was made by both.

The progressive stance of the SNP under Alex Salmond had begun to appeal to Jimmy. Having shifted to a more social democratic position, the party was a substantially different entity to the one that Jimmy had criticised so caustically in the past. As a political activist, Jimmy knew that change was achieved by parties and not individuals. For social and economic change to be delivered, a successful political vehicle was needed. It may not have been the socialist party that he had hoped for in ruminations years before, but of the options available, it was the one to which he was becoming most sympathetic.

For Jimmy, it was the Scottish Parliament that seemed to hold the key to radical social change. The British road to socialism seemed at an impasse and, although there were hurdles on the Scottish route, the prospects looked better. As he had strived for its restoration, he now began to long for its further empowerment. New Labour weren't providing that in Holyrood any more than in Westminster, and the opposition to them and the party that offered that opportunity was the SNP. Unsurprisingly, Jimmy's move to the SNP would soon follow.

Despite Alex Salmond standing down as SNP leader, the friendship between the two continued. Jimmy had been very keen that Salmond return to take the helm once again of the party and lobbied for it extensively. Jimmy encouraged him to run believing that he could win and become First Minister at the next Holyrood elections set for 2007, despite the odds. Salmond seemed to be thinking along similar lines and both being gamblers, they were happy to try and defy the odds. When Salmond finally decided to throw his hat in the ring once again Jimmy was quick to support him publicly.

In August 2004, *The Herald* reported an open letter that Jimmy had sent to Salmond, which he had utilised at SNP leadership hustings and more widely. Jimmy was reported in the paper on 9 August as having stated that 'as a man steeped in the labour movement, it was now time to support self-determination'.

The letter went on to add that:

The SNP is already to the left of New Labour but then who isn't? I know Alex Salmond as a man of the Left, a natural social democrat. It is the restoration of social democratic concepts, as embodied by the welfare state and the NHS so brutally undermined by Thatcher and Blair, which must be at the top of any progressive agenda for Scotland. All of this places a great responsibility on the SNP as the second party in Scotland and on the leadership of the party.*

---

* *The Herald*, 9 August 2004.

Jimmy's public endorsement of Salmond and Sturgeon was followed in 2005 with his support for the SNP candidate in the upcoming Westminster elections in Argyll and Bute. During his discussions with Alex Salmond about his returning as leader, they had agreed it was possible for the SNP to win the next Holyrood elections. However, the future First Minister was also eager to make the point that it wouldn't happen without consolidating support in the Westminster elections, to provide the electoral base from which to advance. As Jimmy had lobbied Salmond to lead the party once again, Salmond lobbied Jimmy to publicly back him.

And so, on 20 April 2005, the SNP announced that Jimmy had formally signed up as a member. He appeared with Salmond at the STUC conference in Dundee, as the campaign for the general election was underway. The SNP were eager to parade their star new recruit, and what better a showcase than at the gathering of the Scottish labour movement. While still dominated by Labour Party members, it was far more radical in its position on Home Rule than the party itself.

Jimmy was quoted in reports as stating:

> To me New Labour has abandoned and betrayed all the principles that were fundamental to the labour movement in Scotland. I have waited a long time to see forces emerging within the New Labour Party that would bring the party back to its roots. But I have been waiting in vain and with every year that passes, Blair and New Labour move further to the right. They are now indistinguishable from the Thatcherite Tories.[*]

---

[*] *The Herald*, 21 April 2005.

He continued with his reasons for joining the SNP, adding:

> The obvious alternative is available to us here in Scotland. The
> SNP is a social democratic party – that means it adheres to the
> values that the labour movement was based on. I want to help
> it in this election and in future elections so that we can reverse
> the damage done by New Labour.

His newly acquired membership was welcomed by Salmond, who
announced:

> He is not only one of Scotland's most respected trade unionists, he
> has also shown himself over many years to be a man true to his
> principles and those of the labour movement. Tony Blair and New
> Labour have betrayed those principles. They have lost the trust
> not only of Jimmy Reid but of millions of Scots. Like Jimmy Reid,
> those Scots will receive a warm welcome in the SNP, which upholds
> the traditional Scottish values of community and compassion.

In many ways, it was a bold and brave decision. Beside his
column pieces, Jimmy had been away from the political fray for
many years. This meant putting his head above the political par-
apet once more, even if his activism and involvement would be
limited. It would open him up both to criticism for joining yet
another political party and to further accusations of treachery
from some on the left. Some family and friends felt he would have
been better staying away and commenting from his position as an
elder statesman of the Scottish political scene.

However, even though he knew the risks and personal criticism that would follow, Jimmy felt it necessary to speak out. When Jimmy felt deeply about something, such as Scargill's leadership of the miners' strike or his reasons for leaving the Labour Party, he felt obliged to say so. People listened to Jimmy, even if the explosion in SNP membership would only occur after his passing. Jimmy's membership was highly symbolic for the SNP, giving them stature as well as growing credibility, which it had previously lacked, within the broader labour movement.

The SNP was still an opposition party with only a remote likelihood of forming a government. But, as both Jimmy and Alex Salmond identified, Scotland was stirring from the stupor that had followed the Parliament's reopening. Jimmy had sensed that something was rousing and that action was needed. Although a referendum for independence was not on the horizon, building up the Scottish Parliament seemed like the best route for social and economic progress.

Jimmy had most certainly not jumped on a bandwagon. Despite his endorsement, the Westminster election of 2005 was hard for the SNP. Salmond's call for Scots voters to follow the path of Jimmy from Labour to the SNP was politely listened to, but mainly ignored. The SNP were squeezed by strategic votes to keep the Tories out and there was an increase in support for the Lib Dems in the aftermath of the Iraq War. The SNP though had survived and Holyrood elections would always be an easier contest for them.

Labour won, although with a reduced majority and a far narrower lead in votes cast. The Tory vote in Scotland was still half of what it was in the UK as a whole, confirming diverging voting patterns across the border, which had been an early factor in Jimmy's support of a Scottish Parliament.

The result was in 2005 was:

SCOTLAND

Labour: 39.5% (41 seats)

Lib Dem: 22.6% (11 seats)

SNP: 17.7% (6 seats)

Conservative: 15.8% (1 seat)

UK

Labour: 35.2% (355 seats)

Conservative: 32.4% (198 seats)

Lib Dem: 22% (62 seats)

Jimmy wasn't active in that election nor would he be for the SNP in coming years, as ill health precluded it. He did give an interview for SNP TV that was used by the party as they sought to utilise social media, and his name was used in other political paraphernalia. But by then he was growing much more infirm. Though he enjoyed Rothesay, many felt he never really settled there and missed the city of his upbringing. As he still loved to return to Glasgow, the family sought to help by arranging trips there as often as possible.

He appeared at some SNP meetings but mostly just chatted and engaged with members, eager to meet a man they had admired over years and were delighted had joined them. But, his days of active political involvement were long gone. He was elected president of the SNP Trade Union Group, whose members were delighted to have a doyen of Scottish trade unionism to give them some added credence.

However, his journey to the SNP and down a Scottish road was to be followed by many Scots in the elections to the Scottish Parliament that were up next in the electoral cycle in 2007. That saw the

SNP break through from the Labour hegemony that had ruled for over two generations and become the largest party, in both votes and seats. It was though only by a whisker of less than 1 per cent and just one seat. The result of the election in Scotland was:

SNP: 37% (47 seats)
Labour: 36.2% (46 seats)
Conservative: 13.4% (17 seats)
Lib Dem: 12.6% (16 seats)
Green: 1.6% (2 seats)
Independent: 0.8% (1 seat)

The crumbling of former Labour strongholds was enough to allow a minority SNP government to be formed and Salmond and Sturgeon were subsequently sworn in as Scotland's First Minister and Deputy First Minster.

Moreover, the local authority elections that took place on the same day and were now under proportional representation saw Labour's power base crumble even further. Control of all but two local authorities was lost by Labour, although they were in administrations in others through coalitions. Their share of the vote remained the highest but only by a fraction, with just 28.1 per cent of the vote to 27.9 per cent for the SNP. However, in the number of councillors elected, they were surpassed by the nationalists who returned 363 to their 348. The days of Labour domination in Scottish council chambers were now gone, as was their control in Holyrood. Labour Scotland was ending and an SNP era was arriving. Jimmy's foresight had once again been proven correct.

Despite being constrained by the absence of a majority, the

SNP in Holyrood still managed to form an administration under Salmond. Labour was seen to be defeated and, with the Tories in Westminster eager to avoid installing Labour, which would have been the only viable alternative, the SNP minority government took power and its administration thrived. Labour had run out of steam in Scotland, where their tenure was seen as lacklustre. A breath of fresh air was sweeping through the corridors of power and it was welcomed by many. There was a genuine desire in Scotland for change, though concerns about independence were reflected in the tentative overall support for the SNP. Meanwhile, south of the border, New Labour had become irreparably tarnished after its actions in Iraq amongst other things.

The SNP was proving to be competent and capable in Holyrood. In contrast, Labour north of the border was having difficulties in coming to terms with defeat. Some in the leadership still seemed to imagine that there was almost a divine right for Labour to rule and that the election had been an aberration which would soon be resolved. That resulted in them adopting an extremely hostile position to the SNP administration and seeming to oppose many of their actions irrespective of their merit. The outcome was that Labour was seen to be opposing progressive moves and support for them diminished further.

SNP actions in government resonated with Jimmy who, writing in the *Scottish Left Review* in 2007, stated: 'They now govern Scotland with policies that can objectively only be described as Social Democratic.'*

The piece was headlined: 'Not scared to be ourselves: the kind

---

* *Scottish Left Review*, Issue 43, November/December 2007.

of Scotland we wish to be is linked both to our national politics and to our sense of national identity. Jimmy Reid looks at the next steps for Scotland's identity.' In the article, he again detailed the reasons for his longstanding support for a Scottish Parliament, echoing comments made decades before and with the same searing insight and biting sarcasm. He criticised those on the left who disparaged nationalism and explained why the Scottish working class were deserting Labour for the SNP.

Breathes there the man with soul so dead who never to himself has said, this is my own, my native land, wrote Walter Scott; a man I wrongfully scandalised with all the brashness of a fourteen year old, but came to revere, as one of the world's first great novelists, before my teens were out. Years later an old Welsh miner told me that a man who cannot love all that's good in the culture of his own nation is incapable of respect for all that's good in the cultures of other nations. In other words, a healthy nationalism spawns a healthy internationalism.

This truth seemed to elude many on the British left who tend to equate nationalism with chauvinism and to pose nationalist against internationalist. This is nonsense. 'Inter' means between and 'nationalist' a sense of your own national identity. Internationalism can therefore only exist as a kind of solidarity or a coming togetherness of peoples from different nations. If there were no nations there would be no nationalists. If there were no nationalists there could be no internationalists.

In Britain, during its imperial phase, love of country became perverted into a menacing chauvinism that was simply a form of brainwashing to justify the enslavement of other nations and their allegedly inferior peoples; particularly in Africa and Asia. The origin of racism in Britain today is rooted in those evil days of Empire. The corruption of empire took a terrible ideological toll on the labour movement in Britain. Scotland's labour movement was not unscathed by this corruption although in our case the hallmark was religious and not racial. The Irish were White Europeans; but as England's first colony that didn't save them. The Irish famine was not an act of God but caused by the ruthlessness of British Colonialism.

When the starving Irish stumbled onto Scottish soil they were greeted with enmity by the Scottish working class and its trade unions. Mick McGahey, president of the Scottish miners, told me of his plan to produce a book about the life of Bob Smillie [sic], one of the founders and charismatic leaders of the miners' union in Scotland and a pioneer of the wider Scottish labour movement. After a few months I asked Mick how his project was going. He told me 'Jimmy we can't publish it. Bob's speeches at the time were viciously anti Irish. Like the racist language currently used by the National Front against Pakistanis today.' Smillie had clearly feared that starving Irish workers could undercut the wages that his union had struggled to achieve for their members over many years of struggle. That was obviously the strategic objective of the mine owners. I wanted Mick to publish. It was the truth from which lessons could be learned. But Mick saw this revelation as bringing shame to the Union he loved. It wasn't published.

Some years ago, Andy Stewart was singing a song about the Scottish soldier fighting 'battles glorious, victorious, far from the Green Hills of home.' I was writing a newspaper column at the time and in it asked Andy what the hell Scottish soldiers were doing fighting battles far from the Green Hills of home. Was it to enslave new lands and peoples for exploitation by the City of London? While they were so engaged were the Scottish landed aristocracy, throwing their families from their homes and holdings, in the Highland Clearances? Weren't the Scottish soldiers fighting the wrong people in the wrong places? Yes, is my verdict. But aren't our Scottish soldiers in Iraq today fighting the wrong people in the wrong place? So, what's changed?

For me, the biggest mistake of the Scottish labour movement in the second half of the twentieth century was its almost complete failure to make any serious analysis of the National Question in Scotland. So cocooned was Scottish Labour in the UK status quo that it didn't think that Scottish Home Rule was an issue. This was in a world where colonialism was disintegrating and small nations were coming into their own. That Scotland would remain unaffected by this clamour for the right to self-determination was an absurd presumption.

In 1966 or thereabouts I returned to Scotland after about ten years domiciled in England; convinced that the main task for the Scottish left was to win the Scottish labour movement for a policy of Home Rule in the form of a devolved or independent Parliament for Scotland. I simply couldn't understand how it was possible to be for the right of self-determination for all small countries in the world – except your own.

Scottish Labour is paying the price for this folly. The custodianship of Scotland's national aspirations literally fell into the hands of the nationalists. They now govern Scotland with policies that objectively can only be described as Social Democratic.

This puts them substantially to the left of New Labour. On matters of policy and principles can Labour lefties oppose Salmond's Government? The answer to that must surely be 'no'.

Written in the autumn of 2007, it was to be one of Jimmy's last political contributions. Once again, Jimmy was prescient in his analysis and prediction of the demise of Scottish Labour. The reverential aura that still surrounded him and his name was used by the SNP in their campaign in the by-election for the Glasgow East seat in the following summer of 2008. Jimmy's limited appearance was closely trailed and the seat was won by the SNP with a narrow majority. Jimmy was quoted in the press as saying that 'the SNP offer a positive vision and fresh thinking of what Scotland can be'. He also added 'the Labour Party is not the party that I voted for in the past, it has let the people of Glasgow down and abandoned its roots'.

There was to be little more political activity by Jimmy thereafter. Age was hampering him and ill health bedevilling him. Jimmy's life and political journey were coming to the end. The British road to socialism had become the Scottish road to independence and he shone the light for many of the Scottish working class who would follow him down it in coming years.

CHAPTER EIGHTEEN

JOURNEY'S END

The latter years were difficult for Jimmy. Old age caught up with him and was far from kind in many ways. He had dementia and his mind had been failing for some time. Friends had noted the odd occasion when speaking at an event that he would lose the thread of his thoughts. It was not the majestic Jimmy of old, and even though those gathered forgave any lapses, it was embarrassing for him and he began to decline the invitations that continued to arrive.

It was hard for Joan and the family. It was deeply distressing for those closest to Jimmy see his decline and cope with some of the behaviour brought about by it. However, in the times when he was well and lucid, his charm and spark still shone.

Jimmy's journey was to end soon after he collapsed in the summer of 2010 at the age of seventy-eight. He was taken across the water to the Inverclyde Royal Hospital, which was uncomfortable for him as his fall was compounded by the disorientation that afflicts dementia sufferers away from familiar surroundings. Suffering from sepsis and other ailments, he was failing and sadly never recovered. Jimmy passed away on 10 August in the hospital that stands on the hills above the banks of his beloved River Clyde; a fitting setting for a man who had been 'Clyde-built'.

The tributes and eulogies that followed were evident of his colossal standing in Scotland. Political friends, foes and commentators alike lavished praise on the man who embodied the spirit of the Clyde. Respect and admiration abounded in newspapers and on TV. The attendance at the funeral service and the people that lined the streets pays testimony to the high regard in which he was held by Scottish people far and wide.

Jimmy had often chosen a lonely political road. The causes he had espoused, whether in the Communist Party, the left of the Labour Party or the SNP, had often been minority views or held at a time of limited public support. He never chose his routes in the hope of personal gain or any guaranteed political advancement, and his views were often met with criticism. Yet he remained hugely popular throughout his life. His integrity, sincerity and outstanding oratory were respected and admired across the land. Even those who disagreed with him recognised his ability and talents.

Jimmy's contribution at UCS, still seared in the memory of many Scots alive today, is what he'll for ever be remembered for. He remains an iconic figure in Scotland where he is fondly remembered by most and revered by many. He joins the pantheon of socialist greats from his native Clydeside, his name now standing alongside the likes of James Maxton, John MacLean and Willie Gallacher as a champion of and for the people.

His belief in socialism and in the Scottish nation remained undiminished from when he had first joined the Communist Party all those years before. Then, as throughout his lifetime, he was driven to action by the grinding poverty that afflicted the area in which he had grown up. He was inspired by the vision of a different society that could be created, based on the idea of wealth being shared out to all, not retained by the few.

The firebrand speeches of Maxton and Gallacher for a socialist society would be matched by him and reverberate in a new era, as further generations faced unemployment and poverty. The calls from George Buchanan and the Rev. James Barr for a Scottish Parliament, to let the Scots decide their own priorities and pursue their own society, would be made in a new context by him to further generations.

Although Jimmy changed his party membership, he never veered from his political principles. His commitment to socialism and a Scottish Parliament remained rock solid throughout. Social and economic conditions altered and the political landscape changed. Hence his move through the political parties. He joined the Communist Party in the shadow of the Second World War, when sympathy for the Soviet Union was widespread and the sins of the regime not fully known. He left when it became clear that they neither were living up to those beliefs nor were capable of delivering them. Seeking to deliver them, he followed the path of the Labour Party until New Labour abandoned the very soul of the cause he held so dear. His membership of the SNP was not a road-to-Damascus-conversion, but simply the route that offered the best path to social and economic progress for Scottish people. Jimmy's political legacy was to live on after his passing, for though his journey had concluded, others were to follow in his footsteps. The move of many working-class voters from Labour to the SNP would become a torrent and the battle between Westminster and Holyrood the political focus for Scotland.

The UK general election in 2010 occurred whist Jimmy was

approaching his final days in Inverclyde Hospital. It resulted in Gordon Brown losing and a Conservative/Liberal Democrat coalition government being formed under the leadership of David Cameron and Nick Clegg. Labour held on in Scotland where, once again, a desire to keep the Tories out and doubts over the relevance of the SNP at Westminster saw strategic voting behaviour. The Tory vote though was again less than half in Scotland than what it was in the UK. The result was:

SCOTLAND
Labour: 41% (42 seats)
Lib Dem: 18.9% (11 seats)
SNP: 19.9% (6 seats)
Conservative: 16.7% (1 seat)

UK
Conservative: 36.1% (306 seats)
Labour: 29% (258 seats)
Lib Dem: 23% (57 seats)

It was, however, to be the last hurrah for the Labour Party in Scotland. Despite the Scottish working class putting their faith in Labour to defend them from Tory rule, another Conservative government, albeit in coalition with the Liberal Democrats, was the outcome. Labour's comfortable win in Scotland underlined just how Westminster failed to represent the clear wishes of the majority of Scottish people or protect them from Tory rule.

Scotland had changed immeasurably over the years, with the demise of the manufacturing industry and the closures of pits, coal mines and steel works. Housing tenure had also evolved with home ownership overtaking council housing. However, as election results showed, the Tories remained hugely unpopular. The Scottish Parliament offered a bulwark to mitigate Tory rule and an alternative vision of how Scotland could be. The country was growing in self-confidence and the Parliament in stature. Scottish Labour's impotence in Westminster saw a further erosion of Labour support while the SNP administration was widely perceived as competent and credible, as well as seeking to protect and promote public services. It was recipe for disaster for Labour when the Scottish Parliament elections came about in 2011.

The electoral system of the Scottish Parliament had been designed to avoid a majority government, and especially a nationalist one. Yet, the perceived impossibility of an SNP majority was what, in fact, transpired.

The result of the Scottish Parliament election was:

SNP: 53.49% (69 seats)
Labour: 28.68% (37 seats)
Conservative: 11.63% (15 seats)
Lib Dem: 3.88% (5 seats)
Green: 1.55% (2 seats)

The SNP won five out of nine seats in Glasgow including the new seat that was made up of Govan and the constituency of Clydebank and Milngavie. The left and working-class vote had shifted solidly to the SNP and it was now game on for a referendum on Scottish independence. With an SNP majority, it could no longer be blocked. The Conservative government under David Cameron's leadership were confident of a comfortable victory in a referendum on independence and believed they could deliver a crushing blow to the SNP. Accordingly, Westminster refused to consider a multi-option referendum that would have allowed for federalism to be considered on the ballot.

In September 2014, however, a referendum on Scottish independence took place. Jimmy wasn't alive to see it, but would almost certainly have supported a Yes vote had he lived. Leading UCS campaigners who had been involved in the occupation with Jimmy publicly backed it. The left was divided, with most of the big unions and the Labour Party supporting a 'No' vote, whereas the young and the working class were overwhelmingly in favour. Campaigning was frenetic and the housing schemes that had been politically moribund for years were mobilised. It was the political activity that Jimmy had believed was needed and which he had always sought to encourage.

There was a huge turnout, including many voters who had not voted for years. An enormous 84.59 per cent of the electorate cast their vote on the matter of Scottish independence, and the result was:

Yes: 44.7%
No: 55.3%

Only four local authority areas – all areas that Jimmy was associated with – voted in favour. Dundee, with a 57 per cent Yes vote was the highest, which was followed by West Dunbartonshire with 54 per cent, Glasgow with 53.5 per cent and North

Lanarkshire. The Yes vote in areas of poverty and deprivation, especially in west and central Scotland, was overwhelming.

The call of Yes campaigners to end Tory rule, not just once, but for ever, resonated amongst those who had suffered more than two generations of Conservative austerity from a government they had overwhelmingly rejected. It was driven partly by fear of what might happen, as well as by hope of what might be. They turned out in their droves from areas where voting was not the norm or hadn't been for many years. The grassroots politics that Jimmy had believed in was undertaken and communities politicised. Many people who either had never voted before or hadn't participated for many years turned out in their droves to the polling booths to vote for a better society.

But it was not enough. The fear of change that many older and middle-class voters felt triumphed. Doubts about the currency and the economy from those with a stake in society overcame the hopes of those with little or none.

Despite the heart wrenching defeat for many, the result confirmed the journey being made by the Scottish working class. The referendum had seen Labour campaign for a No vote and stand on the Better Together platform with the Conservatives. They were to pay a heavy price for it when the general election came about the following year. The transformation of the Scottish working-class vote from Labour to the SNP was complete. Labour lost all but one seat, returning just one MP. The Tories and the Liberal Democrats also returned just one seat each, and the SNP won all fifty-six other seats. However, a Tory government was still returned south of the border.

The result of the 2015 general election in Scotland was:

SNP: 56 (50%)
Labour: 1 (24.3%)
Conservative: 1 (14.9%)
Lib Dem: 1 (7.5%)

The result in the UK was:

Conservative: 330 (36.9%)
Labour: 232 (30.4%)
SNP: 56 (4.7%)
Lib Dem: 8 (7.9%)

The Holyrood elections in 2016 confirmed the SNPs' dominance and supplanting of Labour in working-class areas. Though their overall majority was lost in Holyrood, a majority for independence remained along with the Greens who had been active in the broader Yes campaign. The Tories commenced an election comeback and replaced Labour as the chief opposition in the Scottish Parliament, as unionism strengthened in areas that had voted overwhelmingly No in the referendum.

The result was:

SNP: 63 (48.8%)
Conservative: 31 (24%)
Labour: 24 (18.6%)
Green: 6 (4.7%)
Lib Dem: 5 (3.9%)

The council elections in Scotland that followed in 2017 again saw Labour supplanted by the SNP. Glasgow City Council had an SNP majority for the first time in its history, with Labour losing control after generations in power. West Dunbartonshire, where Jimmy had served on Clydebank Town Council, also saw an SNP minority administration in power.

The Westminster elections in 2017 saw a revitalised Labour Party under Jeremy Corbyn make significant progress south of the border. North of the border, the surge of support for Corbyn saw Labour make modest gains, though the SNP comfortably remained the largest party in terms of both seats and votes, with particularly strong presence in the former Labour heartlands of Clydeside where both the seats that covered Govan and Clydebank remained in nationalist control. Former SNP citadels in the north-east, however, turned Tory, including that of former First Minister Alex Salmond, who had signed Jimmy up for the party a decade and more before. In some ways, with rural areas of Scotland turning Conservative, the political map of Scotland from Jimmy's early involvement in the 1950s was reappearing,

Despite the surge of support for Corbyn and the dismal campaign of Theresa May, it was still a Conservative victory south of the border.

The result in Scotland was:

SNP: 36.9% (35 seats)
Conservative: 28.6% (13 seats)
Labour: 27.1% (7 seats)
Lib Dem: 6.8% (4 seats)

The result in the UK was:

Conservative: 42.4% (317 seats)
Labour: 40% (262 seats)
SNP: 3% (35 seats)
Lib Dem: 7.4 % (12 seats)

Would Jimmy have been persuaded to return to his roots by the more socialist programme of Jeremy Corbyn's Labour Party? Or would he have stayed with the SNP? The SNP, despite having moved slightly to the left and remaining a social democratic party, were still far from the red-blooded socialist party Jimmy sought. However, the Labour Party in Scotland still remained intractably hostile to the question of Scottish independence, as Jimmy had written about a decade before, and seemed a much paler imitation of their London socialist colleagues.

We'll never know what Jimmy would have made of the political climate in 2017. He'd no doubt welcome the re-emergence of socialism, but would despair at the Tories becoming the official opposition in Holyrood and Scotland again being ruled by the right-wing government it had rejected at the polls.

But what we do know is that Jimmy Reid was a truly remarkable man who made a remarkable political journey. He led the Scottish working class through times of fire and fury and did much to support the achievement of Scotland's own Parliament. He dreamt of a better society for all, and lived his life accordingly. He most certainly was 'the best MP Scotland never had' and Scotland's undoubtedly a better place for the huge part he played in its modern history.

ACKNOWLEDGEMENTS

There are many people that I need to thank for their support and assistance in writing this book, none more, though, than the Reid family who allowed me to write about a man I hugely admire. Joan and Julie indulged my questions and were always kind with their responses, and Jimmy's daughter Eileen was generous with her time and her assistance was invaluable.

Brian McGeachan was also hugely generous with his time and massively helpful in his provision of information that always seemed to be at his fingertips. His almost encyclopaedic knowledge about Jimmy's life was remarkable, as was his kindly reading of early drafts. Likewise, David Scott was of great assistance as a conduit to the Reid family and also in his thoughts and suggestions.

My friend, Charlie Reid, though no relation but another huge admirer, must be thanked for his idea for me to write the book. Roddy MacAskill, my son, provided great assistance in interviews and research, as well as constructive comment on it as it evolved.

Sir Alex Ferguson, Bob Thomson, Pat Kelly, Bob Dickie, Jimmy Cloughley, Bob Starrett, John Kay, Ross Wilson, the late Gordon Wilson, Hannah Bardell MP and Alex Salmond all gave their time and provided great assistance by talking about their memories of Jimmy and aspects of his life that they had encountered.

Barclay McBain at *The Herald* and Donald Walker at *The Scotsman* were extremely helpful in providing information on Jimmy's writings and recollections of his time with the press. Staff at the Mitchell Library, Glasgow, Glasgow University Archives and the Working-Class Movement Library, Salford, were all equally obliging and helpful.

At Biteback, my editor Alison Macdonald was remarkably diligent given her lack of direct knowledge of the time or events and was enormously insightful in her suggested amendments. Olivia Beattie was equally supportive in the arrangements necessary to bring this to print.

Finally, my partner, Susan, has been extremely supportive, as well as encouraging, as ever.

SUGGESTED READING

Reid, Jimmy, *As I Please*

Reid, Jimmy, *Reflections of a Clyde-Built Man*

Thompson, Willie, *The Good Old Cause*

Thompson, Willie and Hart, Finlay, *The UCS Work-In*

INDEX